CSS Mastery

Advanced Web Standards Solutions

Second Edition

Andy Budd, Simon Collison, and Cameron Moll

ISBN-13 (pbk): 978-1-4302-2397-9

ISBN-13 (electronic): 978-1-4302-2398-6

Printed and bound in the United States of America 9 8 7 6 5 4 3 2 1

Distributed to the book trade worldwide by Springer-Verlag New York, Inc., 233 Spring Street, 6th Floor, New York, NY 10013. Phone 1-800-SPRINGER, fax 201-348-4505, e-mail orders-ny@springer-sbm.com, or visit www.springeronline.com.

For information on translations, please e-mail info@apress.com or visit www.apress.com.

Apress and friends of ED books may be purchased in bulk for academic, corporate, or promotional use. eBook versions and licenses are also available for most titles. For more information, reference our Special Bulk Sales–eBook Licensing web page at http://www.apress.com/info/bulksales.

The source code for this book is freely available to readers at www.friendsofed.com in the Downloads section.

Credits

Lead Editor:
Ben Renow-Clarke

Project Managers:
Richard Dal Porto and Debra Kelly

Technical Reviewers:
Natalie Downe and Tony White

Copy Editor:
Heather Lang

Editorial Board:
Clay Andres, Steve Anglin, Mark Beckner, Ewan Buckingham, Tony Campbell, Gary Cornell, Jonathan Gennick, Michelle Lowman, Matthew Moodie, Jeffrey Pepper, Frank Pohlmann, Ben Renow-Clarke, Dominic Shakeshaft, Matt Wade, Tom Welsh

Compositor:
v-prompt

Indexer:
BIM Indexing

To Alison, for all the help and support over the last 6 months.

— Andy Budd

Contents at a Glance

Contents vii

Foreword xiv

About the Authors xv

About the Technical Reviewers xvii

Acknowledgments xviii

Introduction xx

Chapter 1: Setting the Foundations 3

Chapter 2: Getting Your Styles to Hit the Target 25

Chapter 3: Visual Formatting Model Overview 51

Chapter 4: Using Backgrounds for Effect 71

Chapter 5: Styling Links 109

Chapter 6: Styling Lists and Creating Nav Bars 133

Chapter 7: Styling Forms and Data Tables 175

Chapter 8: Layout 205

Chapter 9: Bugs and Bug Fixing 245

Chapter 10: Case Study: Roma Italia 275

Chapter 11: Case Study: Climb the Mountains 311

Index 355

Contents

Foreword xiv

About the Authors xv

About the Technical Reviewers xvii

Acknowledgments xviii

Introduction xx

    Who is this book for? xx

    How is this book structured? xx

    Conventions used in this book xxi

Chapter 1: Setting the Foundations 3

    Structuring your code 4

      A brief history of markup 4

        The power of meaning 6

        IDs and class names 7

        Naming your elements 9

        IDs or Classes? 10

        Divs and spans 11

        Microformats 12

        Different versions of HTML and CSS 16

      Document types, DOCTYPE switching, and browser modes 18

      Validation 18

        Browser modes 20

        DOCTYPE switching 21

    Summary 22

Chapter 2: Getting Your Styles to Hit the Target 25

    Common selectors 25

      Pseudo-classes 27

    The universal selector 27

    Advanced selectors 28

      Child and adjacent sibling selectors 28

      Attribute selectors 30

The cascade and specificity 35

    Specificity 35

    Using specificity in your style sheets 37

    Adding a class or an ID to the body tag........................... 38

Inheritance.. 39

Planning, organizing, and maintaining your style sheets 40

    Applying styles to your document 40

    Structuring your code... 42

    Note to self.. 44

    Removing comments and optimizing your style sheets........ 45

Style guides... 45

Summary 48

Chapter 3: Visual Formatting Model Overview 51

Box model recap 51

    IE and the box model 53

    Margin collapsing 54

Positioning recap... 57

    The visual formatting model 57

    Relative positioning 59

    Absolute positioning 60

    Fixed positioning 61

    Floating.. 62

    Line boxes and clearing 63

Summary 69

Chapter 4: Using Backgrounds for Effect................................. 71

Background image basics 72

Rounded-corner boxes.. 75

    Fixed-width rounded-corner boxes................................... 75

    Flexible rounded-corner box 78

Mountaintop corners... 81

    Multiple background images 83

border-radius..85

border-image..86

Drop shadows 88

Easy CSS drop shadows..88

Drop shadows à la Clagnut 91

Box-shadow 91

Opacity 95

CSS opacity 95

RGBa 96

PNG transparency 97

CSS parallax effect 99

Image replacement..102

Fahrner Image Replacement (FIR) 103

Phark 104

Scalable Inman Flash Replacement (sIFR) 104

Summary 106

Chapter 5: Styling Links 109

Simple link styling...109

Fun with underlines 111

Simple link embellishments 111

Fancy link underlines...112

Visited-link styles...113

Styling link targets 113

Highlighting different types of links...115

Highlighting downloadable documents and feeds.......................117

Creating links that look like buttons...118

Simple rollovers 120

Rollovers with images 120

Pixy-style rollovers 121

CSS sprites...123

Rollovers with CSS 3..125

Pure CSS tooltips 128

Summary 130

Chapter 6: Styling Lists and Creating Nav Bars 133

Basic list styling 134

Creating a basic vertical nav bar 135

Highlighting the current page in a nav bar 138

Creating a simple horizontal nav bar.. 139

Creating a graphical nav bar 142

Simplified sliding door tabbed navigation................................. 144

Suckerfish drop-downs... 147

CSS image maps 151

Flickr-style image maps.. 156

Remote rollovers 165

A short note about definition lists 171

Summary 172

Chapter 7: Styling Forms and Data Tables................................... 175

Styling data tables 176

Table-specific elements... 178

Summary and caption 178

thead, tbody, and tfoot 178

col and colgroups.. 179

Data table markup 179

Styling the table.. 181

Adding the visual style.. 182

Simple form layout.. 185

Useful form elements 186

Form labels 187

The basic layout 188

Other elements 189

Embellishments 192

Required fields 193

Complicated form layout 193

    Accessible date input 195

    Multicolumn check boxes 196

        Submit buttons 198

    Form feedback 201

Summary 203

Chapter 8: Layout 205

Planning your layout 206

Setting the foundations 208

    Centering a design using margins 210

Float-based layouts 212

    Two-column floated layout 213

    Three-column floated layout 216

Fixed-width, liquid, and elastic layout 219

Liquid layouts 220

Elastic layouts 223

Liquid and elastic images 226

Faux columns 228

Equal-height columns 231

CSS 3 columns 236

CSS Frameworks vs. CSS Systems 238

Summary 243

Chapter 9: Bugs and Bug Fixing 245

Bug hunting 246

    Common CSS problems 246

        Problems with specificity and sort order 247

        Problems with margin collapsing 249

Bug hunting basics 252

    Try to avoid bugs in the first place 254

    Isolate the problem 254

    Creating minimal test cases 255

Fixing the problem, not the symptoms **256**

Asking for help.. **256**

Having layout.. **256**

What is layout? **257**

What effect does layout have? **258**

Workarounds **260**

Internet Explorer conditional comments... **260**

A warning about hacks and filters **261**

Using hacks and filters sensibly **262**

Applying the IE for Mac band pass filter.. **262**

Applying the star HTML hack **263**

Applying the child selector hack **264**

Common bugs and their fixes **264**

Double-margin float bug **264**

Three-pixel text jog bug.. **265**

IE 6 duplicate character bug... **267**

IE 6 peek-a-boo bug **269**

Absolute positioning in a relative container.. **269**

Stop picking on Internet Explorer **270**

Graded browser support **271**

Summary **273**

Chapter 10: Case Study: Roma Italia **276**

About this case study **276**

The foundation **278**

An eye towards HTML 5.. **279**

reset.css **281**

The 1080 layout and grid **282**

Using grids in web design **283**

Advanced CSS2 and CSS3 features **285**

Dowebsitesneedtolookexactlythesameineverybrowser.com?.................... **285**

Attribute selector .... **288** box-shadow, RGBa, and text-overflow.................................289

Font linking and better web typography............................293

Setting font-size like it's 1999.......................................293

Hanging punctuation 294

Multi-column text layout..296

@font-face..298

Cufón, an interim step towards @font-face......................301

Adding interactivity with Ajax and jQuery.......................303

Ajax...304

jQuery..305

Using Ajax + jQuery for the search feature 307

Summary...310

Chapter 11: Case Study: Climb the Mountains 311

About this case study 312

Style Sheet organization and conventions.......................314

The hard-working screen.css 315

Describing contents 315

Reset 316

IE style sheets using conditional comments 317

Grid flexibility...317

How does the CTM layout work? 318

Navigation control with body classes 319

Highlighting the current page 319

Layering the blockquote 323

Strategically targeting elements 325

Deep descendent selectors..325

The :first-child pseudo-class...329

Adjacent sibling selectors 331

Transparency, shadows, and rounded corners..................332

Our aim...332

Caption image overlay and RGBa transparency................333

Combining classes 336

border-radius 337

box-shadow 339

Positioning lists and revealing content.. 340

Rounding the corners 343

The main elevation chart.. 344

Summary 351

Index 355

Foreword

In our wonderful world of web design, there are 3,647 ways to accomplish the same goal—approximately. And that absurdly fictitious number is increasing every day. Instead of one, correct way of solving a particular problem, we're both blessed and cursed by the abundant choices we have as web designers. It's these choices that make designing for the Web fun and interesting, while at the same time overwhelming. *CSS Mastery* will help cure that overwhelmingitis (a word that I've just invented).

Andy Budd has been writing, designing, and speaking about standards-based web design for years, and we're now lucky to see his clear, easy-to-follow way of teaching essential CSS techniques compiled in this very book. The result is a card catalog of indispensable solutions, tricks, and tips that a web professional such as yourself should not be without.

I've always frowned on publications that suggest a *single*, correct way of accomplishing a goal, and Andy does the complete opposite, offering multiple methods for tasks such as styling links, creating tabbed navigation, utilizing time-saving CSS3 solutions, or creating fixed, fluid, or elastic layouts, as well as giving tips on how to troubleshoot those pesky browser bugs that go along with designing with CSS (to name but a few). Armed with these popular and stylish approaches to common design elements, you'll be better prepared to make your own *informed* decisions.

And as if that wasn't enough, Andy's gone ahead and enlisted the help of two imitable designers to help pull all the pieces together, showing how these essential techniques can work *together*. I've long been a fan of Cameron's and Simon's work, and to see two great case studies covering fluid, bulletproof designs as well as flexible style solutions, respectively, well, that's just a gigantic bonus.

So dig in and start chipping away at those 3,647 ways to master your CSS.

Dan Cederholm

Author, Web Standards Solutions

About the Authors

Andy Budd is one of the founding partners at User Experience Design Consultancy, Clearleft (clearleft.com). As an interaction design and usability specialist, Andy is a regular speaker at international conferences like Web Directions, An Event Apart, and SXSW. Andy curates dConstruct (dconstruct.org), one of the UK's most popular design conferences. He's also responsible for UX London (uxlondon.com), the UK's first dedicated usability, information architecture, and user experience design event.

Andy was an early champion of web standards in the UK and has developed an intimate understanding of the CSS specification and cross-browser support. As an active member of the community, Andy has helped judge several international design awards and currently sits on the advisory board for *.Net* magazine. Andy is also the driving force behind Silverbackapp (silverbackapp.com), a low-cost usability testing tool for the Mac. Andy is an avid Twitter user (@andybudd) and occasionally blogs at andybudd.com.

Never happier than when he's diving in some remote tropical atoll, Andy is a qualified PADI dive instructor and retired shark wrangler.

Cameron Moll has been designing meaningful web interfaces that harmonize utility and presentation since the late 1990s. His work or advice has been featured by *HOW*, *Print*, and *Communication Arts* magazines, Forrester Research, National Public Radio (NPR), and many others. He speaks on user interface design at conferences nationally and internationally, and he is also the author of *Mobile Web Design* (mobilewebbook.com).

Cameron is the founder and president of Authentic Jobs Inc. (authenticjobs.com), a targeted destination for web and creative professionals and the companies seeking to hire them. He is also the proprietor of Cameron Moll LLC, whose products include letterpress typography posters available for purchase at cameronmoll.bigcartel.com. And amid all this craziness, he still finds time to play ball with each of his four boys.

You can also find Cameron online at cameronmoll.com, twitter.com/cameronmoll, flickr.com/photos/authentic, and vimeo.com/cameronmoll.

Simon Collison is cofounder and creative director at Erskine Design (erskinedesign.com), part of a talented team of designers and developers doing exceptional things. Over the last ten years, he's worked on numerous web projects for record labels and bands, visual artists, businesses, government—pretty much the full gamut. He's now working with a broad client list ranging from established magazines to polar explorers.

Colly writes a long-running blog (colly.com), writes about the web at ErskineLabs (erskinelabs.com) and he has written the bestselling *Beginning CSS Web Development* (ISBN: 978-1-59059-689-0) for Apress and coauthored *Web Standards Creativity* (ISBN: 978-1-59059-803-0). He's never happier than when he's experimenting with CSS and HTML, or when talking about it in front of an audience.

In the real world, Colly loves climbing mountains and getting lost in the wildernesses of the UK or Iceland. He drives a 32-year-old car and has a stupid cat called Bearface.

About the Technical Reviewers

Natalie Downe is a perfectionist by nature and works for Brighton's Clearleft as a client-side web developer. An experienced usability consultant and project manager, her first loves remain front-end development and usability engineering. She enjoys Doing Things Right and occasionally dabbling in the dark arts of Python and poking the odd API.

 **Tony White** is a front-end developer and designer living in Memphis, Tennessee. During the day he is the user interface manager for Hilton Hotels, where he nurtures usability, advocates web standards, and lassos HTML with jQuery. He also runs the one-man show Ask the CSS Guy (askthecssguy.com), an after-hours site devoted to peaking under the hood of CSS and JavaScript web design techniques.

Acknowledgments

Thanks to everybody who helped make this book possible, both directly and indirectly.

To my friends and colleagues at Clearleft: Thanks for providing encouragement and feedback throughout the book-writing process. And especially to Natalie Downe for lending your experience and breadth of knowledge to this book: Your support and guidance was invaluable, and I still don't know where you manage to find the time.

To Chris Mills for guiding me through the initial writing process and helping turn my ideas into reality, and to everybody at Apress who worked tirelessly to get this book published on time: Your dedication and professionalism is much appreciated.

To all my colleagues who continue to share their wealth of knowledge in order to make the Web a better place: This book would not have been possible without the previous work of the following people, to name but a few: Cameron Adams, John Allsopp, Rachel Andrew, Nathan Barley, Holly Bergevin, Mark Boulton, Douglas Bowman, The BritPack, Dan Cederholm, Tantek Çelik, Joe Clark, Andy Clarke, Simon Collison, Mike Davidson, Garrett Dimon, Derek Featherstone, Nick Fink, Patrick Griffiths, Jon Hicks, Molly E. Holzschlag, Shaun Inman, Roger Johansson, Jeremy Keith, Ian Lloyd, Ethan Marcotte, Drew McLellan, Eric Meyer, Cameron Moll, Dunstan Orchard, Veerle Pieters, D. Keith Robinson, Richard Rutter, Jason Santa Maria, Dave Shea, Jeffrey Veen, Russ Weakley, Simon Willison, and Jeffrey Zeldman.

To all the readers of my blog and everybody I've met at conferences, workshops, and training events over the last couple of years: Your discussions and ideas helped fuel the content of this book.

And finally, thanks to you for reading. I hope this book helps you take your CSS skills to the next level.

Andy Budd

First, thanks to you for choosing this book. I hope it improves the caliber of work you do, day in and day out. I'm endlessly inspired by the potential of those in our industry, and that includes you.

I echo Andy's words in giving thanks to the many notable individuals that have shaped and refined the Web, making it a better place today than it's ever been. Years from now, these individuals will be just as revered as those men and women who first sent men to the Moon.

A special thanks to Aaron Barker (`aaronbarker.net`) who assisted with several of the jQuery and AJAX examples in my case study.

Most importantly, I give my utmost gratitude to my beautiful wife, Suzanne, and four sons, Everest, Edison, Isaac, and Hudson. Without their love, support and patience, the work I've produced to date would not have been realized.

Cameron Moll

I must thank my friend and colleague Gregory Wood for his ideas and assistance with the "Climb the Mountains" concept. Everything he produces inspires me, and he's the designer I want to be when I grow up. I'd also like to thank all of my colleagues at Erskine Design for their support and for turning a blind eye to my feverish work on projects such as this. Big thanks to Simon Campbell, Jamie Pittock, Glen Swinfield, Phil Swan, Vicky Twycross, and Angela Campbell.

Above all, I should take this opportunity to thank my mum, and those that I have lost since the first edition of this book, my two grandfathers, and especially my dad. I still do this stuff to make you proud, even though you've gone.

Simon Collison

Introduction

There are an increasing number of CSS resources around, yet you only have to look at a CSS mailing list to see the same questions popping up time and again: How do I center a design? What is the best rounded-corner box technique? How do I create a three-column layout?

If you follow the CSS design community, finding the solution is usually a case of remembering which website a particular article or technique is featured on. However, if you are relatively new to CSS, or don't have the time to read all the blogs, this information can be hard to track down.

Even people who are skilled at CSS run into problems with some of the more obscure aspects of CSS such as the positioning model or specificity. This is because most CSS developers are self-taught, picking up tricks from articles and other people's code without fully understanding the specifications. And is it any wonder, as the CSS specification is complex, often contradictory, and written for browser manufacturers rather than web developers?

Then there are the browsers to contend with. Browser bugs and inconsistencies are one of the biggest problems for the modern CSS developer. Unfortunately, many of these bugs are poorly documented, and their fixes verge on the side of folk law. You know that you have to do something a certain way, or it will break in one browser or another. You just can't remember for which browser or how it breaks.

So the idea for a book formed. A book that brings together the most useful CSS techniques in one place, that focuses on real-world browser issues and that helps plug common gaps in people's CSS knowledge. A book that will help you jump the learning curve and have you coding like a CSS expert in no time flat.

Who is this book for?

CSS Mastery is aimed at anybody with a basic knowledge of HTML and CSS. If you have just recently dipped your toes into the world of CSS design, or if you've been developing pure CSS sites for years, there will be something in this book for you. However, you will get the most out of this book if you have been using CSS for a while but don't consider yourself an expert just yet. This book is packed full of practical, real-world advice and examples to help you master modern CSS design.

How is this book structured?

This book eases you in gently, with three chapters on basic CSS concepts and best practices. You will learn how to structure and comment your code, the ins-and-outs of the CSS positioning model, and how floating and clearing really works. You may know a lot of this already, but you will probably find bits you've missed or not understood fully. As such, the first three chapters act as a great CSS primer as well as a recap on what you already know.

With the basics out of the way, the next five chapters cover core CSS techniques such as image, link, and list manipulation; form and data-table design; and pure CSS layout. Each chapter starts simply and then works up to progressively more complicated examples. In these chapters, you will learn how to create rounded-corner boxes, images with transparent drop shadows, tabbed navigation bars, and interactive buttons. With many of these techniques, you will first learn the traditional way of doing them before seeing how you can achieve the same affect using CSS 3. If you want to follow along with the examples in this book, all the code examples can be downloaded from www.cssmastery.com or www.friendsofed.com.

Browser bugs are the bane of many a CSS developer, so all the examples in this book focus on creating techniques that work across browsers. What's more, this book contains a whole chapter devoted to bugs and bug fixing. In this chapter, you will learn all about bug-hunting techniques and how to spot and fix common bugs before they start causing problems. You will even learn what really causes many of Microsoft Internet Explorer's seemingly random CSS bugs.

The last two chapters are the *pièce de résistance*. Simon Collison and Cameron Moll, two of the best CSS designers around, have combined all of these techniques into two fantastic case studies. So you learn not only how these techniques work but also how to put them into practice on a real-life web project.

This book can be read from cover to cover or kept by your computer as a reference of modern tips, tricks, and techniques. The choice is up to you.

Conventions used in this book

This book uses a couple of conventions that are worth noting. The following terms are used throughout this book:

- *HTML* refers to both the HTML and XHTML languages.

- Unless otherwise stated, *CSS* relates to the CSS 2.1 specification.

- *Internet Explorer 6 (IE 6) and below on Windows* refers to Internet Explorer 5.0 to 6.0 on Windows.

- *Modern browsers* are considered to be the latest versions of Firefox, Safari, and Opera along with IE 7 and above.

- It is assumed that all the HTML examples in this book are nested in the `<body>` of a valid document, while the CSS is contained within an external style sheet. Occasionally, HTML and CSS have been placed in the same code example for brevity. However, in a real document, these items need to go in their respective places to function correctly.

Finally, for HTML examples that contain repeating data, rather than writing out every line, the ellipsis character (. . .) is used to denote code continuation:

With the formalities out of the way, let's get started.

Chapter 1

Setting the Foundations

The human race is a naturally inquisitive species. We just love tinkering with things. When I recently bought a new iMac, I had it to bits within seconds, before I'd even read the instruction manual. We enjoy working things out ourselves and creating our own mental models of how we think things behave. We muddle through and only turn to the manual when something goes wrong or defies our expectations.

One of the best ways to learn Cascading Style Sheets (CSS) is to jump right in and start tinkering. In fact, I imagine this is how the majority of you learned to code, by picking things up off blogs, viewing source to see how things worked, and then trying them out on your personal sites. You almost certainly didn't start by reading the full CSS specification, which is enough to put anyone to sleep.

Tinkering is a great way to start, but if you're not careful, you may end up misunderstanding a crucial concept or building in problems for later on. I know; I've done so several times. In this chapter, I am going to review some basic but often misunderstood concepts and show you how to keep your HTML and CSS clear and well structured.

In this chapter you will learn about

- Structuring your code

- The importance of meaningful documentation

- Naming conventions

- When to use IDs and class names

- Microformats

- Different versions of HTML and CSS

- Document types, DOCTYPE switching, and browser modes

Structuring your code

Most people don't think about the foundations of a building. However, without solid foundations, the majority of buildings wouldn't stay standing. While this book is about advanced CSS techniques, much of what you are about to learn would not be possible (or at least would be very difficult) without a well-structured and valid HTML document to work with.

In this section, you will learn why well-structured and meaningful HTML is vital to standards-based development. You will also learn how you can add more meaning to your documents, and by doing so, make your job as a developer easier.

A brief history of markup

The early Web was little more than a series of interlinked research documents using HTML to add basic formatting and structure. However, as the World Wide Web gained in popularity, HTML started being used for presentational purposes. Instead of using heading elements for page headlines, people would use a combination of font and bold tags to create the visual effect they wanted. Tables got co-opted as a layout tool rather than a way of displaying data, and people would use blockquote to add whitespace rather than to indicate quotations. Very quickly, the Web lost its meaning and became a jumble of font and table tags. Web designers came up with a name for this kind of markup; they called it *tag soup* (see Figure 1-1).

```
view-source: - Source of: http://web.archive.org/web/20000815052646/abcnews.go.com/
<!--------------- 11 MAIN CONTENT-------------------->
  <td colspan="2" width="425" valign="top" bgcolor=#eeeee3>
<table width="417" cellspacing="0" cellpadding="4" border=0>
<tr><td width="417" valign="top">
<a href="/sections/politics/DailyNews/DEMCVN_open000813.html"  >
<img
src="http://a4.g.akamaitech.net/7/4/622/001/abcnews.go.com/media/FrontPage/i
width=200 height=150 vspace=0 hspace=3 border=0 alt="Not Looking Back"
align=left></a>
<font face= geneva,arial,helvetica size=5><b>
<a href="/sections/politics/DailyNews/DEMCVN_open000813.html" >
Passing the Torch
</a>
</b></font><br>
<font face=geneva,arial,helvetica size=2>Bill Clinton gave a spirited
defense of his eight years in office and touted the qualifications of his
vice president, Al Gore, who wants to take Clinton&#0146;s place in the
White House. Get full coverage and <a href
="http://abcnews.go.com/sections/politics/DailyNews/DEMCVN_trans_clinton0008
a transcript</a>.</font>
```

Figure 1-1. The markup for the lead story from abcnews.com on August 14, 2000, uses tables for layout and large, bold text for headings. The code lacks structure and is difficult to understand

As web pages became more and more presentational, the code became increasingly difficult to understand and maintain. WYSIWYG (What You See Is What You Get) editors offered authors an escape from these complexities and promised a brave new world of visual layout. Unfortunately, rather than making things simpler, these tools added their own complicated markup to the mix. Editors like FrontPage or Dreamweaver allowed users to build complex table layouts at the click of a button, cluttering the code with nested tables and "spacer GIFs" (see Figure 1-2). Sadly, these layouts were extremely fragile and prone to breaking. Because the markup was littered with meaningless code, it was easy to delete the wrong tag and watch the whole layout crumble. Furthermore, due to the complexity of the code, bug hunting was almost impossible. It was often easier to code the page from scratch than hunt around in the hope of fixing the bug. Things were further complicated if you were working on a large site. Because the presentation of the site was locked into the individual pages, you had to craft complicated "find and replace" routines to make even the smallest sitewide change. I've broken more than one site in my time because of a hastily constructed "find and replace" routine. Consequently, your page templates would go out of sync extremely quickly, and a simple change could mean hand editing every page on your site.

Tables were never meant for layout, so David Siegel invented a clever hack to make them work. In order to prevent tables from horizontally or vertically collapsing, Siegel suggested using a 1-pixel transparent GIF. By putting these hidden images in their own table cells and then scaling them vertically or horizontally, you could artificially enforce a minimum width on the cells, thus preserving the layout. Also known as a "shim GIF" because of the file name given to them in Dreamweaver, they were an extremely common sight in old school table-based layouts. Thankfully, the practice has now died out, so you no longer see these presentational elements cluttering up your code.

Rather than being seen as a simple markup language, HTML gained a reputation for being complicated, confusing, and prone to errors. Consequently, many people were afraid of touching the code, which resulted in an overreliance on visual editors and spawned a whole generation of designers that didn't understand how to code.

By the turn of the millennium, the web design industry was in a mess, and something needed to be done.

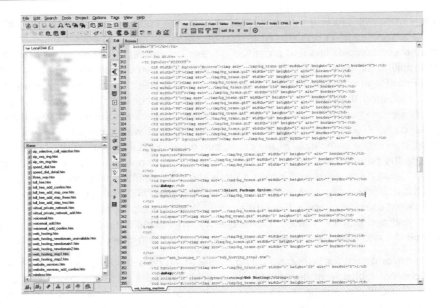

Figure 1-2. A screenshot of Homesite showing a complicated table-based layout using lots of spacer GIFs (courtesy of Jeff L.).

Then along came Cascading Style Sheets. CSS allowed authors to control how a page looked through an external style sheet, making it possible to separate the content from presentation. Now, sitewide changes could be made in one place and would propagate throughout the system. Presentational tags like the font tag could be ditched, and layout could be controlled using CSS instead of tables. Markup could be made simple again, and people began to develop a newfound interest in the underlying code.

Meaning started to creep back into documents. Browser default styles could be overridden, so it became possible to mark up something as a heading without it being big, bold, and ugly. Lists could be created that didn't display as a series of bullet points, and blockquotes could be used without the associated styling. Developers started to use HTML elements because of what they meant rather than how they looked   (see Figure 1-3).

```
view-source: - Source of: http://abcnews.go.com/
<div id="main_story" class="clearthis">
<div id="main_photo" align="right">
<a href="/International/wireStory?id=947057"><img width="126"
src="http://a.abcnews.com/images/International/BAG12007171046.jpeg"
id="BAG12007171046.jpeg" height="188" /></a></div>

<div id="main_headline">

<h2 class="replace">
<a href="/International/wireStory?id=947057">Iraq Bomb Toll Grows; New
Attacks Kill 22</a>
</h2>
<p>New suicide bombings killed at least 22 people in the Baghdad area on
Sunday, while relatives struggled to identify charred bodies from a fiery
suicide attack near a Shiite mosque in Musayyib that...</p>

</div>
</div>
```

Figure 1-3. The markup for the lead story on abcnews.com from earlier this year is well structured and easy to understand. While it does contain some presentational markup, the code is a significant improvement on the code in Figure 1-1.

The power of meaning

Meaningful markup provides the developer with several important benefits. Meaningful pages are much easier to work with than presentational ones. For example, say you need to change a quotation on a page. If the quotation is marked up correctly, it is easy to scan through the code until you find the first blockquote element. However, if the quotation is just another paragraph element, it will be a lot harder to find. For a more complicated, but no less realistic example, say that you needed to add an extra column to your homepage. You could simply drop the content in at the right point and then update the widths in your CSS. To do the same in a table-based layout you'd need to add an extra column in your table, change the colspan settings, alter the widths on all the cells, and change the widths of all your shim gifs. In effect, you'd have to change the entire structure of your page to accommodate this simple change.

As well as being easy for humans to understand, meaningful markup—otherwise known as semantic markup—can be understood by programs and other devices. Search engines, for instance, can recognize a headline because it is wrapped in h1 tags and assign more importance to it. Screen reader users can rely on headings as supplemental page navigation.

Most importantly for the context of this book, meaningful markup provides you with a simple way of targeting the elements you wish to style. It adds structure to a document and creates an underlying framework to build upon. You can style elements directly without needing to add other identifiers, and thus avoid unnecessary code bloat.

HTML includes a rich variety of meaningful elements, such as

- h1, h2, and so on
- ul, ol, and dl

- strong and em

- blockquote and cite

- abbr, acronym, and code

- fieldset, legend, and label

- caption, thead, tbody, and tfoot

As such, it is always a good idea to use an appropriate meaningful element where one exists.

Every few years the CSS versus tables argument seems to flare up on blogs, mailing lists, or developer forums. The discussion is usually sparked when developers who have grown accustomed to the table-based approach rebel against the idea of having to learn a new skill. I can sympathies with this reaction, as CSS-based layout does seem difficult at first, especially when your current process seems to work. However, the benefits of CSS have been debated numerous times and include things like less code bloat, faster downloads, and easier maintenance to name just three. Most professional developers have come to see the benefits of web standards, and it's rare to see an agency of any size or quality doing things the old-fashioned way. So if you're still using table based layout, you're going to find it increasingly difficult to get work with agencies. Thankfully, these old habits are dying out, and there is a whole new generation of developers who have never had to suffer the inconvenience of table-based layout.

IDs and class names

Meaningful elements provide an excellent foundation, but the list of available elements isn't exhaustive. HTML 4 was created as a simple document markup language rather than an interface language. Because of this, dedicated elements for things such as content areas or navigation bars just don't exist. You could create your own elements using XML, but for reasons too complicated to go into, it's not very practical.

HTML 5 hopes to solve some of these problems by providing developers with a richer set of elements to work with. These include structural elements like header, nav, article, section, and footer as well as well as new UI features like data inputs and the menu element. In preparation for HTML 5, many developers have started adopting these as naming conventions for their ID and class names.

The next best thing is to take existing elements and give them extra meaning with the addition of an ID or a class name. This adds additional structure to your document and provides useful hooks for your styles. So you could take a simple list of links, and by giving it an ID of nav, create your own custom navigation element.

```
<ul id="nav">
  <li><a href="/home/">Home</a></li>
  <li><a href="/about/">About Us</a></li>
  <li><a href="/contact/">Contact</a></li>
</ul>
```

An ID is used to identify a specific element, such as the site navigation, and must be unique to that page. IDs are useful for identifying persistent structural elements such as the main navigation or content areas. They are also useful for identifying one-off elements—a particular link or form element, for example.

While a single ID name can only be applied to one element on a page, the same class name can be applied to any number of elements on a page. This makes classes much more powerful. Classes are useful for identifying types of content or similar items. For instance, you may have a page that contains multiple news stories.

```
<div id="story-id-1">
  <h2>Salter Cane win Best British Newcomer award</h2>
    <p>In a surprise turn of events, alt folk group, Salter Cane, won↵
Best British Newcomer and the Grammys this week…</p>
</div>


<div id="story-id-2">
  <h2>Comic Sans: The Movie wins best documentary at the BAFTAs </h2>
    <p>The story of this beloved typeface one the best documentary↵
category. Director Richard Rutter was reported to be speechless…</p>
</div>
```

Rather than giving each story a separate ID, you would give them all a class of news.

```
<div class="news">
  <h2>Salter Cane win Best British Newcomer award</h2>
    <p>In a surprise turn of events, alt folk group, Salter Cane, won↵
Best British Newcomer and the Grammys this week…</p>
</div>
```

```
<div class="news">
    <h2>"Comic Sans: The Movie" wins best documentary at the BAFTAs </h2>
        <p>The story of this beloved typeface one the best documentary↵
category. Director Richard Rutter was reported to be speechless…</p>
</div>
```

Naming your elements

When naming your IDs and classes, it is important that you keep the names as "unpresentational" as possible. For instance, if you want all of your form notification messages to be red, you could give them a class of red. This is fine as long as there are no other red elements on the page. However, say you wanted to style required form labels red as well. You are now forced to guess to which element that class could refer, and things are already starting to get confusing. Imagine how confusing the code could become if you used presentational elements across the whole site? This gets even more complicated if you decide to change the presentation of your form notifications from red to yellow. Now, you either have to go back and change all your class names, or you have an element called red that looks yellow.

Instead, it makes sense to name your elements based on what they are rather than how they look. That way your code will have more meaning and never go out of sync with your designs. So in the previous example, rather than giving your notifications a class of red, you should give them a more meaningful name like .warning or .notification (see Figure 1-4). The great thing about meaningful class names is that you can reuse them across your site. For instance, you could also use the class of .notification on other types of messages, and style them completely differently based on where they are in the document.

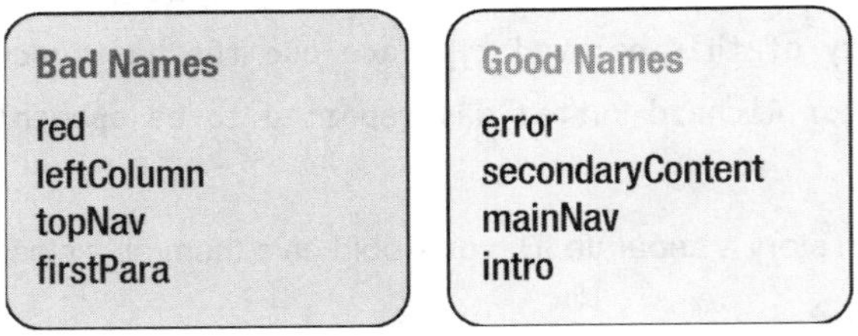

Bad Names	Good Names
red	error
leftColumn	secondaryContent
topNav	mainNav
firstPara	intro

Figure 1-4. Good and bad ID names

When writing class and ID names, you need to pay attention to case sensitivity, as browsers assume .andybudd is a different class from .andyBudd. The best way to handle this issue is simply to be consistent with your naming conventions. I always keep all my class and ID names lowercase and separate multiple words with a hyphen for legibility. So andy-budd is more legible than andyBudd.

IDs or Classes?

It is often difficult to decide if an element should have an ID or class name. As a general rule, classes should be applied to conceptually similar items that could appear in multiple places on the same page, whereas IDs should be applied to unique elements. However, you then get into a debate about which elements are conceptually similar and which elements are unique.

For instance, imagine you have a site that contains primary navigation in the header, page-based navigation at the bottom of the search results page, and tertiary navigation in the footer. Do you give each of these a separate ID like main-nav, page-nav, and footer-nav, or do you give them all a class of nav and style them based on their position in the document? I used to prefer the former approach, as it felt slightly more targeted. However, it comes with its own set of problems. What happens if I decide that I now need search results navigation at the top and the bottom of the search page or that I need two levels of navigation in the footer?

If you use a lot of IDs, you will start to run out of unique names very quickly and end up creating extremely long and complicated naming conventions. So these days, I tend to prefer class names and only use IDs if I'm targeting something extremely specific and know that I'll never want to use that name for something different elsewhere on the site. Or to put it another way, you should only use an ID if you're absolutely sure the item will appear only once. If you think you will need similar items in the future, use a class. By keeping your naming conventions general and using classes you don't end up with long chains of ID selectors all with very similar styles.

```
#andy, #rich, #jeremy, #james-box, #cennydd, #paul, #natalie, #sophie {
    font-size: 1.6em;
    font-weight: bold;
    border: 1px solid #ccc;
}
```

You can simply create a generic class for them all.

```
.staff {
    font-size: 1.6em;
    font-weight: bold;
    border: 1px solid #ccc;
}
```

Due to the flexibility of classes, they can be very powerful. At the same time, they can be overused and even abused. Novice CSS authors often add classes to nearly everything in an attempt to get fine-grained control over their styles. Early WYSIWYG editors also had the tendency to add classes each time a style was applied. Many developers picked up this bad habit when using generated code to learn CSS. This affliction is described as *classitis* and is, in some respects, as bad as using table-based layout because it adds meaningless code to your document.

```
<h2 class="news-head">Andy wins an Oscar for his cameo in Iron Man</h2>
  <p class="news-text">
  Andy Budd wins the Oscar for best supporting actor in Iron Man↵
  after his surprise cameo sets Hollywood a twitter with speculation.
  </p>
  <p class="news-text"><a href="news.php" class="news-tink">More</a></p>
```

In the preceding example, each element is identified as being part of a news story by using an individual news-related class name. This has been done to allow news headlines and text to be styled differently from the rest of the page. However, you don't need all these extra classes to target each individual element. Instead, you can identify the whole block as a news item by wrapping it in a div (code) with a class name of news. You can then target news headlines or text by simply using the cascade.

```
<div class="news">
  <h2>Andy wins an Oscar for his cameo in Iron Man </h2>
    <p>Andy Budd wins the Oscar for best supporting actor in Iron Man↵
  after his surprise cameo sets Hollywood a twitter with speculation.</p>
    <p><a href="news.php">More</a></p>
</div>
```

Anytime you find yourself repeating words in your class names like news-head and news-link or section-head and section-foot, it would be worth looking to see if you can break those elements into their constituent parts. This makes your code much more componentized and hence much more flexible.

Removing extraneous classes in this way will help simplify your code and reduce page weight. I will discuss CSS selectors and targeting your styles shortly. However, this overreliance on class names is almost never necessary. If you find yourself adding lots of classes, it's probably an indication that your HTML document is poorly structured.

Divs and spans

One element that can help add structure to a document is the div element. Many people mistakenly believe that a div element has no semantic meaning. However, div actually stands for *division* and provides a way of dividing a document into meaningful areas. So by wrapping your main content area in a div and giving it a class of content, you are adding structure and meaning to your document.

To keep unnecessary markup to a minimum, you should only use a div element if there is no existing element that will do the job. For instance, if you are using a list for your main navigation, there is no need to wrap it in a div.

```
<div class="nav">
  <ul>
    <li><a href="/home/">Home</a></li>
    <li><a href="/about/">About Us</a></li>
    <li><a href="/contact/">Contact</a></li>
  </ul>
</div>
```

You can remove the div entirely and simply apply your class to the list instead:

```
<ul class="nav">
    <li><a href="/home/">Home</a></li>
    <li><a href="/about/">About Us</a></li>
    <li><a href="/contact/">Contact</a></li>
</ul>
```

Using too many divs is often described as *divitus* and is usually a sign that your code is poorly structured and overly complicated. Some people new to CSS will try to replicate their old table structure using divs. But this is just swapping one set of extraneous tags for another. Instead, divs should be used to group related items based on their meaning or function rather than their presentation or layout.

Whereas divs can be used to group block-level elements, spans can be used to group or identify inline elements:

```
<h2>Andy wins an Oscar for his cameo in Iron Man </h2>
  <p>Published on <span class="date">February 22nd, 2009</span>
by <span class="author">Harry Knowles</span></p>
```

Although the goal is to keep your code as lean and mean(ingful) as possible, sometimes you cannot avoid adding an extra nonsemantic div or span to the page to display the way you want. If this is the case, don't fret too much over it. We live in a transitional period, and CSS 3 will give us much greater control of our documents. In the meantime, real-world needs often have to come before theory. The trick is knowing when you have to make a compromise and if you are doing it for the right reasons.

Microformats

Due to the scarcity of elements in HTML it's very difficult to highlight certain types of information such as people, places, or dates. To combat this, a group of developers decided to create a set of standardized naming conventions and markup patterns to represent this data. These naming conventions were based on existing data formats such as vCard and iCalendar and became known as *microformats*. As an example, here are my contact details, marked up in the hCard format.

```
<div class="vcard">
  <p><a class="url fn" href="http://andybudd.com/">Andy Budd</a>
    <span class="org">Clearleft Ltd</span>
    <a class="email" href="mailto:info@andybudd.com">info@andybudd.com</a>↵
  </p>
  <p class="adr">
    <span class="locality">Brighton</span>,
    <span class="country-name">England</span>
  </p>
</div>
```

Microformats allow you to mark up data in a way that makes it accessible to other programs and services. Some people have written scripts that can extract event information marked up in hCalendar format and import it directly into a calendar application (see Figures 1-5 and 1-6).

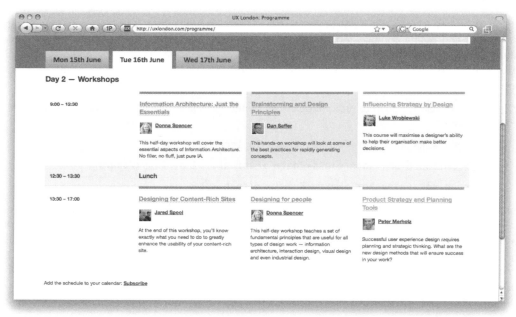

Figure 1-5. The schedule for the UX London conference is marked up in hCalendar format.

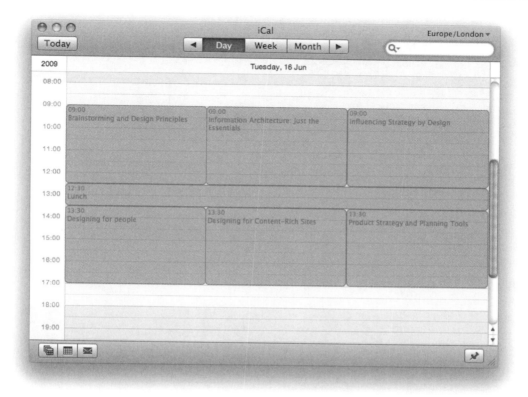

Figure 1-6. This means that visitors can add the whole schedule to their calendar application at the click of a button.

Other people have written plug-ins that allow Firefox to extract contact information marked up in hCard format and send it to your mobile phone via Bluetooth (see Figure 1-7 and 1-8).

Figure 1-7. The contact details on the Clearleft website are also marked up in hCard format.

Figure 1-8. Using Operator or the older Tails add-on in Firefox, you can import these contact details directly into your address book.

There are currently 9 official microformats, along with a further 14 draft formats. These include

- hCalendar for dates, calendars and events

- hCard for people and organizations

- XFN for relationships between people

- hProduct for product descriptions (draft)

- hRecipe for ingredients and cooking instructions (draft)

- hReview for product and event reviews (draft)

- hAtom for episodic content like blog posts (draft)

Many large websites already support microformats. For instance, Google Maps uses the hCard format for address information on its map search results. Similarly, Yahoo! supports microformats on a number of properties including the popular Flickr photo-sharing site. In fact, Yahoo! released 26 million microformats into the wild when they used the hListing format in their Kelkoo shopping search engine. It's extremely easy to add microformatted data to your website, so it's something I recommend doing wherever possible.

We're only just scratching the surface with what can be achieved with microformats. If you want to learn more, check out "Microformats: Empowering Your Mark-up for Web 2.0" by John Allsopp. Alternatively head over to http://microformats.org to view the official specifications.

Different versions of HTML and CSS

CSS comes in various versions, or levels, so it's important to know which version to use. CSS 1 became a recommendation at the end of 1996 and contains very basic properties such as fonts, colors, and margins. CSS 2 was released in 1998 and added advanced concepts such as floating and positioning to the mix, as well as new selectors like the child, adjacent sibling, and universal selectors.

Time moves very slowly at the World Wide Web Consortium (W3C), so while work on CSS 3 started before the turn of the millennium, the final release is still some way off. To help speed development and browser implementation, CSS 3 has been broken down into modules that can be released and implemented independently. CSS 3 contains some exciting new additions, including an advanced layout module, brand new background properties, and a host of new selectors. Some of these modules are scheduled for release as soon as the second half of 2009. Sadly, we've been here before, and several modules have been on the verge of release only to be pushed back into "last call" or "working draft" status, so it's difficult to know how many will actually make the grade. Hopefully, by 2011, we'll see a number of these modules become official recommendations. More worryingly, some modules don't appear to have been started, while others haven't been updated for several years. Due to this glacial pace of development, it seems unlikely the CSS 3 will ever be fully complete.

The good news is that, despite the numerous delays, many browser vendors have already implemented some of the more interesting parts of the CSS 3 specification. As such, it is possible to start using many of these exciting selectors today,

Because of the expected length of time between the release of CSS 2 and CSS 3, work started in 2002 on CSS 2.1. This revision of CSS 2 intends to fix some errors and provide a much more accurate picture of CSS browser implementation. CSS 2.1 is slowly nearing completion and is thus the recommended version of CSS to use.

HTML 4.01 became a recommendation at the end of 1999 and is the version of HTML that most people use. In January 2000 the W3C created an XML version of HTML 4.01 and named it XHTML 1.0. The main difference between XHTML 1.0 and HTML 4.01 is that it follows the XML coding conventions. This means that, unlike in regular HTML, all XHTML attributes must contain quote marks, and all elements must be closed. So while the following code is legitimate in HTML, it's not in XHTML:

```
<h2>Peru Celebrates Guinea Pig festival

    <p><img src=pigonastick.jpg alt=Roast Guinea Pig>

    <p>Guinea pigs can be fried, roasted, or served in a casserole.
```

Instead, in XHTML 1.0 it would have to be written link this.

```
<h2>Peru Celebrates Guinea Pig festival</h2>

    <p><img src="pigonastick.jpg" alt="Roast Guinea Pig" /></p>

    <p>Guinea pigs can be fried, roasted, or served in a casserole.</p>
```

XHTML 1.1 was an attempt to take XHTML even closer to XML. There was very little practical difference between the two languages. However there was one big theoretical difference. While it was still considered acceptable to serve up an XHTML 1.0 page as an HTML document, XHTML 1.1 pages were supposed to be sent to the browsers as if they were XML. This meant that if your XHTML 1.1 page contained a single error, such as an unencoded ampersand, web browsers weren't supposed to display the page. This obviously isn't ideal for most website owners, so XHTML 1.1 never really took off.

There is still some debate as to whether you should serve up an XHTML 1.0 pages as if it were HTML or if you're better sticking with HTML 4.01. However, it's clear that you shouldn't be using XHTML 1.1 unless you're using the correct mime type and are happy for your page not to display if it contains an error.

HTML 5 is relatively new, and as a draft specification is changing all the time. However, it has a lot of momentum and several popular browsers have already started building in support. HTML 5 grew out the frustration developers had with the slow and archaic development of XHTML 2. So a group of them decided to draft their own specification. This proved so successful that HTML 5 became an official W3C project, and the development of XHTML 2 was sidelined.

As mentioned previously, the goal of HTML5 was to produce a modern markup language that better reflected the type of information being published on the web. So it introduces new structural elements like header, nav, article, sections and footer. It also contains a host of new form additions that should make building web applications a lot easier.

Document types, DOCTYPE switching, and browser modes

A document type definition (DTD) is a set of machine-readable rules that define what is and isn't allowed in a particular version of HTML or XML. Browsers are supposed to use these rules when parsing a web page to check the validity of the page and act accordingly. Browsers know which DTD to use, and hence which version of HTML you are using, by analyzing the page's DOCTYPE declaration.

A DOCTYPE declaration is a line or two of code at the start of your HTML document that describes the particular DTD being used. In this example, the DTD being used is for XHTML 1.0 Strict:

```
<!DOCTYPE html PUBLIC "-//W3C//DTD XHTML 1.0 Strict//EN"
"http://www.w3.org/TR/xhtml1/DTD/xhtml1-strict.dtd">
```

DOCTYPE declarations will typically, but not always, contain a URL to the specified DTD file. So HTML5, for instance, doesn't require a URL. Browsers tend to not read these files, choosing instead to recognize common DOCTYPE declarations.

DOCTYPEs currently come in two flavors, strict and transitional. As the name suggests, transitional DOCTYPEs are aimed at people transitioning from older versions of the language. As such, the transitional versions of HTML 4.01 and XHTML 1.0 still allow the use of deprecated elements like the font element. The strict versions of these languages ban the use of deprecated elements to separate content from presentation.

Validation

As well as being semantically marked up, an HTML document needs to be written using valid code. If the code is invalid, browsers will try to interpret the markup themselves, sometimes getting it wrong. Worse still, if an XHTML document is being sent with the correct MIME type, browsers that understand XML simply won't display an invalid page. Because browsers need to know which DTD to use in order to process the page correctly, a DOCTYPE declaration is required for the page to validate.

You can check to see if your HTML is valid by using the W3C validator, a validator bookmarklet, or a plug-in like the Firefox Web Developer Extension. Many HTML editors now have validators built in, and you can even install a copy of the W3C validator locally on your computer. The validator will tell you if your page validates, and if not, why not (see Figure 1-9).

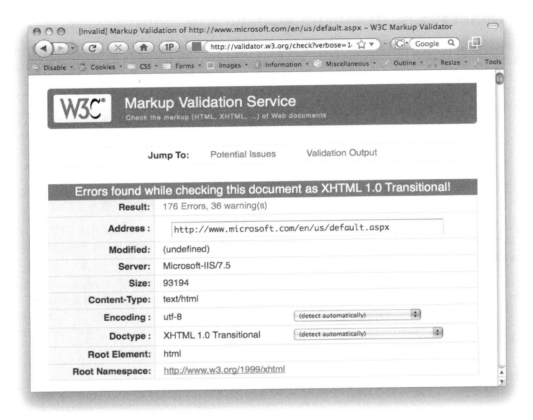

Figure 1-9. The microsoft.com homepage contains 176 HTML errors and 36 CSS errors.

Validation is important because it can help you track down bugs in your code. As such, it is a good idea to get into the habit of validating early and often. However, validation isn't an end unto itself, and many otherwise good pages fail to validate due to small errors such as unencoded ampersands, or because of legacy content. So although validation is important, in the real world, a degree of common sense is required.

> *Various code validation tools are available. You can validate your site online by going to http://validator.w3.org/ and entering your URL. However, if you are going to validate often—which is a good idea—typing your URL each time can become a little tedious. Instead, I use a handy validation bookmarklet, or favelet, which is a small piece of JavaScript that can be stored in the bookmarks or favorites folder in your browser. Clicking the bookmark will trigger the JavaScript action. In the case of the validator bookmarklet, it runs the page you are currently on through the W3C validator and displays the results. You can find the validator bookmarklet along with many other handy web development bookmarklets from http://favelets.com/.*
>
> *If you use Firefox, you can download and install a wide variety of plug-ins. Among the numerous validator plug-ins available, my personal favorite is the Web Developers Extension plug-in. As well as allowing you to validate your HTML and CSS, it enables you to do a wide variety of other useful tasks like outlining various HTML elements, turning off stylesheets, and even editing styles in the browser. The Firefox Web Developer Extension can be downloaded from http://chrispederick.com/work/web-developer/ and is a must-have for any CSS developer using Firefox. Another great tool is the Firefox Validator Extension, which you can download from http://users.skynet.be/mgueury/mozilla/.*
>
> *There is also a developer toolbar for Internet Explorer 6 and 7, which can be downloaded from http://tinyurl.com/7mnyh. Although it is not as feature rich as the Firefox toolbar, it is still extremely useful. Internet Explorer 8 includes its own set of developer tools built directly into the browser, as does Safari 4.*

As well as being important for validation, browsers use DOCTYPE declarations for another purpose.

Browser modes

When browser manufacturers started to create standards-compliant browsers, they wanted to ensure backward compatibility. To accomplish this, they created two rendering modes: standards mode and quirks mode. In standards mode, the browser renders a page according to the specifications, and in quirks mode pages are displayed in a looser, more backward-compatible fashion. Quirks mode typically emulates the behavior of older browsers such as Microsoft Internet Explorer 4 and Netscape Navigator 4 to prevent older sites from breaking.

The most obvious example of the difference between these modes revolves around the Internet Explorer (IE) on Windows proprietary box model. When Internet Explorer 6 debuted, the correct box model was used in standards mode, while the older, proprietary box model was used in quirks mode. To maintain backward compatibility with sites built for IE 5 and below, Opera 7 and above also uses IE's faulty box model in quirks mode.

Other differences in rendering are subtler and specific to certain browsers. However, they include things like not requiring the # symbol for hex color values, assuming lengths without units in CSS are pixels, and increasing the font size by one step when using keywords.

Mozilla and Safari have a third mode called "almost standards mode," which is the same as standards mode, except for some subtle differences in the way tables are handled.

You can tell what mode a page is rendering in by using the Web Developer Extension in Firefox. A green tick will be displayed in the toolbar if the site is rendering in standards mode, while a red cross shows that the page is being rendered in quirks mode. The development tools in Internet Explorer 8 also show which mode the browser is rendering in.

DOCTYPE switching

The browser chooses which rendering method to use based on the existence of a DOCTYPE declaration and the DTD being used. If an XHTML document contains a fully formed DOCTYPE, it will normally be rendered in standards mode. For an HTML 4.01 document, a DOCTYPE containing a strict DTD will usually cause the page to render in standards mode. A DOCTYPE containing a transitional DTD and URI will also cause the page to render in standards mode, while a transitional DTD without a URI will cause the page to render in quirks mode. A badly formed or nonexistent DOCTYPE will cause both HTML and XHTML documents to be rendered in quirks mode.

The effect of choosing a rendering mode based on the existence of a DOCTYPE is known as *DOCTYPE switching*, or *DOCTYPE sniffing*. Not all browsers follow these exact rules, but they give you a good idea of how DOCTYPE switching works. For a more complete list, the chart at http://hsivonen.iki.fi/doctype/ shows the various rendering modes different browsers use depending on the DOCTYPE declaration in use.

DOCTYPE switching is a hack used by browsers to distinguish legacy documents from more standards-compliant ones. Despite writing valid CSS, if you choose the wrong DOCTYPE, your pages will be rendered in quirks mode and behave in a buggy and unpredictable way. As such, it is important to include a fully formed DOCTYPE declaration on every page of your site and choose a strict DTD when using HTML.

```
<!DOCTYPE HTML PUBLIC "-//W3C//DTD HTML 4.01//EN"
    "http://www.w3.org/TR/html4/strict.dtd">


<!DOCTYPE html PUBLIC "-//W3C//DTD XHTML 1.0 Strict//EN"
    "http://www.w3.org/TR/xhtml1/DTD/xhtml1-strict.dtd">


<!DOCTYPE html>
```

Many HTML editors will automatically add a DOCTYPE declaration for you. If you are creating an XHTML document some older editors may also add an XML declaration before the DOCTYPE declaration:

```
<?xml version="1.0" encoding="utf-8"?>
```

An XML declaration is an optional declaration used by XML files to define things such as the version of XML being used and the type of character encoding. Unfortunately, IE 6 automatically switches to quirks mode if the DOCTYPE declaration is not the first element on a page. This was fixed in IE 7, but unless you are serving your pages as XML documents, it is best to avoid using an XML declaration.

Summary

In this chapter, you learned all about how semantic naming conventions and meaningful markup can make your code easier to read and maintain. You also learned the difference between IDs and class names and which ones to use when. You know about the different versions of CSS and HTML available and how the browsers decide how to handle those differences.

In the next chapter, you will recap some of the basic CSS selectors as well as learn about a host of new CSS 3 selectors. You will learn all about specificity and the cascade, as well as how to organize and plan your style sheets for easy maintenance.

Chapter 2

Getting Your Styles to Hit the Target

A valid and well-structured document provides the foundations to which your styles are applied. To be able to style a particular HTML element using CSS, you need to have some way of targeting that element. In CSS the part of a style rule that does this is called the *selector*.

In this chapter, you will learn about

- Common selectors
- Advanced selectors
- New CSS 3 selectors
- The wonderful world of specificity and the cascade
- Planning and maintaining your style sheets
- How to comment your code

Common selectors

The most common kinds of selectors are type and descendant selectors. Type selectors are used to target a particular type of element, such as a paragraph or a heading element. You do this by simply specifying the name of the element you wish to style. Type selectors are sometimes also referred to as *element* or *simple* selectors.

```
p {color: black;}
h1 {font-weight: bold;}
```

Descendant selectors allow you to target the descendants of a particular element or group of elements. A descendant selector is indicated by a space between two other selectors. In this example, only paragraph elements that are descendants of a blockquote will be indented, while all other paragraphs will remain unchanged.

```
blockquote p {padding-left: 2em;}
```

These two types of selector are great for applying generic styles that apply across the board. To be more specific and target selected elements, you can use ID and class selectors. As the names suggest, these selectors will target elements with the corresponding ID or class name. ID selectors are identified using a hash character; class selectors are identified with a period. The first rule in this example will make the text in the introductory paragraph bold, and the second rule will make the date grey:

```
#intro {font-weight: bold;}
.date-posted {color: #ccc;}
```

```
<p id="intro">Happy Birthday Andy</p>
<p class="date-posted">24/3/2009</p>
```

As I mentioned previously, many CSS authors develop an overreliance on class and ID selectors. If they want to style headlines one way in the main content area and another way in the secondary content area, there is the tendency to create two classes and apply a class to each headline. A much simpler approach is to use a combination of type, descendant, ID, and/or class selectors:

```
#main-content h2 {font-size: 1.8em;}
#secondaryContent h2 {font-size: 1.2em;}
```

```
<div id="main-content">
  <h2>Articles</h2>

    ...

</div>
<div id="secondary-content">
  <h2>Latest news</h2>

    ...

</div>
```

This is a very simple and obvious example. However, you will be surprised how many elements you can successfully target using just the four selectors discussed so far. If you find yourself adding lots of extraneous classes to your document, it is probably a warning sign that your document is not well structured. Instead, think about how these elements differ from each other. Often, you will find that the only difference is where they appear on the page. Rather than give these elements different classes, think about applying a class or an ID to one of their ancestors, and then targeting them using a descendant selector.

Pseudo-classes

There are instances where you may want to style an element based on something other than the structure of the document—for instance, the state of a link or form element. This can be done using a pseudo-class selector.

```
/* makes all unvisited links blue */
a:link {color:blue;}
```

```
/* makes all visited links green */
a:visited {color:green;}
```

```
/* makes links red when hovered or activated.
focus is added for keyboard support */
a:hover, a:focus, a:active {color:red;}
```

```
/* makes table rows red when hovered over */
tr:hover {background-color: red;}
```

```
/* makes input elements yellow when focus is applied */
input:focus {background-color:yellow;}
```

:link and :visited are known as *link* pseudo-classes and can only be applied to anchor elements. :hover, :active, and :focus are known as *dynamic* pseudo-classes and can theoretically be applied to any element. Most modern browsers support this functionality. Unsurprisingly, IE 6 only pays attention to the :active and :hover pseudo-classes when applied to an anchor link, and ignores :focus completely. IE7 supports :hover on arbitrary elements but ignores :active and :focus.

Last, it's worth pointing out that pseudo-classes can be strung together to create more complex behaviors, such as styling the hover effect on visited links different from those on unvisited links.

```
/* makes all visited linkes olive on hover */
a:visited:hover {color:olive;}
```

The universal selector

The universal selector is possibly one of the most powerful and least used of all the selectors. The universal selector acts like a wild card, matching all the available elements. Like wild cards in other languages, the universal selector is denoted by an asterisk. The universal selector is often used to style every element on a page. For instance, you can remove the default browser padding and margin on every element using the following rule:

```
* {
  padding: 0;
  margin: 0;
}
```

When combined with other selectors, the universal selector can be used to style all the descendants of a particular element or skip a level of descendants. You will see how this can be put to practical effect a little later in this chapter.

Advanced selectors

CSS 2.1 and CSS 3 have a number of other useful selectors. Unfortunately, while most modern browsers support these advanced selectors, older browsers like IE 6 do not. Luckily, CSS was created with backward compatibility in mind. If a browser doesn't understand a selector, it ignores the whole rule. That way, you can apply stylistic and usability embellishments in more modern browsers and not worry about it causing problems in older browsers. Just remember to avoid using these more advanced selectors for anything critical to the function or layout of your site.

Child and adjacent sibling selectors

The first of these advanced selectors is the child selector. Whereas a descendant selector will select all the descendants of an element, a child selector only targets the element's immediate descendants, or *children*. In the following example, the list items in the outer list will be given a custom icon while list items in the nested list will remain unaffected (see Figure 2-1):

```
#nav>li {
  background: url(folder.png) no-repeat left top;
  padding-left: 20px;
}

<ul id="nav">
  <li><a href="/home/">Home</a></li>
  <li><a href="/services/">Services</a>
    <ul>
      <li><a href="/services/design/">Design</a></li>
      <li><a href="/services/development/">Development</a></li>
      <li><a href="/services/consultancy/">Consultancy</a></li>
    </ul>
  </li>
  <li><a href="/contact/">Contact Us</a></li>
</ul>
```

Figure 2-1. The child selector styles the children of the list but not its grandchildren.

The child selector is supported by IE 7 and above. However, there is a small bug in IE 7 that causes problems if there are HTML comments between the parent and child.

It is possible to fake a child selector that works in IE 6 and below by using the universal selector. To do this, you first apply to all of the descendants the style you want the children to have. You then use the universal selector to override these styles on the children's descendants. So to fake the previous child selector example you would do this:

```
#nav li {
  background: url(folder.png) no-repeat left top;
  badding-left: 20px;
}

#nav li * {
  background-image: none;
  padding-left: 0;
}
```

Sometimes, you may want to style an element based on its proximity to another element. The adjacent sibling selector allows you to target an element that is preceded by another element that shares the same parent. Using the sibling selector, you could make the first paragraph following a top-level heading bold, gray, and slightly larger than the subsequent paragraphs (see Figure 2-2):

```
h2 + p {
  font-size: 1.4em;
  font-weight: bold;
  color: #777;
}
<h2>Peru Celebrates Guinea Pig festival</h2>
  <p>The guinea pig festival in Peru is a one day event to celebrate
these cute local animals. The festival included a fashion show where
animals are dressed up in various amusing costumes.</p>
  <p>Guinea pigs can be fried, roasted, or served in a casserole. Around
65 million guinea pigs are eaten in Peru each year.</p>
```

Peru Celebrates Guinea Pig festival

The guinea pig festival in Peru is a one day event to celebrate these cute local animals. The festival included a fashon show where animals are dressed up in various amusing costumes.

Guinea pigs can be fried, roasted or served in a casserole. Around 65 million guinea pigs are eaten in Peru each year.

Figure 2-2. The adjacent sibling selector can be used to style the first paragraph after a headline, allowing you to do away with extraneous classes.

As with the child selector, this fails in IE 7 if comments appear between the elements you are targeting.

Attribute selectors

As the name suggests, the attribute selector allows you to target an element based on the existence of an attribute or the attribute's value. This allows you to do some very interesting and powerful things.

For example, when you hover over an element with a `title` attribute, most browsers will display a tooltip. You can use this behavior to expand the meaning of things such as acronyms and abbreviations:

```
<p>The term <acronym title="self-contained underwater breathing↵
apparatus">SCUBA</acronym> is an acronym rather than an abbreviation↵
as it is pronounced as a word.</p>
```

However, there is no way to tell that this extra information exists without hovering over the element. To get around this problem, you can use the attribute selector to style `acronym` elements with titles differently from other elements—in this case, by giving them a dotted bottom border. You can provide more contextual information by changing the cursor from a pointer to a question mark when the cursor hovers over the element, indicating that this element is different from most.

```
acronym[title] {
   border-bottom: 1px dotted #999;
}


acronym[title]:hover, acronym[title]:focus {
   cursor: help;
}
```

In addition to styling an element based on the existence of an attribute, you can apply styles based on a particular value. For instance, sites that are linked to using a `rel` attribute of `nofollow` gain no added ranking benefit from Google. The following rule displays an image next to such links, possibly as a way of showing disapproval of the target site:

```
a[rel="nofollow"] {
   background: url(nofollow.gif) no-repeat right center;
   padding-right: 20px;
}
```

All modern browsers including IE 7 support these selectors. However, because IE 6 doesn't support attribute selectors, you could potentially use them to apply one style to IE 6 and a different style to more capable browsers. For instance, Andy Clarke makes use of this technique by presenting black and white version of his site to IE 6 (see Figure 2-3) and a color one to all other browsers (see Figure 2-4).

Figure 2-3. Andy Clarke serves up a black and white version of his site to IE 6 using attribute selectors, among other techniques.

Figure 2-4. More modern browsers get a color version.

```
#header {
  background: url(branding-bw.png) repeat-y left top;
}
[id="header"] {
  background: url(branding-color.png) repeat-y left top;
}
```

Some attributes can have more than one value, separated by spaces. The attribute selector allows you to target an element based on one of those values. For instance, the XFN microformat allows you to define the relationship you have with a site by adding keywords to the rel attribute of an anchor link. So I can say that a particular site belongs to a work colleague of mine by adding the co-worker keyword to the links in my blogroll. I can then show readers that I work with that person by displaying a particular icon next to that co-worker's name.

```
.blogroll a[rel~="co-worker"] {
  background: url(co-worker.gif) no-repeat left center;
}


<ul class="blogroll">
  <li>
  <a href="http://adactio.com/" rel="friend met colleague co-worker">↵
Jeremy Keith</a>
  </li>
  <li>
  <a href="http://clagnut.com/" rel="friend met colleague co-worker">↵
Richard Rutter</a>
  </li>
  <li>
  <a href="http://hicksdesign.com/" rel="friend met colleague">↵
John Hicks</a>
  </li>
  <li>
  <a href="http:// stuffandnonsense.co.uk/" rel="friend met colleague">↵
Andy Clarke</a>
  </li>
```

```
</ul>
```

The cascade and specificity

With even a moderately complicated style sheet, it is likely that two or more rules will target the same element. CSS handles such conflicts through a process known as the *cascade*. The cascade works by assigning an importance to each rule. Author style sheets are those written by the site developers and are considered the most important. Users can apply their own styles via the browser and these are considered the next most important. Finally, the default style sheets used by your browser or user agent are given the least importance so you can always override them. To give users more control, they can override any rule by specifying it as !important even a rule flagged as !important by the author. This is to allow for specific accessibility needs such as using a medium contrast user style sheet if you have a certain forms of dyslexia.

So the cascade works in the following order of importance:

- User styles flagged as !important
- Author styles flagged as !important
- Author styles
- User styles
- Styles applied by the browser/user agent

Rules are then ordered by how specific the selector is. Rules with more specific selectors override those with less specific ones. If two rules are equally specific, the last one defined takes precedence.

Specificity

To calculate how specific a rule is, each type of selector is assigned a numeric value. The specificity of a rule is then calculated by adding up the value of each of its selectors. Unfortunately, specificity is not calculated in base 10 but a high, unspecified, base number. This is to ensure that a highly specific selector, such as an ID selector, is never overridden by lots of less specific selectors, such as type selectors. However, if you have fewer than 10 selectors in a specific selector, you can calculate specificity in base 10 for simplicity's sake.

The specificity of a selector is broken down into four constituent levels: a, b, c, and d.

- If the style is an inline style, a equals 1.
- b equals the total number of ID selectors.
- c equals the number of class, pseudo-class, and attribute selectors.
- d equals the number of type selectors and pseudo-element selectors.

Using these rules, it is possible to calculate the specificity of any CSS selector. Table 2-1 shows a series of selectors, along with their associated specificity.

Table 2-1. Specificity examples

Selector	Specificity	Specificity in Base 10
Style=""	1,0,0,0	1000
#wrapper #content {}	0,2,0,0	200
#content .datePosted {}	0,1,1,0	110
div#content {}	0,1,0,1	101
#content {}	0,1,0,0	100
p.comment .dateposted {}	0,0,2,1	21
p.comment{}	0,0,1,1	11
div p {}	0,0,0,2	2
p {}	0,0,0,1	1

At first glance, all this talk of specificity and high but undefined based numbers may seem a little confusing, so here's what you need to know. Essentially, a rule written in a style attribute will always be more specific than any other rule. A rule with an ID will be more specific than one without an ID, and a rule with a class selector will be more specific than a rule with just type selectors. Finally, if two rules have the same specificity, the last one defined prevails.

Specificity can be extremely important when fixing bugs, as you need to know which rules take precedence and why. For instance, say you had this set of rules. What color do you think the two headlines will be?

```
#content div#main-content h2 {
  color: gray;
}
#content #main-content>h2 {
  color: blue;
}
body #content div[id="main-content"] h2 {
  color: green;
}
#main-content div.news-story h2 {
  color: orange;
}
```

```
#main-content [class="news-story"] h2 {
  color: yellow;
}
div#main-content div.news-story h2.first {
  color: red;
}


<div id="content">
 <div id="main-content">
    <h2>Strange Times</h2>
      <p>Here you can read bizarre news stories from around the globe.</p>
    <div class="news-story">
      <h2 class="first">Bog Snorkeling Champion Announced Today</h2>
        <p>The 2008 Bog Snorkeling Championship was won by Conor Murphy↵
        with an impressive time of 1 minute 38 seconds.</p>
    </div>
  </div>
</div>
```

The answer, surprisingly, is that both headlines are gray. The first selector has the highest specificity because it's made up of two ID selectors. Some of the later selectors may look more complicated, but as they only contain one ID, they will always lose out against the more specific selectors.

If you ever come across a CSS rule that just doesn't seem to be working, you could be suffering from a specificity clash. Try making your selectors more specific by adding the ID of one of its parents. If that fixes the problem, you'll probably find that there is a more specific rule somewhere in your style sheet overriding what you're trying to do. If that's the case, you'll probably want to go back through your code and clean up the specificity clashes to keep your code as lean as possible.

Using specificity in your style sheets

Specificity is very useful when writing CSS, as it allows you to set general styles for common elements and then override them for more specific elements. For instance, say you want most of the text on your site black, except for your intro text, which you want gray. You could do something like this:

```
p {color: black;}
p.intro  {color: grey;}
```

This is fine for smaller sites. However, on larger sites you will find more and more exceptions will start to creep in. Maybe you want to have the introductory text on your news stories blue and the introductory text on your home page on a gray background. Each time you create a more specific style, you will probably need to override some of the general rules. This can lead to quite a bit of extra code. It can also start to get very complicated, as one element may be picking up styles from a variety of places.

To avoid too much confusion, I try to make sure my general styles are very general while my specific styles are as specific as possible and never need to be overridden. If I find that I have to override general styles several times, it's simpler to remove the declaration that needs to be overridden from the more general rules and apply it explicitly to each element that needs it.

Adding a class or an ID to the body tag

One interesting way to use specificity is to apply a class or an ID to the body tag. By doing this, you can then override styles on a page-by-page or even a site-wide basis. For instance, if you wanted all your news pages to have a specific layout, you could add a class name to the body element and use it to target your styles:

```
body.news {
    /* do some stuff */
}


<body class="news">
    <p>My, what a lovely body you have.</p>
</body>
```

Sometimes, you'll need to override these styles on a particular page, such as your news archive page. In this case, you can add an ID to the body tag to target that specific page.

```
body.news {
    /* do some stuff */
}


body#archive {
    /* do some different stuff */
}


<body id="archive" class="news">
    <p>My, what a lovely body you have.</p>
</body>
```

Using a class for the type of page and an ID for the specific page gives you a huge amount of control over the design and layout of your site. As such, this is one of my favorite techniques for writing maintainable code.

Inheritance

People often confuse inheritance with the cascade. Although they seem related at first glance, the two concepts are actually quite different. Luckily, inheritance is a much easier concept to grasp. Certain properties, such as color or font size, are inherited by the descendants of the elements those styles are applied to. For instance, if you were to give the body element a text color of black, all the descendants of the body element would also have black text. The same would be true of font sizes. If you gave the body a font size of 1.4 ems, everything on the page should inherit that font size. I say *should* because IE for Windows and Netscape have problems inheriting font sizes in tables. To get around this, you will either have to specify that tables should inherit font sizes or set the font size on tables separately.

If you set the font size on the body, you will notice that this style is not picked up by any headings on the page. You may assume that headings do not inherit text size. But it is actually the browser default style sheet setting the heading size. Any style applied directly to an element will always override an inherited style. This is because inherited styles have a null specificity.

Inheritance is very useful, as it lets you avoid having to add the same style to every descendant of an element. If the property you are trying to set is an inherited property, you may as well apply it to the parent element. After all, what is the point of writing this:

```
p, div, h1, h2, h3, ul, ol, dl, li {color: black;}
```

when you can just write this:

```
body {color: black;}
```

Just as sensible use of the cascade can help simplify your CSS, good use of inheritance can help to reduce the number and complexity of the selectors in your code. It you have lots of elements inheriting various styles, though, determining where the styles originate can become confusing.

Figure 2-5. Firebug is a handy add-on to Firefox that allows you to interrogate various elements to see where their rendered styles originate from.

Planning, organizing, and maintaining your style sheets

The larger, more complicated, and graphically rich your sites become, the harder your CSS is to manage. In this section, I will look at ways to help you manage your code, including grouping your styles into logical sections and adding comments to make your code easier to read.

Applying styles to your document

You can add styles directly to the head of a document by placing them between style tags; however, this is not a very sensible way to apply styles to a document. If you want to create another page using the same styles, you would have to duplicate the CSS on the new page. If you then wanted to change a style, you would have to do it in two places rather than one. Luckily, CSS allows us to keep all our styles in one or more external style sheets. There are two ways to attach external style sheets to a web page. You can link to them or you can import them:

```
<link href="/css/basic.css" rel="stylesheet" type="text/css" />
<style type="text/css">
<!--
@import url("/css/advanced.css");
-->
</style>
```

You do not have to confine importing to an HTML document. You can also import one style sheet from another style sheet. This allows you to link to your basic style sheet from the HTML page and then import your more complicated styles into that style sheet:

```
@import url(/css/layout.css);
@import url(/css/typography.css);
@import url(/css/color.css);
```

Breaking your CSS into multiple style sheets used to be a common approach and was the method I recommended in the first edition of this book. However, recent browser benchmarking has shown that importing style sheets can be slower than linking to them.

There are two other speed related problems when using multiple CSS files. First off, multiple files will result in more packets being sent from the server, and it's the number, rather than the contents, of these packets that affects download time. Furthermore, browsers are only able to download a limited number of concurrent files from the same domain at any one time. For older browsers, this limit used to be a paltry two files, although modern browsers have upped this to eight. So in an older browser, if you have three style sheets, you would have to wait for the first two files to download before it starts downloading the third. Because of these reasons, a single, well-structured CSS file can help improve download speeds considerably.

A single CSS file also allows you to keep all your code in one place. I used to recommend splitting up your code for easy maintenance. However, it was always difficult to decide if a specific declaration related to the layout or the typography of the site. Often, it could relate to both, and you'd end up making arbitrary decisions where to put them. This approach also meant having to keep multiple style sheets open and continually swapping between files. With features like code folding being built into most modern CSS editors, it's now much easier to edit a single page than it used to be. So for these reasons, I tend to prefer a single CSS file over several smaller ones. That being said, it really does depend on the site in question, so there are no hard and fast rules here.

When writing your own style sheets, you will have a good idea how they are structured, what problems you have encountered, and why things have been done a certain way. But if you come back to that style sheet in six months, there is a good chance you will have forgotten much of this. Additionally, you may need to hand your CSS to somebody else for implementation, or another developer may have to edit your code in the future. It is therefore a good idea to comment your code.

Adding comments in CSS is very simple. A CSS comment starts with /* and ends with */. This type of commenting is known as C-style commenting, as it is the type of comment used in the C programming language. Comments can be single or multiline and can appear anywhere within the code.

```css
/* Body Styles */
body {
  font-size: 67.5%; /* Set the font size */
}
```

If your CSS files become very long, finding the style you want can be difficult. One way to speed things up is to add a flag to each of your comment headers. A *flag* is simply an extra word preceding your header text that does not naturally appear in your CSS files. A search for your flag followed by the first couple of letters in your comment header will take you right to the part of the file you're looking for. So in this example, a search for "@group typ" will take you straight to the typography section of your style sheet:

```css
/* @group typography */
```

If you happen to use the OS X editor, CSS Edit, this format is used to create a simple yet effective means of navigating your style sheet.

Structuring your code

It is a good idea to break your style sheets down into sensible chucks for ease of maintenance. At Clearleft, we usually start with the most general styles first. These include styles that are applied to the body tag and should be inherited by everything on the site. Next are any global resets we may need, followed by links, headings, and other elements.

Once the general styles are covered, we start to get a little more specific and tackle our helper styles. These are general classes that are used across the site and include things like forms and error messages. We then move onto structural elements like layout and navigation.

As we move through the style sheet, we slowly layer styles on top of each other, getting more and more specific as we go. Now that the page furniture is out of the way, we turn our attention to page-specific components. Lastly we include any overrides and exceptions at the bottom of the document. The whole document structure ends up looking like this:

- General styles
  - Body styles
  - Resets
  - Links
  - Headings
  - Other elements

- Helper styles

    - Forms
    - Notifications and errors
    - Consistent items

- Page structure

    - Headers, footers, and navigation
    - Layout
    - Other page furniture

- Page components

    - Individual pages

- Overrides

I use a large, stylized comment block to visually separate each section.

```
/* @group general styles
---------------------------------------------------------------*/
```

```
/* @group helper styles
---------------------------------------------------------------*/
```

```
/* @group page structure
---------------------------------------------------------------*/
```

```
/* @group page components
---------------------------------------------------------------*/
```

```
/* @group overrides
---------------------------------------------------------------*/
```

Not everything naturally falls into a well-defined block, so some judgment is required. Keep in mind that the more you can break up and objectify your code, the easier it is to understand and the quicker you can find the rules you are looking for.

Because my style sheets tend to have a similar structure, I save time by creating my own precommented CSS templates to use on all my projects. You can save even more time by adding a few common rules that you use in all of your sites, to create a sort of prototype CSS file. That way, you will not have to reinvent the wheel each time you start a new project. A sample prototype CSS file can be found in the code download for this book at cssmastery.com

Note to self

With large, complicated projects, it is often useful to annotate your CSS files with temporary comments to aid development. These could be reminders of things you need to do before launch or look-up tables for common values such as column widths.

If there are a lot of colors in your design, you will probably find yourself constantly flicking back and forth between your graphics application and text editor to check hex values. This can be a pain at times so several people have suggested the need for CSS variables. While this is an interesting idea it would take CSS one step closer to a proper programming language and potentially alienate non-programmers. As such, I tend to use a low-fi approach instead. All I do is add a little color look-up table at the top of my style sheet so I can constantly refer to it during development. Once I'm finished developing the page, I'll usually strip this out.

```
/* Color Variables

@colordef #434343;  dark gray
@colordef #f2f6e4;  light green
@colordef #90b11f; dark green
@colordef #369; dark blue
*/
```

To make your comments more meaningful, you can use keywords to distinguish important comments. I use @todo as a reminder that something needs to be changed, fixed, or revisited later on, @bugfix to document a problem with the code or a particular browser, and @workaround to explain a nasty workaround:

```
/* :@todo Remember to remove this rule before the site goes live */
/* @workaround: I managed to fix this problem in IE by setting a small
negative margin but it's not pretty */
/* @bugfix: Rule breaks in IE 5.2 Mac  */
```

In programming terms, these keywords are called *gotchas* and can prove very helpful in the later stages of development. In fact, all these terms form part of a project known as CSSDoc (http://cssdoc.net) that aims to develop a standardized syntax for commenting your style sheets.

Removing comments and optimizing your style sheets

Comments can increase the size of your CSS files quite considerably. Therefore, you may want to strip comments from your live style sheets. Many HTML/CSS and text editors have a search-and-replace option, making it pretty easy to remove comments from your code. Alternatively, you could use one of several online CSS optimizers such as the one found at www.cssoptimiser.com Not only does an optimizer remove comments, but it also strips out whitespace, helping to shave off a few extra bytes from your code. If you do choose to strip comments from your live style sheets, remember to retain a commented version for your production environment. The best way of managing this process is to create a deployment script that strips comments automatically when you make your changes go live. However, as this is an advanced technique, it's probably best left to fairly large, sophisticated sites.

Instead, the best way of reducing file size would be to enable server-side compression. If you are using an Apache server, talk to your hosts about installing mod_gzip or mod_deflate. All modern browsers can handle files compressed with GZIP, and decompress them on the fly. These Apache modules will detect whether your browser can handle such files, and if it can, send a compressed version. Server-side compression can reduce your HTML and CSS files by around 80 percent, reducing your bandwidth and making your pages much faster to download. If you don't have access to these Apache modules, you still may be able to compress your files by following the tutorial found at http://tinyurl.com/8w9rp.

Style guides

Most websites will have more than one person working on them, and larger sites can involve several teams all working on different aspects of the site. It is possible that programmers, content managers, and other front-end developers may need to understand how elements of your code and design function. Therefore, it is a very good idea to create some form of style guide.

A style guide is a document, web page, or microsite that explains how the code and visual design of a site is pieced together. At its most basic level a style guide should outline the general design guidelines like the appropriate treatment for headlines and other typographic elements, how the grid structure works and what color pallet to use. A good style guide will also look at the treatment of repeating elements like articles, news items, and notifications to define how they should and shouldn't be implemented. More detailed style guides may even include information on coding standards like the version of XHTML/CSS used, the chosen accessibility level, browser support details, and general coding best practices (see Figure 2-6).

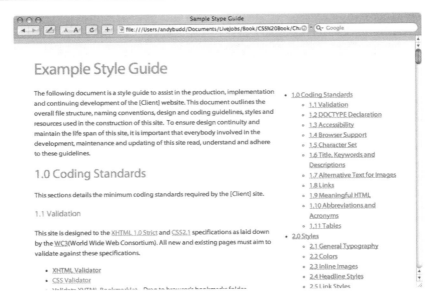

Figure 2-6. An example style guide

Style guides are a great way of handing a project over to those responsible for maintaining or implementing the site. By setting down some simple guidelines, you can help ensure the site develops in a controlled way, and help lessen the fragmentation of your styles over time. Style guides are also a great way of introducing new employees or contractors to an unfamiliar and potentially complicated system.

Unfortunately, keeping your style guide up-to-date can take a considerable amount of effort so they often go out of sync with the live site very quickly. Because of this we prefer to use a form of living style guide that we've called a "pattern portfolio" (see Figure 2-7).

A pattern portfolio is a page or series of pages that use the live style sheets to display every possible permutation and combination of styles on a site, from heading levels and text styles through to specific content and layout types. These pages can provide your back-end and front-end developers with an extremely valuable resource, allowing them to build page combinations that haven't even been conceived of yet. As they draw from the live styles, they can also act as a useful form of regression testing, allowing you to check that any changes to your CSS haven't caused and untoward problems.

Figure 2-7. An extract from the pattern portfolio of the WWF International site. The actual page is around five times the length and contains every typographic and layout permutation allowed on the site.

Summary

In this chapter, you have reacquainted yourself with the common CSS 2.1 selectors as well as learned about some powerful new CSS 3 selectors. You now have a better understanding of how specificity works and how you can use the cascade to structure your CSS rules and help them hit the target. You have also learned how to comment and structure your style sheets for maintainability.

In the next chapter, you will learn about the CSS box model, how and why margins collapse, and how floating and positioning really works.

Chapter 3

Visual Formatting Model Overview

Three of the most important CSS concepts to grasp are floating, positioning, and the box model. These concepts control the way elements are arranged and displayed on a page, forming the basis of CSS layout. If you are used to controlling layout with tables, these concepts may seem strange at first. In fact, most people will have been developing sites using CSS for some time before they fully grasp the intricacies of the box model, the difference between absolute and relative positioning, and how floating and clearing actually work. Once you have a firm grasp of these concepts, developing sites using CSS becomes that much easier.

In this chapter you will learn about

- The intricacies and peculiarities of the box model

- How and why margins collapse

- The difference between absolute and relative positioning

- How floating and clearing work

Box model recap

The box model is one of the cornerstones of CSS and dictates how elements are displayed and, to a certain extent, how they interact with each other. Every element on the page is considered to be a rectangular box made up of the element's content, padding, border, and margin (see Figure 3-1).

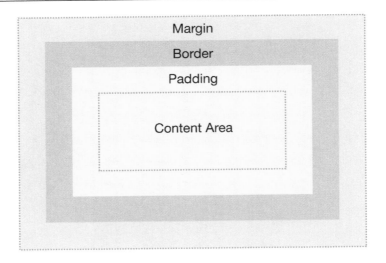

Figure 3-1. An illustration of the box model

Padding is applied around the content area. If you add a background to an element, it will be applied to the area formed by the content and padding. As such, padding is often used to create a gutter around content so that it does not appear flush to the side of the background. Adding a border applies a line to the outside of the padded area. These lines come in various styles such as solid, dashed, or dotted. Outside the border is a margin. Margins are transparent and cannot be seen. They are generally used to control the spacing between elements.

> *CSS 2.1 also contains the outline property. Unlike the border property, outlines are drawn over the top of an element's box, so they don't affect its size or positioning. Because of this, outlines can be useful when fixing bugs, because they won't alter the layout of your page. Outlines are supported by most modern browsers including IE 8 but are not supported in IE 7 and below.*

Padding, borders, and margins are optional and default to zero. However, many elements will be given margins and padding by the user-agent style sheet. You can override these browser styles by setting the element's `margin` or `padding` back to zero. You can do this on a case-by-case basis or for every element by using the universal selector:

```
* {
    margin: 0;
    padding: 0;
}
```

Just remember that this technique is fairly indiscriminant, so it can have adverse effects on elements like the option element. As such it's probably safer to zero down the padding and margins explicitly using a global reset.

In CSS, width and height refer to the width and height of the content area. Adding padding, borders, and margins will not affect the size of the content area but will increase the overall size of an element's box. If you wanted a box with a 10-pixel margin and a 5-pixel padding on each side to be 100 pixels wide, you would need to set the width of the content to be 70 pixels (see Figure 3-2):

```
#myBox {
    margin: 10px;
    padding: 5px;
    width: 70px;
}
```

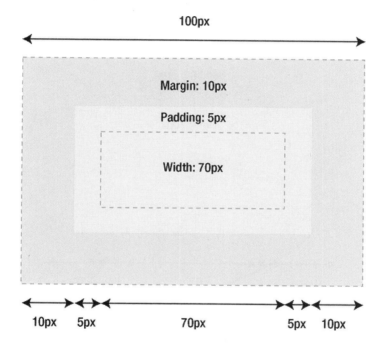

Figure 3-2. The correct box model

Padding, borders, and margins can be applied to all sides of an element or individual sides. Margins can also be given a negative value and can be used in a variety of techniques.

IE and the box model

Unfortunately, older versions of Internet Explorer, along with IE 6 in quirks mode, use their own, nonstandard box model. Instead of measuring just the width of the content, these browsers take the width property as the sum of the width of the content, padding, and borders. This actually makes a lot of sense, because in the real-world boxes have a fixed size, and the padding goes on the inside. The more padding you add, the less room there will be for the content. However, despite the logic, the fact that these versions of IE disregard the specification can cause significant problems. For instance, in the previous example the total width of the box would only be 90 pixels in IE 5.x. This is because IE 5.x will consider the 5 pixels of padding on each side as part of the 70-pixel width, rather than in addition to it (see Figure 3-3).

> The CSS 3 box-sizing property allows you to define which box model to use, although this feature is unlikely to be widely used except in some very specific circumstances.

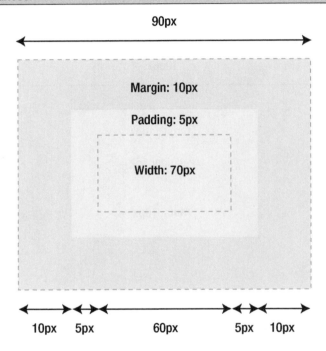

Figure 3-3. IE's proprietary box model can cause elements to be smaller than intended.

Luckily, there are several ways you can tackle this issue, the details of which can be found in Chapter 9. However, by far the best solution is to avoid the problem altogether. You can do this by never adding padding to an element with a defined width. Instead, try adding padding or margins to the element's parent or children.

Margin collapsing

Margin collapsing is a relatively simple concept. In practice, however, it can cause a lot of confusion when you're laying out a web page. Put simply, when two or more vertical margins meet, they will collapse to form a single margin. The height of this margin will equal the height of the larger of the two collapsed margins.

When two elements are above one another, the bottom margin of the first element will collapse with the top margin of the second element (see Figure 3-4).

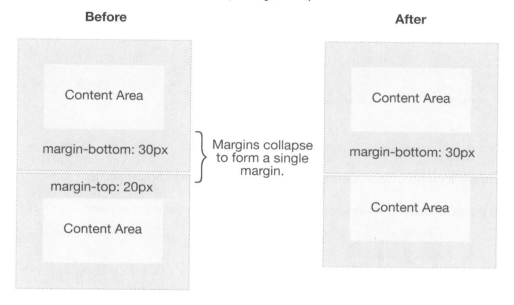

Figure 3-4. Example of an element's top margin collapsing with the bottom margin of the preceding element

When one element is contained within another element, assuming there is no padding or border separating margins, their top and/or bottom margins will also collapse together (see Figure 3-5).

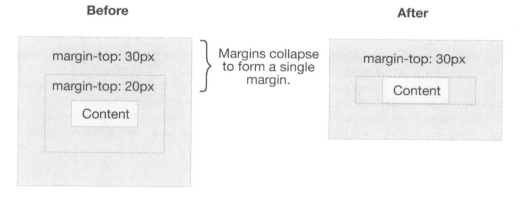

Figure 3-5. Example of an element's top margin collapsing with the top margin of its parent element

It may seem strange at first, but margins can even collapse on themselves. Say you have an empty element with a margin but no border or padding. In this situation, the top margin is touching the bottom margin, and they collapse together (see Figure 3-6).

Figure 3-6. Example of an element's top margin collapsing with its bottom margin

If this margin is touching the margin of another element, it will itself collapse (see Figure 3-7).

Figure 3-7. Example of an empty element's collapsed margin collapsing with another empty element's margins

This is why a series of empty paragraph elements take up very little space, as all their margins collapse together to form a single small margin.

Margin collapsing may seem strange at first, but it actually makes a lot of sense. Take a typical page of text made up of several paragraphs (see Figure 3-8). The space above the first paragraph will equal the paragraph's top margin. Without margin collapsing, the space between all subsequent paragraphs will be the sum of their two adjoining top and bottom margins. This means that the space between paragraphs will be double the space at the top of the page. With margin collapsing, the top and bottom margins between each paragraph collapse, leaving the spacing the same everywhere.

Without Margin Collapsing

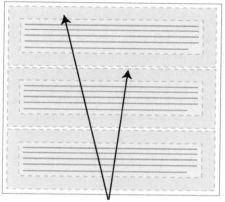

The space between paragraphs is double the space at the top.

With Margin Collapsing

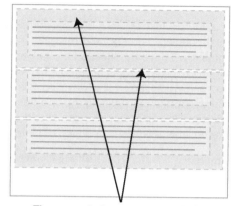

The space between paragraphs is the same as the space at the top.

Figure 3-8. Margins collapse to maintain consistent spacing between elements.

Margin collapsing only happens with the vertical margins of block boxes in the normal flow of the document. Margins between inline boxes, floated, or absolutely positioned boxes never collapse.

Positioning recap

Now that you are familiar with the box model, let's take a look at the visual formatting and positioning models. Understanding the nuances of both of these models is vitally important, as together they control how every element is arranged on a page.

The visual formatting model

People often refer to elements such as p, h1, or div as block-level elements. This means they are elements that are visually displayed as blocks of content, or *block boxes*. Conversely, elements such as strong and span are described as inline elements because their content is displayed within lines as *inline boxes*.

It is possible to change the type of box generated by using the display property. This means you can make an inline element such as an anchor behave like a block-level element by setting its display property to block. It is also possible to cause an element to generate no box at all by setting its display property to none. The box, and thus all of its content, is no longer displayed and takes up no space in the document.

There are three basic positioning schemes in CSS: normal flow, floats, and absolute positioning. Unless specified, all boxes start life being positioned in the normal flow. As the name suggests, the position of an element's box in the normal flow will be dictated by that element's position in the HTML.

Block-level boxes will appear vertically one after the other; the vertical distance between boxes is calculated by the boxes' vertical margins.

Inline boxes are laid out in a line horizontally. Their horizontal spacing can be adjusted using horizontal padding, borders, and margins (see Figure 3-9). However, vertical padding, borders, and margins will have no effect on the height of an inline box. Similarly, setting an explicit height or width on an inline box will have no effect either. The horizontal box formed by a line is called a *line box*, and a line box will always be tall enough for all the line boxes it contains. There is another caveat, though—setting the line height can increase the height of this box. Because of these reasons, the only way you can alter the dimensions of an inline box is by changing the line height or horizontal borders, padding, or margins.

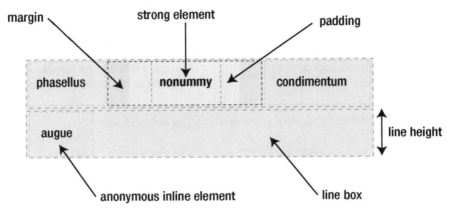

Figure 3-9. Inline elements within a line box

Helpfully, CSS2.1 allows you to set the display property of an element to be inline-block. As the name suggests, this declaration makes the element line up horizontally as if it were an inline element. However, the contents of the box behave as though the box were a block-level, including being able to explicitly set widths, heights, vertical margins, and padding. Historically, this property has been poorly supported; hence, it's relative obscurity. Thankfully, inline-block is now supported by Firefox 3.0 and above, IE 8, and the latest versions of Safari and Opera, so I think we are going to see inline-block being used to create more interesting layouts over the next few years.

In the same way that HTML elements can be nested, boxes can contain other boxes. Most boxes are formed from explicitly defined elements. However, there is one situation where a block-level element is created even if it has not been explicitly defined—when you add some text at the start of a block-level element like a div. Even though you have not defined the text as a block-level element, it is treated as such:

```
<div>
    some text
    <p>Some more text</p>
</div>
```

In this situation, the box is described as an anonymous block box, since it is not associated with a specifically defined element.

A similar thing happens with the lines of text inside a block-level element. Say you have a paragraph that contains three lines of text. Each line of text forms an anonymous line box. You cannot style anonymous block or line boxes directly, except through the use of the :first-line pseudo element, which obviously has limited use. However, it is useful to understand that everything you see on your screen creates some form of box.

Relative positioning

Relative positioning is a fairly easy concept to grasp. If you relatively position an element, it will stay exactly where it is. You can then shift the element relative to its starting point by setting a vertical or horizontal position. If you set the top position to be 20 pixels, the box will appear 20 pixels below the top of its original position. Setting the left position to 20 pixels will create a 20-pixel space on the left of the element, moving the element to the right (see Figure 3-10).

```
#myBox {
    position: relative;
    left: 20px;
    top: 20px;
}
```

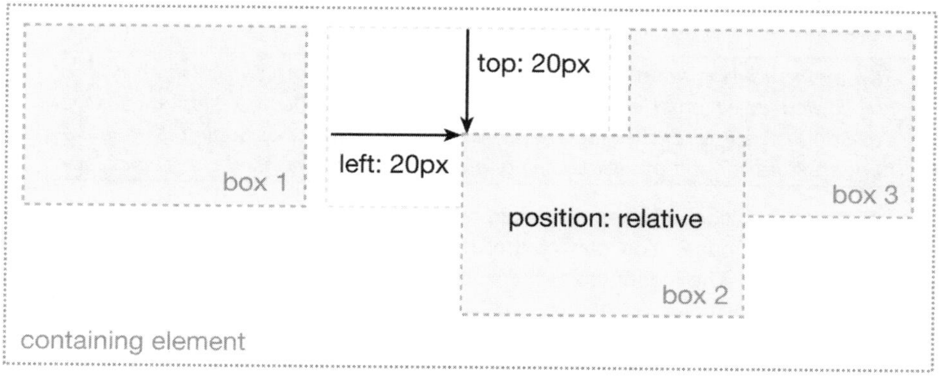

Figure 3-10. Relatively positioning an element

With relative positioning, the element continues to occupy the original space, whether or not it is offset. As such, offsetting the element can cause it to overlap other boxes.

Absolute positioning

Relative positioning is actually considered part of the normal flow-positioning model, as the position of the element is relative to its position in the normal flow. By contrast, absolute positioning takes the element out of the flow of the document, thus taking up no space. Other elements in the normal flow of the document will act as though the absolutely positioned element was never there (see Figure 3-11).

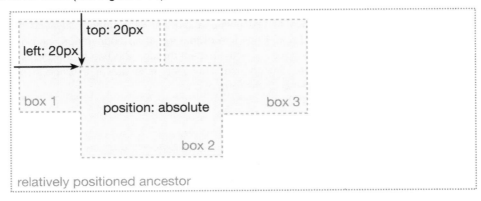

Figure 3-11. Absolutely positioning an element

An absolutely positioned element is positioned in relation to its nearest positioned ancestor. If the element has no positioned ancestors, it will be positioned in relation to the initial containing block. Depending on the user agent, this will either be the canvas or the HTML element.

As with relatively positioned boxes, an absolutely positioned box can be offset from the top, bottom, left, or right of its containing block. This gives you a great deal of flexibility. You can literally position an element anywhere on the page.

> *The main problem people have with positioning is remembering which type of positioning is which. Relative positioning is "relative" to the element's initial position in the flow of the document, whereas absolute positioning is "relative" to nearest positioned ancestor or, if one doesn't exist, the initial container block.*

Because absolutely positioned boxes are taken out of the flow of the document, they can overlap other elements on the page. You can control the stacking order of these boxes by setting a property called z-index. The higher the z-index, the higher up the box appears in the stack.

Positioning an absolutely positioned element in relation to its nearest positioned ancestor allows you to do some very interesting things. For instance, say you wanted to align a paragraph of text at the bottom right of a large box. You could simply give the container box a relative position and then absolutely position the paragraph in relation to this box:

```css
#branding {
  width: 70em;
  height: 10em;
  position: relative;
}


#branding .tel {
  position: absolute;
  right: 1em;
  bottom: 1em;
  text-align: right;
}
```

```html
<div id="branding">
    <p class="tel">Tel: 0845 838 6163</p>
</div>
```

> *Absolutely positioning a box in relation to a relatively positioned ancestor works well in most modern browsers. However, there is a bug in IE 5.5 and IE 6 on Windows. If you try to set the position of the absolutely positioned box relative to the right or bottom of the relatively positioned box, you need to make sure the relatively positioned box has some dimensions set. If not, IE will incorrectly position the box in relation to the canvas instead. You can read more about this bug and possible fixes in Chapter 9. The simple solution is to set the width and height of your relative box to avoid this problem.*

Absolute positioning can be a useful tool when laying out a page, especially if it is done using relatively positioned ancestors. It is entirely possible to create a design solely using absolute positioning. For this to work, these elements need to have fixed dimensions, so you can position them where you want without the risk of overlapping.

Because absolutely positioned elements are taken out of the flow of the document, they have no effect on boxes in the normal flow. If you were to enlarge an absolutely positioned box—by increasing the font size, for instance—the surrounding boxes wouldn't reflow. As such, any change in size can ruin your finely tuned layout by causing the absolutely positioned boxes to overlap.

Fixed positioning

Fixed positioning is a subcategory of absolute positioning. The difference is that a fixed element's containing block is the viewport. This allows you to create floating elements that always stay at the same position in the window. An example of this is shown at the old snook.ca website (see Figure 3-12). The weblog comment form has been given a fixed position to keep it anchored at the same place on screen when the page is scrolled. This really helps improve usability, and you don't have to scroll all the way to the bottom of the page to leave a comment.

Figure 3-12. At the old snook.ca website, the comment field on the right side of the screen used a fixed position to stay at the same position in the viewport.

Unfortunately, IE 6 and below do not support fixed positioning. IE 7 partially supports this property, but the implementation is fairly buggy. To get around these problems, Jonathan Snook used JavaScript to replicate the effect in IE.

Floating

The last visual formatting model is the float model. A floated box can either be shifted to the left or the right until its outer edge touches the edge of its containing box or another floated box. Because floated boxes aren't in the normal flow of the document, block boxes in the regular flow of the document behave as if the floated box wasn't there.

As shown in Figure 3-13, when you float Box 1 to the right, it's taken out of the flow of the document and moved to the right until its right edge touches the right edge of the containing block.

Figure 3-13. Example of an element being floated right

In Figure 3-14, when you float Box 1 to the left, it is taken out of the flow of the document and moved left until its left edge touches the left edge of the containing block. Because it is no longer in the flow, it takes up no space and actually sits on top of Box 2, obscuring it from view. If you float all three boxes to the left, Box 1 is shifted left until it touches its containing box, and the other two boxes are shifted left until they touch the preceding floated box.

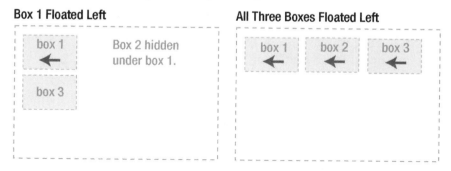

Figure 3-14. Example of elements being floated left

If the containing block is too narrow for all of the floated elements to fit horizontally, the remaining floats will drop down until there is sufficient space (see Figure 3-15). If the floated elements have different heights, it is possible for floats to get "stuck" on other floats when they drop down.

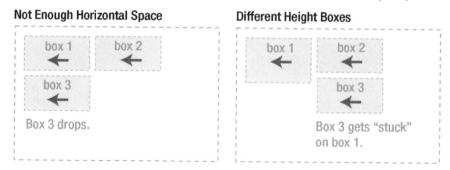

Figure 3-15. If there is not enough available horizontal space, floated elements will drop down until there is.

Line boxes and clearing

You learned in the previous section that floating an element takes it out of the flow of the document where it no longer exerts an effect on non-floated items. Actually, this isn't strictly true. If a floated element is followed by an element in the flow of the document, the element's box will behave as if the float didn't exist. However, the textural content of the box retains some memory of the floated element and moves out of the way to make room. In technical terms, a line box next to a floated element is shortened to make room for the floated element, thereby flowing around the floated box. In fact, floats were created to allow text to flow around images (see Figure 3-16).

No Boxes Floated

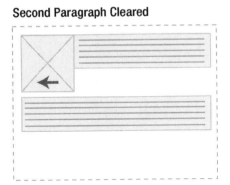

Image Floated Left

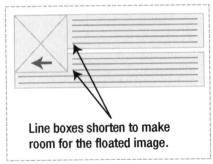

Line boxes shorten to make
room for the floated image.

Figure 3-16. Line boxes shorten when next to a float.

To stop line boxes flowing around the outside of a floated box, you need to apply a clear property to the element that contains those line boxes. The clear property can be left, right, both, or none, and it indicates which side of the box should not be next to a floated box. I always used to think that the clear property was some magic flag that automatically negated the previous float. However, the reality is much more interesting. When you clear an element, the browser adds enough margin to the top of the element to push the element's top border edge vertically down, past the float (see Figure 3-17).

Second Paragraph Cleared

Second Paragraph Cleared

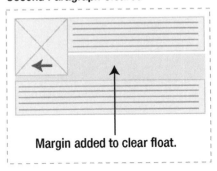

Margin added to clear float.

Figure 3-17. Clearing an element's top margin to create enough vertical space for the preceding float

As you've seen, floated elements are taken out of the flow of the document and have no effect on surrounding elements. However, clearing an element essentially clears a vertical space for all the preceding floated elements.

This can be a useful layout tool as it allows surrounding elements to make space for floated elements. This solves the problem you saw earlier with absolute positioning, where changes in vertical height do not affect surrounding elements and can break your design.

Let's have a look at floating and clearing in a little more detail. Say you have a picture that you want to float to the left of a block of text. You want this picture and text to be contained in another element with a background color and border. You would probably try something like this:

```css
.news {
  background-color: gray;
  border: solid 1px black;
}

.news img {
  float: left;
}

.news p {
  float: right;
}
```

```html
<div class="news">
    <img src="/img/news-pic.jpg" alt="my pic" />
    <p>Some text</p>
</div>
```

However, because the floated elements are taken out of the flow of the document, the wrapper div takes up no space. How do you visually get the wrapper to enclose the floated element? You need to apply a clear somewhere inside that element (see Figure 3-18). Unfortunately, as there are no existing elements in the example to clear, you could add an empty element under the last paragraph, and clear that.

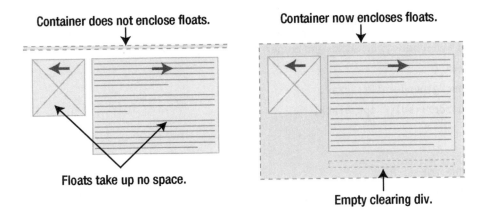

Figure 3-18. Because floats take up no space, they are not enclosed by container elements. The addition of an empty clearing element forces the container element to enclose the floats.

```
.news {
  background-color: gray;
  border: solid 1px black;
}

.news img {
  float: left;
}

.news p {
  float: right;
}

.clear {
  clear: both;
}
```

```
<div class="news">
    <img src="/img/news-pic.jpg" alt="my pic" />
    <p>Some text</p>
    <br class="clear" />
</div>
```

This gets the result we want, but at the expense of adding extraneous code to our markup. Often there will be an existing element you can apply the clear to, but sometimes you may have to bite the bullet and add meaningless markup for the purpose of layout.

Instead of clearing the floated text and image, you could choose to float the container div as well:

```
.news {
    background-color: gray;
    border: solid 1px black;
    float: left;
}

.news img {
    float: left;
}

.news p {
    float: right;
}

<div class="news">
    <img src="/img/news-pic.jpg" alt="my pic" />
    <p>Some text</p>
</div>
```

This creates the desired result. Unfortunately, the next element is now going to be affected by the float. To solve this problem, some people choose to float nearly everything in a layout and then clear those floats using an appropriate meaningful element, often the site footer. This helps reduce or eliminate the need for extraneous markup. However, floating can be complicated, and some older browsers may choke on heavily floated layouts. As such, many people prefer to add that extra bit of markup.

The overflow property defines how an element is supposed to behave if the enclosed content is too big for the stated dimensions. By default the content will spill out of the box, overflowing into the neighboring space. One useful side-effect of applying an overflow property of hidden or auto is that it will automatically clear any floats contained within. So this can be a useful way of clearing an element without adding any extra markup. This method is not appropriate in all situations, since setting the box's `overflow` property will affect how it behaves. More specifically, this method can force scroll bars or clip content under certain circumstances.

Then too, some people have taken to clearing floats using CSS-generated content or JavaScript. The basic concept for both methods is the same. Rather than add a clearing element directly to the markup, you add it to the page dynamically. For both methods, you need to indicate where the clearing element goes, and this is usually done with the addition of a class name:

```
<div class="news clear">
    <img src="/img/news-pic.jpg" alt="my pic" />
    <p Some text</p>
</div>
```

Using the CSS method, you use the `:after` pseudo-class in combination with the content declaration to add new content at the end of the specified existing content. In this case, I'm adding a period, as it is a fairly small and unobtrusive character. You don't want the new content to take up any vertical space or be displayed on the page, so you need to set `height` to `0` and `visibility` to `hidden`. Because cleared elements have space added to their top margin, the generated content needs to have its `display` property set to `block`. Once this is done, you can then clear your generated content:

```
.clear:after {
  content: ".";
  height: 0;
  visibility: hidden;
  display: block;
  clear: both;
}
```

This method works in most modern browsers but fails in Internet Explorer 6 and below. Various workarounds are available, many of which are documented at www.positioniseverything.net/easyclearing.html. The most common of these involves using the Holly Hack (see Chapter 8) to trick IE 5 and 6 into applying "Layout" (see Chapter 9) and incorrectly clearing the floats.

```
.clear {
display: inline-block;
}
/* Holly Hack Targets IE Win only \*/
* html .clear {height: 1%;}
.clear {display: block;}
/* End Holly Hack */
```

However, due to its complexity this method may not be suitable for everybody so has been included primarily for historical reasons.

An explanation of the JavaScript method is beyond the scope of this book but is worth a brief mention. Unlike the previous method, the JavaScript method works on all major browsers when scripting is turned on. However, if you use this method, you need to make sure that the content is still readable when scripting is turned off.

Summary

In this section, you learned about the box model and how padding, margin, width, and height affect the dimensions of a box. You also learned about the concept of margin collapsing and how this can affect your layouts. You were introduced to the three formatting models in CSS: normal flow, absolute positioning, and floating. You learned the difference between inline and block boxes, how to absolutely position an element within a relatively positioned ancestor, and how clearing really works.

Now that you are armed with this knowledge, let's start putting it to good use. In the following chapters of this book, you will be introduced to a number of core CSS concepts and you'll see how they can be used to create a variety of useful and practical techniques. So open your favorite text editor, and let's get coding.

Chapter 4

Using Backgrounds for Effect

Now that you are all up to speed with the theory, let's start putting it into practice. Today's Web is a very visual medium. The humble image tag has allowed web designers to turn dull and uninspiring documents into graphically rich experiences. Graphic designers quickly seized on the image tag (originally intended as a way to add visual content to a website) as a way of visually embellishing a page. In fact, if it wasn't for the invention of the image tag, the profession of web designer may never have evolved.

Unfortunately, we've used the image tag to clutter our pages with purely presentational images. Luckily, CSS gives us the ability to display an image on a page without it being part of the markup. This is achieved by adding an image as a background to an existing element. Through a series of practical examples, this chapter will show you how background images can be used to create a variety of interesting and useful techniques.

In this chapter, you will learn about

- Fixed- and flexible-width rounded-corner boxes

- The sliding doors technique

- Multiple background images and the `border-radius` property

- CSS drop shadows

- Opacity and RGBa

- Getting PNGs to work in older versions of Internet Explorer

- Parallax scrolling

- Image replacement

Background image basics

Applying a background image is easy. Say you want your website to have a nice tiled background. You can simply apply the image as a background to the body element:

```
body {
  background-image:url(/img/pattern.gif);
}
```

The default browser behavior is to repeat background images horizontally and vertically so that the image tiles across the whole of the page. For more control, you can choose whether your background image tiles vertically, horizontally, or not at all.

Gradients are very fashionable at the moment, so you may want to apply a vertical gradient to your page instead. To do this, create a tall but narrow gradient graphic. You can then apply this graphic to the body of the page and let it tile horizontally.

```
body {
  background-image: url(/img/gradient.gif);
  background-repeat: repeat-x;
}
```

Because the gradient has a fixed height, it will stop abruptly if the content of the page is longer than the height of the image. You could choose to create a really long image, possibly one that fades to a fixed color. However, it is always difficult to predict how long a page will become. Instead, simply add a background color as well. Background images always sit on the top of the background color, so when the image runs out the color will be displayed. If you choose a background color that is the same as the bottom of the gradient, the transition between image and background color will be seamless.

```
body {
  background-image: url(/img/gradient.gif);
  background-repeat: repeat-x;
  background-color: #ccc;
}
```

Tiling images can be useful in some situations. However, most of the time, you will want to add nontiled images to your page. For instance, say you want your web page to start with a large branding image. You could simply add the image directly into the page, and in many situations, this would be the correct thing to do. Yet if the image contains no information and is purely presentational, you may want to separate the image from the rest of your content. You can do this by creating a hook for the image in your HTML and applying the image using CSS. In the following example, I have added an empty div to the markup and given it an ID of branding. You can then set the dimensions of the div to be the same as the branding image, apply it as a background, and tell it not to repeat.

```
#branding {
  width: 700px;
  height: 200px;
  background-image:url(/img/branding.gif)
  background-repeat: no-repeat;
}
```

Last, it is possible to set the position of your background image. Say you want to add a bullet to every headline on your site, as shown in Figure 4-1. You could do something like this:

```
h1 {
  padding-left: 30px;
  background-image: url(/img/bullet.gif);
  background-repeat: no-repeat;
  background-position: left center;
}
```

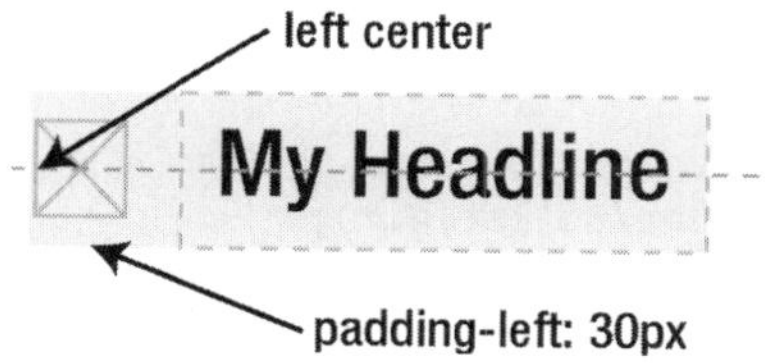

Figure 4-1. Creating a bullet using a background image

The last two keywords indicate the positioning of the image. In this case, the image will be positioned to the left of the element and vertically centered. As well as using keywords, you can set a background image's position using units such as pixels or percentages.

If you set a background position using pixels or ems, the top-left corner of the image is positioned from the top-left corner of the element by the specified number of pixels. So if you were to specify a vertical and horizontal position of 20 pixels, the top-left corner of the image will appear 20 pixels from the top-left corner of the element. However, background positioning using percentages works slightly differently. Rather than positioning the top-left corner of the background image, percentage positioning uses a corresponding point on the image. So if you set a vertical and horizontal position of 20 percent, you are actually positioning a point 20 percent from the top left of the image, 20 percent from the top left of the parent element (see Figure 4-2).

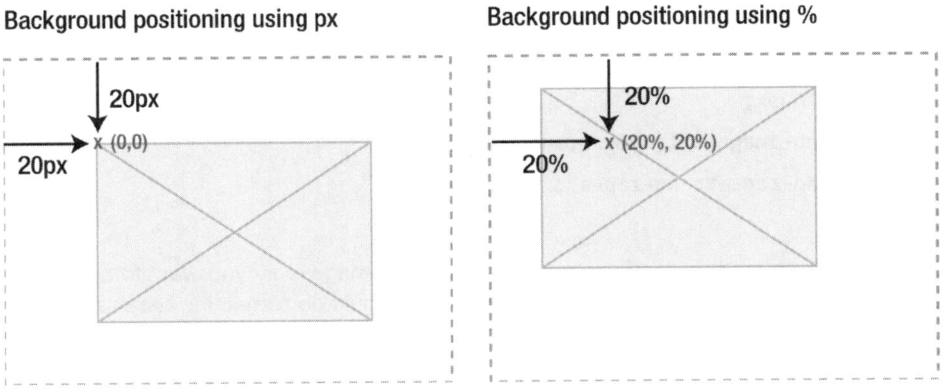

Background positioning using px

Background positioning using %

Figure 4-2. When positioning background images using pixels, the top-left corner of the image is used. When positioning using percentages, the corresponding position on the image is used.

If you want to position the previous bullet example using percentages instead of keywords, setting the vertical position to 50 percent would vertically center the bullet image:

```
h1 {
    padding-left: 30px;
    background-image: url(/img/bullet.gif);
    background-repeat: no-repeat;
    background-position: 0 50%;
}
```

The specification says that you are not supposed to mix units such as pixels or percentages with keywords. This seems like a nonsensical rule, and it's one that many modern browsers deliberately ignore. However, mixing units and keywords fails to work on certain browsers and will most likely invalidate your CSS. As such, it is best not to mix units with keywords at this time.

To save time, CSS also provides a shorthand version of the background property. This allows you to set all the properties in one go, rather than having to set them all individually.

```
h1 {
    background: #ccc url(/img/bullet.gif) no-repeat left center;
}
```

While background images are a simple concept to grasp, they form the basis of many advanced CSS techniques.

Rounded-corner boxes

One of the first criticisms leveled against CSS-based designs was that they were very square and boxy. To get around this, people started creating designs that incorporated more organic curved shapes. Rounded-corner boxes very quickly became one of the most sought-after CSS techniques around. There are various ways of creating rounded-corner boxes. Each approach has its strengths and weaknesses, and the one you choose depends largely on your circumstances.

Fixed-width rounded-corner boxes

Fixed-width rounded-corner boxes are the easiest to create. They require only two images: one for the top of the box and one for the bottom. For example, say you want to create a box style like the one in Figure 4-3.

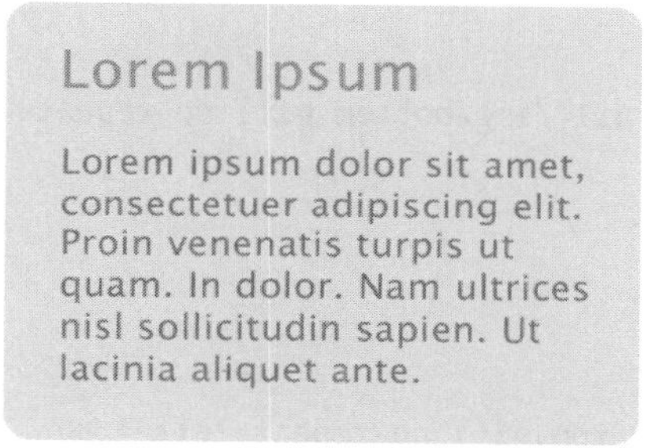

Lorem Ipsum

Lorem ipsum dolor sit amet, consectetuer adipiscing elit. Proin venenatis turpis ut quam. In dolor. Nam ultrices nisl sollicitudin sapien. Ut lacinia aliquet ante.

Figure 4-3. A simple rounded-corner box style

The markup for the box looks something like this:

```
<div class="box">
  <h2>Headline</h2>
    <p>Content</p>
</div>
```

In your favorite graphics package, you need to create two images like those in Figure 4-4: one for the top of the box and one for the bottom. The code and images for this and all the other examples in this book can be downloaded from www.cssmastery.com or www.friendsofed.com.

top.gif   bottom.gif

Figure 4-4. The top and bottom curve graphics

You then apply the top image to the heading element and the bottom image to the bottom of the box div. Because this box style just has a solid fill, you can create the body of the box by adding a background color to the box div.

```
.box {
  width: 418px;
```

```
  background: #effce7 url(/img/bottom.gif) no-repeat  left bottom;
}


.box h2 {
  background: url(/img/top.gif) no-repeat left top;
}
```

You will not want your content to butt up against the sides of the box, so you also need to add some padding to the elements inside the div:

```
.box {
  width: 418px;
  background: #effce7 url(/img/bottom.gif) no-repeat  left bottom;
  padding-bottom: 1px;
}


.box h2 {
  background: url(/img/top.gif) no-repeat left top;
  margin-top: 0;
  padding: 20px 20px 0 20px;
}


.box p {
  padding: 0 20px;
}
```

This is great for a simple box with a solid color and no borders. But what if you want to create a fancier style, such as the one in Figure 4-5?

Lorem Ipsum

Lorem ipsum dolor sit amet, consectetuer adipiscing elit. Proin venenatis turpis ut quam. In dolor. Nam ultrices nisl sollicitudin sapien. Ut lacinia aliquet ante.

Figure 4-5. Example of a stylized rounded-corner box

You can actually use the same approach, but this time, instead of setting a background color on the box, you can set a repeating background image. For this to work, you will need to apply the bottom curve image to another element. In this case, I used the last paragraph element in the box:

```
.box {
  width: 424px;
  background: url(/img/tile2.gif) repeat-y;
}

.box h2 {
  background: url(/img/top2.gif) no-repeat left top;
  padding-top: 20px;
}

.box .last {
  background: url(/img/bottom2.gif) no-repeat left bottom;
  padding-bottom: 20px;
}

.box h2, .box p {
  padding-left: 20px;
  padding-right: 20px;
}

<div class="box">
  <h2>Headline</h2>
    <p class="last">Content</p>
</div>
```

Figure 4-6 shows the resulting styled box. Because no height has been given to the box, it will expand vertically as the text size is increased.

Figure 4-6. Styled fixed-width box. The height of the box expands as the text size is increased.

Flexible rounded-corner box

The previous examples will all expand vertically if you increase your text size. However, they do not expand horizontally, as the width of the box has to be the same as the width of the top and bottom images. If you want to create a flexible box, you will need to take a slightly different approach. Instead of the top and bottom curves consisting of a single image, they need to be made up of two overlapping images (see Figure 4-7).

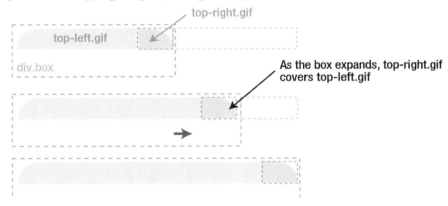

Figure 4-7. Diagram showing how the top graphics expand to form a flexible rounded-corner box

As the box increases in size, more of the larger image will be revealed, thus creating the illusion that the box is expanding. This concept is sometimes referred as the *sliding doors technique* because one image slides over the other, hiding it from view. More images are required for this method to work, so you will have to add a couple of extra, nonsemantic elements to your markup.

```
<div class="box">
  <div class="box-outer">
```

```
        <div class="box-inner">
          <h2>Headline</h2>
            <p>Content</p>
        </div>
      </div>
    </div>
```

This method requires four images: the top two images make up the top curve, and the bottom two images make up the bottom curve and the body of the box (see Figure 4-8). As such, the bottom images need to be as tall as the maximum height of the box. We will name these images top-left.gif, top-right.gif, bottom-left.gif, and bottom-right.gif.

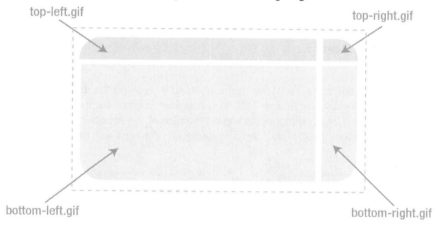

top-left.gif

top-right.gif

bottom-left.gif

bottom-right.gif

Figure 4-8. The images required to create the flexible rounded-corner box

First, you apply the bottom-left.gif to the main box div and bottom-right.gif to the outer div. Next you apply top-left.gif to the inner div and finally top-right.gif to the heading. Last, it is a good idea to add some padding to space out the contents of the box a little.

```
.box {
  width: 20em;
  background: #effce7 url(/img/bottom-left.gif) no-repeat left bottom;
}


.box-outer {
  background: url(/img/bottom-right.gif) no-repeat right bottom;
  padding-bottom: 1em;
}
```

```
.box-inner {
  background: url(/img/top-left.gif) no-repeat left top;
}


.box h2 {
  background: url(/img/top-right.gif) no-repeat right top;
  padding-top: 1em;
}


.box h2, .box p {
  padding-left: 1em;
  padding-right: 1em;
}
```

In this example, I have set the width of the box in ems, so increasing the text size in your browser will cause the box to stretch (see Figure 4-9). You could, of course, set the width in percentages and have the box expand or contract depending on the size of the browser window. This is one of the main principles behind elastic and liquid layouts, something I will be covering later in the book.

Figure 4-9. Flexible rounded-corner boxes expand both horizontally and vertically as the text is resized.

The addition of a couple of extra nonsemantic elements is not ideal. If you only have a couple of boxes, it is probably something you can live with. But if you are concerned you could always add the extra elements using JavaScript (and the DOM) instead. For more details on this topic, see the excellent article by Roger Johansson of 456 Berea Street at www.456bereastreet.com/archive/

200505/transparent_custom_corners_and_borders.

Mountaintop corners

Mountaintop corners are a simple yet very flexible concept, first coined by Dan Cederholm of www.simplebits.com, author of the best-selling friends of ED book *Web Standards Solutions* (friends of ED, 2004 and updated 2009). Suppose you want to create a variety of different-colored rounded-corner boxes. Using the previous methods you would have to create different corner graphics for each color theme. This may be okay if you only had a couple of themes, but say you wanted to let your users create their own themes? You'd probably have to create the corner graphics dynamically on the server, which could get very complicated.

Fortunately, there is another way. Instead of creating colored corner graphics, you can create curved, bitmap corner masks (see Figure 4-10). The masked area maps to the background color you are using while the actual corner area is transparent. When placed over a colored box, they give the impression that the box is curved (see Figure 4-11).

Figure 4-10. In a bitmapped corner mask, the white mask will cover the background color, creating a simple curved effect.

As these corner masks need to be bitmapped, subtle curves work best. If you try to use a large curve, it will appear jagged and unsightly.

The basic markup is similar to the previous method; it requires four elements to apply the four corner masks to:

```
<div class="box">
  <div class="box-outer">
    <div class="box-inner">
      <h2>Headline</h2>
        <p>Content</p>
    </div>
  </div>
</div>
```

The CSS is also very similar:

```
.box {
  width: 20em;
  background: #effce7 url(/img/bottom-left.gif) ↵
  no-repeat left bottom;
}

.box-outer {
  background: url(/img/bottom-right.gif) no-repeat right bottom;
  padding-bottom: 5%;
}

.box-inner {
  background: url(/img/top-left.gif) no-repeat left top;
}

.box h2 {
  background: url(/img/top-right.gif) no-repeat right top;
  padding-top: 5%;
}
```

```
.box h2, .box p {
  padding-left: 5%;
  padding-right: 5%;
}
```

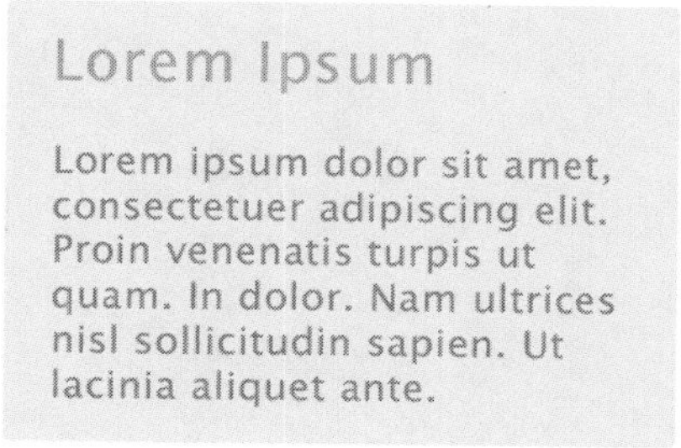

> Lorem Ipsum
>
> Lorem ipsum dolor sit amet,
> consectetuer adipiscing elit.
> Proin venenatis turpis ut
> quam. In dolor. Nam ultrices
> nisl sollicitudin sapien. Ut
> lacinia aliquet ante.

Figure 4-11. Mountaintop corner box

The main difference, apart from using different images, is the addition of a background color on the main box div. If you want to change the color of the box, you can simply change the color value in the CSS without having to re-create any new graphics. This method is only suitable for creating very simple boxes; however, it provides a great deal of flexibility and can be used over and over again on different projects.

Multiple background images

The previous examples are great, but most of them rely on the addition of nonsemantic markup to your code. These extra elements are needed because you can only add one background image per element. Wouldn't it be great if you could add multiple background images instead? Well, through the magic of CSS 3 you can. What's more, the syntax is extremely simple and takes the same form as regular background images. The main difference is that instead of defining one background image to use, you can use as many images as you like. Here's how it's done:

```
.box {
  background-image: url(/img/top-left.gif),
                                    url(/img/top-right.gif),
                                    url(/img/bottom-left.gif),
                                    url(/img/bottom-right.gif);
  background-repeat: no-repeat,
                               no-repeat,
                               no-repeat,
                               no-repeat;
```

83

```
background-position: top left,

                                    top right,
                                    bottom left,
                                    bottom right;

}


<div class="box">
    <h2>Headline</h2>
        <p>Content<p>
</div>
```

You start by defining all the images you want to use with the background-image property. Next, you set whether you want them to repeat on not. Last, you set their positions using the background-position property. You can see the results in Figure 4-12. Safari has supported multiple background images as far back as version 1.3, and the latest versions of Firefox and Opera have now started to catch up. Internet Explorer doesn't yet support multiple background images, but don't let that stop you from using this technique in situations where it doesn't matter if IE users see square corners instead.

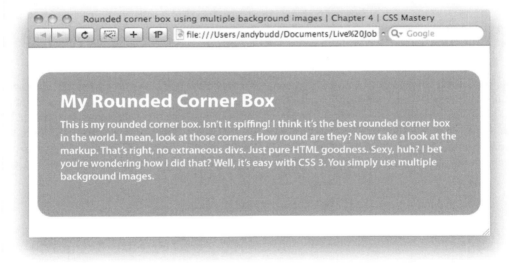

Figure 4-12. A rounded corner box made using CSS 3 multiple backgrounds

border-radius

In these days of high-definition computer games with on-the-fly texture mapping, you would think that browsers would be able to draw a simple rounded corner box themselves, without the need of raster graphics. Well, now they can, thanks to the new CSS 3 `border-radius` property. All you need to do is set the radius of the desired border and let the browser do the rest (see Figure 4-13).

```
.box {
    border-radius: 1em;
}
```

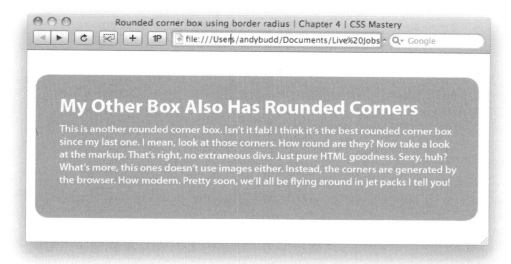

Figure 4-13. A rounded corner box made using the CSS 3 border-radius property

Because this property is new, there is still some disagreement about how it should actually work. So until this property gets wider adoption, you'll need to use browser-specific extensions to invoke it. Currently, both Firefox and Safari support this property, so I'll use the `-moz` and `-webkit` prefixes.

```
.box {
    -moz-border-radius: 1em;
    -webkit-border-radius: 1em;
    border-radius: 1em;
}
```

Browser manufacturers are always experimenting with new extensions to CSS. Some of these may come from yet to be implemented versions of CSS, while others may find their way into the specifications at a later date. Some extensions may never become part of the formal specification, such as those used by Safari for rendering UI elements on the iPhone.

So as not to confuse other user agents or invalidate your code, these extensions can be invoked by adding a vendor-specific prefix to your selector, property, or value. For instance, Mozilla uses the –moz prefix, while Safari uses the –webkit prefix. There are similar prefixes for IE, Opera, and all the major browsers. Each browser has its own set of special features you can access using these prefixes, so you'll probably need to check which ones are available on the vendors developer site.

Using this mechanism, you can try out new CSS 3 features before they become an official recommendation. However, make sure you use these extensions with care, as the format of these experimental features may differ between browsers and could change or disappear by the time the specification becomes an official recommendation.

border-image

Last on my list of new CSS 3 tricks is the `border-image` property. This excellent addition to CSS allows you to define a single image to act as the border of an element. What good is a single image, you may ask? The beautify of this property is that it allows you to slice up that image into nine separate sectors, based on some simple percentage rules, and the browser will automatically use the correct sector for the corresponding part of the border. Known as nine-slice scaling, this technique helps avoid the distortion you'd normally get when resizing rounded corner boxes. It's a little difficult to visualize, so I think an example is in order.

Imagine you had a 100-pixel high image of a curved box, like the one in Figure 4-14. If you draw two lines 25 percent from the top and bottom of the box, then another two lines 25 percent from the left and the right, you will have divided the box up into nine sectors.

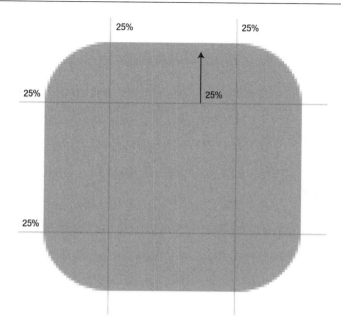

Figure 4-14. The source file for our border image, with the division points draw on for illustration purposes.

The border-image property will automatically use the images in each sector for the corresponding border. So the image in the top-left sector will be used for the top-left border, and the image in the middle-right sector for the right-hand-side border. I want my borders to be 25 pixels wide, so I set that as the width in my CSS. If the images aren't big enough, they will automatically tile, creating an expandable box (see Figure 4-15). Here is how you achieve this effect in code:

```
.box {
  -webkit-border-image: url(/img/corners.gif)
  25% 25% 25% 25% / 25px round round;
}
```

Safari has supported this property for a while, through the use of the Webkit-specific extension, as shown in this example. Firefox 3.5 and Opera 9.5 now also support border-image, which opens up its use to a much wider audience.

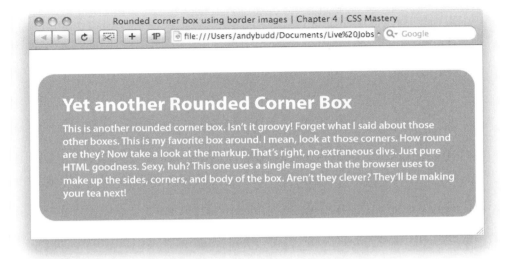

Figure 4-15. A rounded corner box using the border-image property

Drop shadows

Drop shadows are a popular and attractive design feature, adding depth and interest to an otherwise flat design. Most people use a graphics package like Photoshop to add drop shadows directly to an image. However, using the power of CSS, it is possible to apply simple drop shadow effects without altering the underlying image.

There are various reasons you may want to do this. For instance, you may allow nontechnical people to administer your site who have no experience using Photoshop, or you may simply be uploading images from a location where you do not have access to Photoshop, such as an Internet cafe. By having a predefined drop shadow style, you can simply upload a regular image and have it displayed on your site with a drop shadow.

One of the nicest benefits of using CSS is that it is nondestructive. If you decide that you want to remove the drop shadow effect later on, you can simply alter a couple of lines in your CSS files rather than having to reprocess all of your images.

Easy CSS drop shadows

This very simple drop shadow method was first described by Dunstan Orchard of www.1976design.com. It works by applying a large drop shadow graphic to the background of a wrapper div. The drop shadow is then revealed by offsetting the image using negative margins.

The first thing you need to do is create the drop shadow graphic. I created my drop shadow graphic using Adobe Photoshop. Create a new Photoshop file, the dimensions of which are as large as the maximum size of your image. I created a file that's 800 pixels by 800 pixels just to be on the safe side. Unlock the background layer and fill it with the color you want your shadow to sit on. In my case I simply kept the background layer white. Create a new layer and fill it with white. Now move this layer up and left by 4 or 5 pixels and then apply a 4- or 5-pixel-wide drop shadow to this layer. Save this image for web and call it shadow.gif (see Figure 4-16).

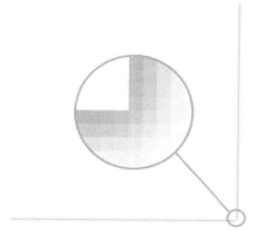

Figure 4-16. The shadow.gif zoomed in so you can see the 5-pixel drop shadow

The markup for this technique is very simple:

```
<div class="img-wrapper"><img src="dunstan.jpg" width="300" ↵
height="300" alt="Dunstan Orchard" /></div>
```

To create the effect, you first need to apply your shadow graphic to the background of the wrapper div. Because divs are block-level elements, they stretch horizontally, taking up all the available space. In this situation we want the div to wrap around the image. You can do this by explicitly setting a width for the wrapper div, but doing so reduces the usefulness of this technique. Instead, you can float the div, causing it to shrink-wrap on modern browsers, with one exception—IE 5.x on the Mac. You may want to hide these styles from IE 5.x on the Mac. For more information on hiding rules from various browsers, see Chapter 8, which discusses hacks and filters.

```
.img-wrapper {
background: url(/img/shadow.gif) no-repeat bottom right;
clear: right;
float: left;
}
```

To reveal the shadow image and create the drop shadow effect (see Figure 4-17), you need to offset the image using negative margins:

```
.img-wrapper img {
margin: -5px 5px 5px -5px;
}
```

Figure 4-17. Image with a drop shadow applied

You can create a good, fake photo border effect by giving the image a border and some padding
(see Figure 4-18):

```
.img-wrapper img {
  background-color: #fff;
  border: 1px solid #a9a9a9;
  padding: 4px;
  margin: -5px 5px 5px -5px;
}
```

Figure 4-18. The final result of our simple drop shadow technique

This works for most modern, standards-compliant browsers. However, we need to add in a couple of simple rules to get it working correctly in IE 6:

```
.img-wrapper {
  background: url(/img/shadow.gif) no-repeat bottom right;
  clear: right;
  float: left;
  position: relative;
}


.img-wrapper img {
  background-color: #fff;
  border: 1px solid #a9a9a9;
  padding: 4px;
  display: block;
  margin: -5px 5px 5px -5px;
  position: relative;
}
```

The drop shadow effect now works in IE 6.

Drop shadows *à la* Clagnut

Richard Rutter of www.clagnut.com came up with a similar method for creating drop shadows. Instead of using negative margins, his technique uses relative positioning to offset the image:

```
.img-wrapper {
  background: url(/img/shadow.gif) no-repeat bottom right;
  float:left;
  line-height:0;
}


.img-wrapper img {
  background:#fff;
  padding:4px;
  border:1px solid #a9a9a9;
  position:relative;
  left:-5px;
  top:-5px;
}
```

Box-shadow

While the previous techniques server their purpose, they are all a little cumbersome. Wouldn't it be good if browsers could create their own drop shadows, doing away with the need of Photoshop filters and raster graphics? Well you guessed it, CSS 3 allows us to do this as well, using the handy box-shadow property. This property takes four values: the vertical and horizontal offsets, the width (and hence blurriness) of the shadow, and the color. So in the following example, I am offsetting the shadow by three pixels, making it six pixels wide and medium gray (see Figure 4-19).

```
img {
    box-shadow: 3px 3px 6px #666;
}
```

Figure 4-19. A lovely drop shadow using the box-shadow effect

Because this is another one of those experimental CSS 3 properties, you will need to use the Safari and Firefox extensions for now. However, it hopefully won't be long until this property is more widely supported.

```
img {
    -webkit-box-shadow: 3px 3px 6px #666;
    -moz-box-shadow: 3px 3px 6px #666;
    box-shadow: 3px 3px 6px #666;
}
```

One of the most exciting things about this property is the fact that it works in conjunction with the border-radius property (see Figure 4-20). This means you can now programmatically create drop shadows on rounded corner boxes without even having to open up your graphics package!

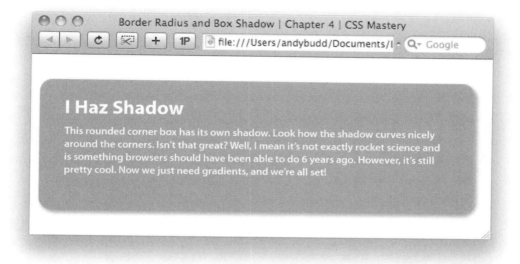

Figure 4-20. A drop shadow on a rounded corner box

We used this effect quite liberally on the UX London 2009 website, serving up drop shadows to modern browsers (see Figure 4-21), and regular boxes to less-capable browsers (see Figure 4-22).

Figure 4-21. The UX London website as seen by Firefox. Notice the solid box shadows created using CSS 3.

Figure 4-22. The UX London website again, this time viewed on Internet Explorer. The design is bereft of shadows, but most users won't notice anything is missing.

Opacity

The clever use of opacity can give your designs an extra dimension. It can also be used to layer elements over each other, so you get a hint of what lies beneath. As well as being a cool trick, this can also be used to improve the usability on your site.

CSS opacity

CSS opacity has been available in most modern browsers for quite some time, so I'm surprised that it's not used more often. Unsurprisingly, it isn't supported by older version of Internet Explorer. However, a quick bit of IE-specific code will fix that problem. As an example of its use, imagine you wanted to pop up an alert message to your users, layering it over the existing document so they could still see what was underneath (see Figure 4-23).

```
.alert {
  background-color: #000;
  border-radius: 2em;
  opacity: 0.8;
  filter: alpha(opacity=80); /*proprietary IE code*/
}
```

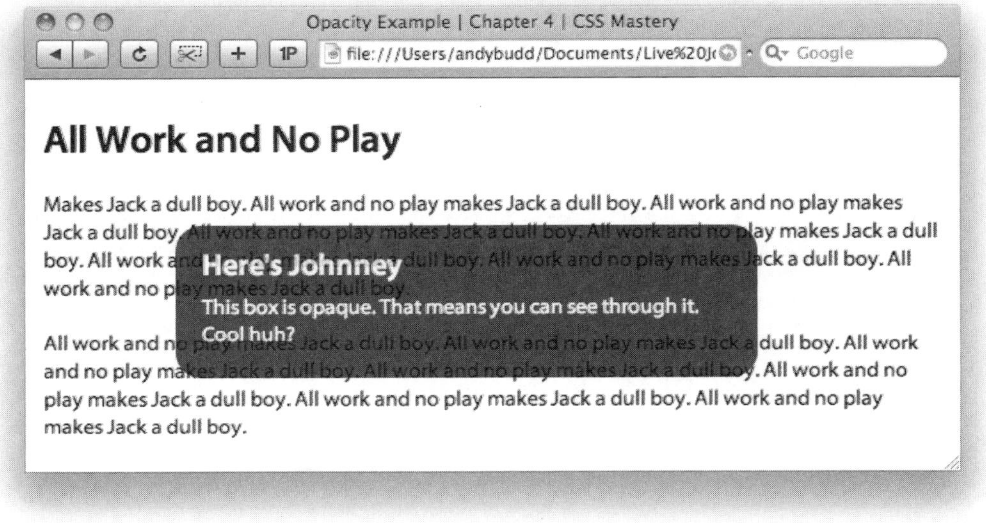

Figure 4-23. A rounded corner alert box with 80 percent opacity

The one big problem with CSS opacity is that it's inherited by the contents of the element you're applying it to, as well as the background. So if you look closely at Figure 4-23, you'll see that the text on the page is showing through the alert text as well. This doesn't matter if you're using a very high opacity in combination with high-contrast text. However, with lower opacities, the content of your box can start to get unreadable. This is where RGBa comes in.

RGBa

RGBa is a mechanism for setting color and opacity in one go. RGB stands for "Red," "Green," and "Blue," while the "a" stands for "alpha transparency." To use RGBa in the previous example, you would do something like this:

```
.alert {
  background-color: rgba(0,0,0,0.8);
  border-radius: 2em;
}
```

The first three numbers represent the red, green, and blue values of the color. In this case, the alert box is going to be black, so these are all set to 0. As with opacity, the last number is the decimal value of opacity, so 0.8 means this background will be 80 percent opaque, or to put it another way, 20 percent transparent. A value of 1 would make the alert 100 percent opaque, while a value of 0 would make it fully transparent. The results of this technique are shown in Figure 4-24.

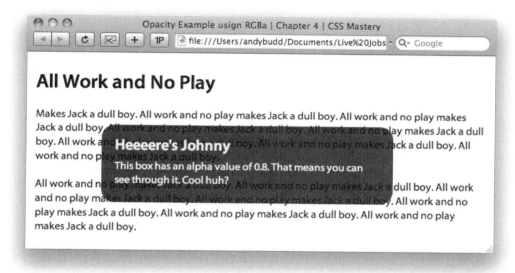

Figure 4-24. A rounded corner alert box with 80 percent opacity using RGBa

PNG transparency

One of the biggest benefits of the PNG file format is its support for alpha transparency. This allows you to get really creative with your designs (see Figure 4-25). Unfortunately, Internet Explorer 6 doesn't natively support PNG transparency, although IE 7 and 8 do. However, there are a couple of ways you can get older versions of Internet Explorer to play ball.

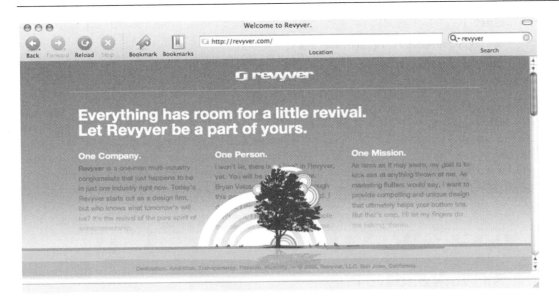

Figure 4-25. The old Revyver site had a beautiful example of PNG transparency at the bottom of the viewport. As the page scrolled, you would get glimpses of the content show through the branches of the tree and arcs of the rainbow.

The best-known way of forcing PNG transparency support in IE 6 is to use the proprietary AlphaImageLoader filter. To do this, you need to include the following line of code in your CSS.

```
filter:progid:DXImageTransform.Microsoft.AlphaImageLoader
(src=/img/my-image.png', sizingMethod='crop');
```

Unfortunately, using this code will invalidate your CSS, so your best option is to filter this off into a separate IE 6–specific style sheet.

```
.img-wrapper div {
    filter:progid:DXImageTransform.Microsoft.AlphaImageLoader
    (src='/img/shadow2.png', sizingMethod='crop');
    background: none;
}
```

The first rule uses a proprietary filter to load in the PNG and enforce alpha transparency. The original background image will still be displayed, so the second rule simply hides the original background image.

Internet Explorer has another piece of proprietary code called a *conditional comment* that will let you serve up a particular stylesheet to specific versions of IE. In this case, you only want IE 6 to see the new stylesheet, so you can place the following code in the head of the page:

```
<!--[if ie 6]>
<link rel="stylesheet" type="text/css" href="ie6.css"/>
<![endif]-->
```

> Don't worry too much about conditional comments at this stage; you will learn all about them in detail in Chapter 8.

The problem with this technique is that it forces you to include this line of code for every alpha-transparent PNG you want to use. As such, it is somewhat cumbersome to use.

The other alternative is to use a technique known as the IE PNG fix. This involves using a little-known, Microsoft-specific extension to CSS called *behaviors*. By downloading the appropriate .htc file and pointing to it in your IE 6–specific stylesheet, you can enable PNG transparency on any element you want.

```
img, div {
    behavior: url(iepngfix.htc);
}
```

For more information on this technique and to download the .htc file, visit www.twinhelix.com/css/iepngfix.

CSS parallax effect

Background images aren't only about creating rounded corner boxes and drop shadows. We can have a lot of fun with them as well. Clearleft did just that when we launched our Silverback usability testing application. If you go to www.silverbackapp.com and resize the browser window, you will notice a strange effect (see Figure 4-26). The background images move at slightly different speeds, giving the impression that the page has depth. This phenomenon is known as parallax scrolling and was the mainstay of many old school computer games.

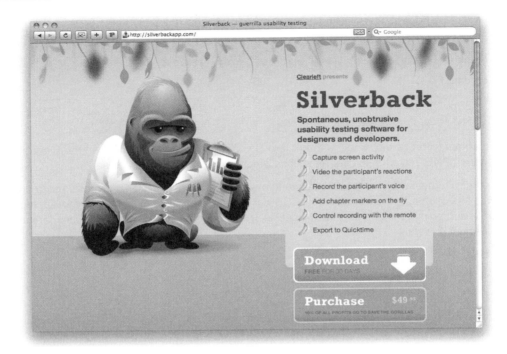

Figure 4-26. Change the window size on www.silverbackapp.com and see what happens.

To achieve this effect, you first need to create a couple of different background images. We created one image of our vines on a green background and then two further images of vines on an alpha transparent background. This allowed the midground and foreground images to flow over each other and the background, without obscuring the view.

The main background will be applied to the body element. However, assuming we're not using CSS 3 multiple-background images, we'll need to add two new elements to attach our backgrounds to. The content of the page then needs to sit in front of these elements so you can interact with it. You could place the foreground div in front of the content, but this would partially block your content and make it difficult to interact with. So the markup structure will look something like this:

```
<body>
  <div class="midground">
    <div class="foreground">
      <p>Your content will go here!</a>
    </div>
  </div>
</body>
```

The first thing you need to do is add the main background to the body element. You want this image to tile horizontally, so you will need to set the `image-repeat` property to `repeat-x`. You also want the body element to take on the color of the background, which in this instance is light green. Last, you want to offset your image horizontally by 20 percent, relative to the size of the window. This is where the magic happens. As the window resizes, the position of the background image will change, and it will appear to move across the screen.

```
body {
    background-image: url(/img/bg-rear.jpg);
    background-repeat: repeat-x;
    background-color:#d3ff99;
    background-position: 20% 0;
}
```

You now need to do the same with the midground and foreground images, choosing higher percentages so they move faster relative to each other and give that sense of depth. We decided to set the midground's position to 40 percent, and the foreground position to a whopping 150 percent. You can obviously play around with these positions to generate the effect that is right for you.

```
body {
    background-image: url(/img/bg-rear.jpg);
    background-repeat: repeat-x;
    background-color:#d3ff99;
    background-position: 20% 0;
}

.midground {
    background-image: url(/img/bg-mid.png);
    background-repeat: repeat-x;
    background-color: transparent;
    background-position: 40% 0;
}

.foreground {
    background-image: url(/img/bg-front.png);
    background-repeat: repeat-x;
    background-color: transparent;
    background-position: 150% 0;
}
```

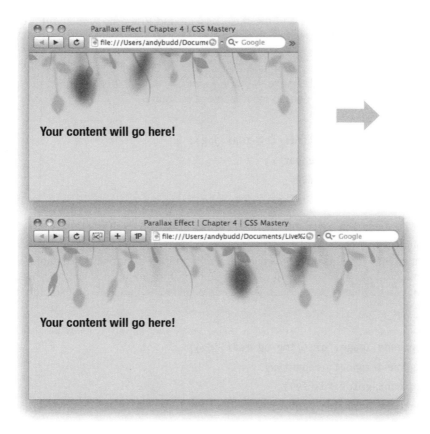

Figure 4-27. As the window size changes, the background vines appear to move at different speeds, giving a sense of depth.

Image replacement

HTML text is great. Search engines can read it; you can copy and paste it; and it enlarges if you increase the text size in your browser. It is, therefore, a good idea to use HTML text instead of text as images wherever possible. Unfortunately, web designers have only a limited selection of fonts to play with. Also, while you can control your typography to a certain extent using CSS, some things just are not possible with live text. Because of this, there are occasions, usually for branding reasons, when you will want to use images of text instead.

Rather than embed these images directly in the page, CSS authors came up with the idea of *image replacement*. Essentially, you add your text to the document as normal, and then, using CSS, you hide the text and display a background image in its place. That way, search engines still have the HTML text to find, and the text will be available if you disable CSS.

This seemed like a great idea for a while, until various flaws emerged. Some of the more popular methods are inaccessible to screen readers, and most do not work with images turned off but CSS turned on. As a result, many CSS authors have stopped using image replacement methods and have reverted to using plain text. While I advocate avoiding image replacement where possible, I still believe there can be situations where it is appropriate, such as when you need to use a particular font because of corporate branding guidelines. To do this, you should have a good grasp of the various techniques available and understand their limitations.

Fahrner Image Replacement (FIR)

Created by Todd Fahrner, Fahrner Image Replacement (FIR) is the original, and probably the most popular, image replacement technique. I am going to explain this method because of its historical significance and because it is one of the easiest methods to understand. However, this method has some serious accessibility implications, which I will come to in a moment, and should thus be avoided.

The basic concept is very simple. You wrap the text you want to replace in a span tag:

```
<h2>
    <span>Hello World</span>
</h2>
```

You then apply your replacement image as a background image to the heading element:

```
h2 {
    background:url(hello_world.gif) no-repeat;
    width: 150px;
    height: 35px;
}
```

and hide the contents of the span by settings its display value to none:

```
span {
    display: none;
}
```

This method works like a charm, but it is this last rule that causes problems. Many of the most popular screen readers ignore elements that have their display value set to none or their visibility to hidden. Therefore, they will completely ignore this text, causing a huge accessibility problem. So a technique intended to improve the accessibility of a site actually has the opposite effect. For this reason, it is best not to use this technique.

Phark

Mike Rundle of www.phark.net invented a screen-reader–friendly image replacement technique that has the added benefit of dropping the extra, nonsemantic `div`:

```
<h2>
  Hello World
</h2>
```

Instead of using the `display` property to hide the text, the Phark method applies a very large, negative text indentation to the headline:

```
h2 {
  text-indent: -5000px;
  background:url(/img/hello_world.gif) no-repeat;
  width: 150px;
  height:35px;
}
```

This method works well and solves the screen reader issue. However, as with the FIR method, this method does not work when images are turned off but CSS is turned on. This is an edge case and probably only applicable to people on very slow connections or those using their cell phones as a modem. There is an argument that site visitors do have the ability to turn images on and they just choose not to. However, it is worth bearing in mind that certain people may not see the replaced text, so it is best to avoid using this method for crucial information or navigation.

Scalable Inman Flash Replacement (sIFR)

One of the main problems image replacement tries to solve is the lack of fonts available on most computers. Rather than swap the text out with images of text, Mike Davidson and Shaun Inman took an altogether more inventive approach.

Flash allows you to embed fonts into a SWF file, so instead of swapping the text out for an image, they decided to swap the text out and replace it with a Flash file. The swapping is done using JavaScript by looping through the document and grabbing any text within a particular element or with a particular class name. The JavaScript then swaps the text for a small Flash file. The really clever part comes next. Rather than creating a separate Flash file for each chunk of text, this technique places the swapped text back into a single, duplicated Flash file. Thus, all you need to do to trigger your image replacement is add a class, and the combination of Flash and JavaScript will do the rest. Another benefit is that the text in Flash files can be made selectable, meaning that it can be copied and pasted with ease.

Shaun Inman released his Flash image replacement method and dubbed it Inman Flash Replacement, or IFR for short. IFR is a very lightweight method. Details about this method, including the source code, can be found at www.shauninman.com/plete/2004/04/ifr-revisited-and-revised.

Mike Davidson built extensively on this method, creating the Scalable Inman Flash Replacement (sIFR) method. This method extends IFR by allowing things such as multiline text replacement and text resizing. sIFR is now being maintained and developed by Mark Wubben and contains lots of interesting new features.

To use sIFR on your site, you first need to download the latest version from http://novemberborn.net/sifr3. Installing sIFR on your site is fairly simple, although it's worth reading through the documentation first. The first thing you need to do is open the Flash file, embed the font you want to use, and export the movie. For sIFR to work properly, you next need to apply the enclosed print and screen styles or create your own. Next, add the sifr.js JavaScript file to every page you want sIFR to work on. This file is highly configurable and allows you to specify which elements to replace, the text color, padding, case, and a variety of other stylistic elements. However, padding and line-height both affect the size of the text, so in practice, this isn't easy. Once you are finished, upload all the files to your server and watch your tired old fonts be replaced with dynamic Flash content.

The main problem with these techniques involves load times. The pages have to load fully before JavaScript can replace the text. Consequently, there is usually a brief flicker before all the text has been replaced with the Flash equivalent (see Figure 4-28).

Figure 4-28. Notice how the headlines at www.fortymedia.com only display once the page has loaded. This is a sure sign that sIFR is being used on this site.

Although this flicker is not a huge problem, it is noticeable and can give the impression that the page is loading slowly. Also, some pages can feel a little sluggish if there is a lot of Flash replacement going on. Furthermore users can get a "flash of unstyled content," which can look buggy and disorientating. As such, it's a good idea to keep any replacement to a minimum and limit this technique to main headlines only. sIFR is a great way to bring richer typography to the web and is perfect for relatively small sites with consistent typographic treatment. However, sIFR can be extremely fiddly when applied to large sites with multiple heading sizes, styles, and colors. It also gets tricky if some headings span multiple lines or have background colors. So my advice would be to avoid using sIFR for large projects and limit it to your personal site.

Summary

In this chapter, you have learned how background images can be applied to elements to produce a variety of interesting techniques, such as flexible rounded-corner boxes and pure CSS drop shadows. You have also seen how the onset of new CSS 3 properties like border-radius and box-shadow are beginning to make these effects redundant. You have learned all about opacity and seen how to force PNG support in Internet Explorer along with several methods of image replacement.

In the next chapter, you will learn how background images and links can be combined to create some interesting interactive effects.

Chapter 5

Styling Links

The humble anchor link is the foundation of the World Wide Web. It is the mechanism that allows web pages to interconnect and people to explore and navigate. The default styling for anchor links is fairly uninspiring, but with a little sprinkling of CSS you can do some amazing things.

In this chapter you will learn about

- Ordering your link selectors based on the cascade
- Creating stylized link underlines
- Styling external links using attribute selectors
- Making links behave like buttons
- Creating visited-link styles
- Creating pure CSS tooltips

Simple link styling

The easiest way to style a link is to use the anchor type selector. For instance, this rule will make all anchors red:

```
a {color: red;}
```

However, anchors can act as internal references as well as external links, so using a type selector is not always ideal. Take this situation, for example. The first anchor contains a fragment identifier, and when the user clicks that anchor, the page will jump to the second named anchor:

```
<p><a href="#mainContent">Skip to main content</a></p>

...

<h1><a name="mainContent">Welcome</a></h1>
```

While you probably only want the link to be styled red, the contents of the headline will be styled red also. To avoid this, CSS has two special selectors called link pseudo-class selectors. The :link pseudo-class selector is used to target links that have not been visited, and the :visited pseudo-class selector is used to target visited links. In this example, all unvisited links will be blue, and all visited links will be green:

```
a:link {color: blue;}        /* Makes unvisited links blue */

a:visited {color: green;}  /* Makes visited links green */
```

The other two selectors you can use for styling links are the :hover and :active dynamic pseudo-class selectors. The :hover dynamic pseudo-class selector is used to target elements when they are hovered over, and the :active dynamic pseudo-class selector targets elements when they are activated. In the case of links, activation occurs when the link is clicked. In this example, links will turn red when hovered over or clicked:

```
a:hover, a:active { color: red;}
```

To ensure your pages are as accessible as possible, it is always a good idea to add a :focus pseudo-class to your links when defining hover states. This will allow your links to take on the same styles when they are tabbed to using the keyboard as they have when hovered over using the mouse.

```
a:hover, a:focus { color: red;}
```

Other elements can also use the :hover, :active, or :focus pseudo-class selectors. For instance, you could add a :hover pseudo-class on your table rows, an :active pseudo-class on your submit buttons, or a :focus pseudo-class on your input fields to highlight various forms of interactivity. Unfortunately, IE 7 and below don't support the use of pseudo-class selectors on anything other than links, but all modern browsers do.

```
/* makes table rows yellow when hovered over */
tr:hover {
  background: yellow;
}


/* makes submit buttons in some browsers yellow when pressed */
input[type="submit"]:active {
  background:yellow;
}
```

```
/* makes inputs yellow when selected */
input:focus {
  background:yellow;
}
```

One of the first things most people learn to use these selectors for is turning off the underline for links, and then turning them back on when they are hovered over or clicked. This can be done by setting the `text-decoration` property to `none` for unvisited and visited links and to `underline` for hovered or active links:

```
a:link, a:visited {text-decoration: none;}

a:hover, a:focus, a:active {text-decoration: underline;}
```

In the previous example, the order of the selectors is very important. If the order is reversed, the hover and active styles won't work.

```
a:hover, a:focus, a:active {text-decoration: underline;}

a:link, a:visited {text-decoration: none;}
```

The reason for this is the cascade. In Chapter 1, you learned that when two rules have the same specificity, the last rule to be defined wins out. In this situation, both rules have the same specificity so the `:link` and `:visited` styles will override the `:hover` and `:active` styles. To make sure this doesn't happen, it's a good idea to apply your link styles in the following order:

```
a:link, a:visited, a:hover, a:focus, a:active
```

An easy way to remember this order is the phrase "Lord Vader Hates Furry Animals," where *L* stands for *link*, *V* stands for *visited*, *H* for *hover*, *F* for *focus*, and *A* for *active*.

Fun with underlines

From a usability and accessibility standpoint, it is important that your links are distinguishable by some means other than color. The reason for this is that many people with visual impairments find it difficult to distinguish between poorly contrasting colors, especially at small text sizes. For instance, people with color blindness cannot distinguish between certain color combinations with similar levels of brightness or saturation. Because of this, links are underlined by default.

Simple link embellishments

Designers tend to dislike link underlines, as they add too much weight and visual clutter to a page. If you decide to remove link underlines, you could choose to make links bold instead. That way, your page will look less cluttered, but the links will still stand out:

```
a:link, a:visited {
  text-decoration: none;
  font-weight: bold;
}
```

You can then reapply the underlines when the links are hovered over or activated, reinforcing their interactive status:

```
a:hover, a:focus, a:active {
    text-decoration: underline;
    font-weight: bold;
}
```

However, it is possible to create a low-impact underline using borders instead. In the following example, the default underline is removed and replaced with a less obtrusive dotted line. When the link is hovered over or clicked, this line turns solid to provide the user with visual feedback that something has happened:

```
a:link, a:visited {
    text-decoration: none;
    border-bottom: 1px dotted #000;
}


a:hover, a:focus, a:active {
    border-bottom-style: solid;
}
```

Fancy link underlines

You can create some very interesting effects by using images to create your link underlines. For instance, I have created a very simple underline graphic comprised of diagonal lines (see Figure 5-1).

Figure 5-1. Simple underline graphic

You can then apply this image to your links using the following code:

```
a:link, a:visited {
    color:#666;
    text-decoration: none;
    background: url(/img/underline1.gif) repeat-x left bottom;
}
```

You can see the resulting styled link in Figure 5-2.

This is a link

Figure 5-2. Custom link underline

You do not have to stop with link and visited styles. In this example, I have created an animated GIF for the hover and active states, which I apply using the following CSS:

```
a:hover, a:focus, a:active {
  background-image: url(/img/underline1-hover.gif);
}
```

When you hover over or click the link, the diagonal lines appear to scroll from left to right, creating an interesting pulsing or poling effect. Not all browsers support background image animations, but those that do not will usually display the first frame of the animation, ensuring that the effect degrades nicely in older browsers.

> Remember to use animation carefully, as it can cause accessibility problems for some users. If in doubt, always remember to check the Web Content Accessibility Guidelines (WCAG 1.0) at www.w3.org/TR/WAI-WEBCONTENT.

Visited-link styles

Designers and developers often forget about the visited-link style and end up styling visited links the same as unvisited ones. However, a separate visited-link style can help orientate users, showing them which pages or sites they have already visited and avoiding unnecessary backtracking.

You can create a very simple visited-link style by adding a check box to every visited link:

```
a:visited {
  padding-right: 20px;
  background: url(/img/check.gif) no-repeat right middle;
}
```

Styling link targets

As well as linking to a specific document, you can use a link containing a fragment identifier to point people to a particular part of a page. You do this by adding a hash character, followed by the ID of the element you want to link to, at the end of your href. This can be extremely useful if you want point to a specific comment in a long comment thread. For instance, say I wanted to link to the third comment on this page.

```
<a href="http://example.com/story.htm#comment3">

    A great comment by Simon

</a>
```

When you click the preceding link, you will be taken to the appropriate document, and the page will scroll down to the comment3 element. Unfortunately, if the page is quite busy, it is often difficult to tell to which element the link has sent you. To get around this problem, CSS 3 allows you to style the target element using the :target pseudo-class. In this next example, I am going to highlight the target element by giving it a yellow background (see Figure 5-3).

```
.comment:target {

    background-color: yellow;

}
```

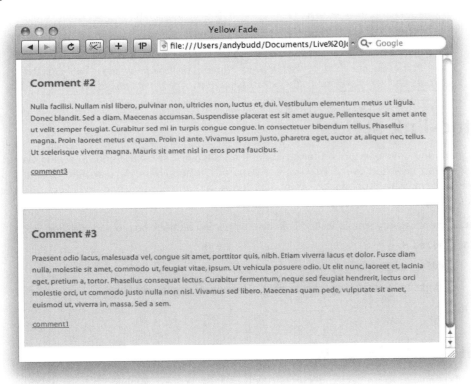

Figure 5-3. The third comment is highlighted with a yellow background when linked to, thanks to the :target selector.

If you wanted to be even cleverer, you could choose to give the element an animated background image that fades from yellow to white, thus simulating the yellow fade technique popularized by companies like 37 Signals.

```
.comment:target {
    background-image: url(img/fade.gif);
}
```

The `target` selector is supported by all recent versions of Safari and Firefox, but isn't supported by Internet Explorer at the time of writing.

Highlighting different types of links

On many sites, it is difficult to tell if a link points to another page on that site or to a different site altogether. We have all clicked a link expecting it to go to another page in the current site, only to be whisked away somewhere different and unexpected. To combat this problem, many sites will open external links in a new window. However, opening a new window is not a good idea as doing so takes control away from the user and potentially litters the desktops with unwanted windows. This can also cause problems for users of screen readers if the new window is not announced. Furthermore, new windows effectively break the back button, as it is impossible go back to the previous screen.

A better solution would be to indicate external links somehow and let the user decide to leave the site, open the link in a new window, or more probably these days, open it in a new tab. You can do this by adding a small icon next to any external links. Sites like www.wikipedia.com already do this, and an icon convention for offsite links has started to appear: a box with an arrow (see Figure 5-4).

Figure 5-4. External link icon

The easiest way to include an external link icon on your page is to add a class to any external links and apply the icon as a background image. In this example, I have created space for the icon by giving the link a small amount of right padding and then applied the icon as a background image at the top right of the link (see Figure 5-5).

```
.external {
    background: url(/img/externalLink.gif) no-repeat right top;
    padding-right: 10px;
}
```

115

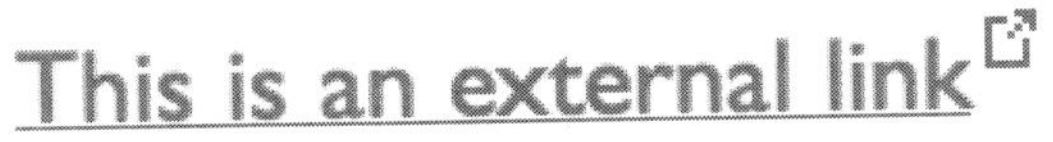

This is an external link 🔗

Figure 5-5. External link styling

Although this method works, it is not a particularly smart or elegant way of doing things, as you have to manually add your class to each external link. What if there was a way to get CSS to determine whether something was an external link for you? Well, in fact there is: using attribute selectors.

As you learned in Chapter 1, attribute selectors allow you to target an element based on the existence or value of an attribute. CSS 3 extends the ability with substring matching. As the name suggests, these selectors allow you to target an element by matching your chosen text to part of the attribute's value. CSS 3 is not an official specification yet, so using these advanced selectors may invalidate your code. However, the majority of standards-compliant browsers support these nifty CSS 3 selectors.

This technique works by first targeting any links that start with the text http: using the [att^=val] attribute selector:

```
a[href^="http:"] {
    background: url(/img/externalLink.gif) no-repeat right top;
    padding-right: 10px;
}
```

This should highlight all external links. However, it will also pick up internal links using absolute rather than relative URLs. To avoid this, you need to reset any links to your own site by removing the external link icon. This is done by matching links that point to your domain name, removing the external link icon, and resetting the right padding (see Figure 5-6).

```
a[href^="http://www.yoursite.com"],
a[href^="http://yoursite.com"] {
    background-image: none;
    padding-right: 0;
}
```

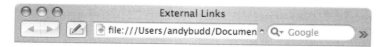

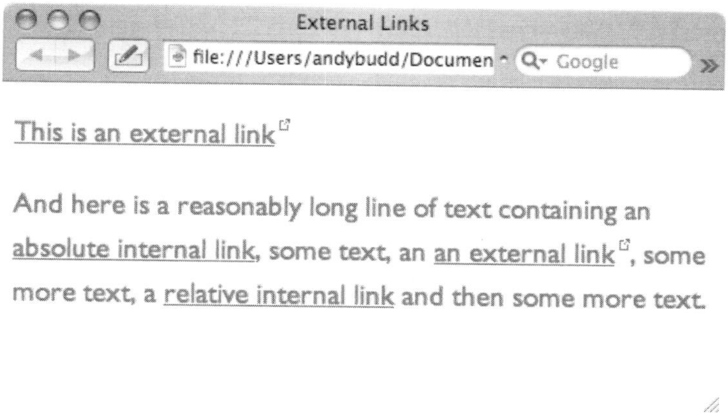

External Links
file:///Users/andybudd/Documen
Google
This is an external link
And here is a reasonably long line of text containing an absolute internal link, some text, an an external link, some more text, a relative internal link and then some more text.

Figure 5-6. A page showing external links styled differently from internal ones

Most modern browsers support this technique, but older browsers such as IE 6 and below will simply ignore it.

If you like, you could extend this technique to highlight email links as well. In this example, I am adding a small email icon to all `mailto` links:

```
a[href^="mailto:"] {
  background: url(img/email.png) no-repeat right top;
  padding-right: 10px;
}
```

You could even highlight nonstandard protocols such as the AOL instant messaging protocol (AIM), with a little AIM buddy icon (see Figure 5-7):

```
a[href^="aim:"] {
  background: url(img/im.png) no-repeat right top;
  padding-right: 10px;
}

<a href="aim:goim?screenname=andybudd">instant message</a>
```

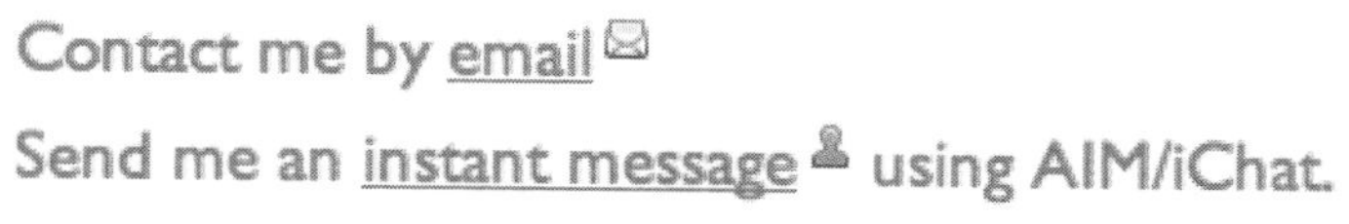
Contact me by email
Send me an instant message using AIM/iChat.

Figure 5-7. Email and instant message link styles

Highlighting downloadable documents and feeds

Another common frustration is clicking a link thinking it will take you to a page and discovering that the site has started downloading a PDF or Microsoft Word document. Luckily, CSS can help us distinguish these types of links as well. This is done using the [att$=val] attribute selector, which targets attributes that end in a particular value, such as .pdf or .doc:

```css
a[href$=".pdf"] {
   background: url(img/pdfLink.gif) no-repeat right top;
   padding-right: 10px;
}


a[href$=".doc"] {
   background: url(img/wordLink.gif) no-repeat right top;
   padding-right: 10px;
}
```

So in a similar way to the previous examples, you can highlight links to word documents or PDFs with their own separate icon, warning people that they are clicking are downloads rather than links to another page.

Last, many people have RSS feeds on their websites. The idea is for people to copy these links into their feed readers. However, inadvertently clicking one of these links may take you to a page of seemingly meaningless data. To avoid possible confusion, you could highlight RSS feeds using a similar method, with your own RSS icon:

```css
a[href$=".rss"], a[href$=".rdf"] {
   background: url(img/feedLink.gif) no-repeat right top;
   padding-right: 10px;
}
```

All these techniques can help to improve the user experience on your site. By warning users about offsite links or downloadable documents, you let them know exactly what to expect when they click a link, and avoid unnecessary backtracking and frustration.

> Unfortunately, IE 6 and below don't support the attribute selector. Luckily, you can create a similar effect by adding a class to each element using JavaScript and the DOM. One of the best ways to do this is with Simon Willison's excellent getElementBySelector function; you can find more details at http://simonwillison.net/2003/Mar/25/getElementsBySelector/. Alternatively, jQuery allows you to do something very similar.

Creating links that look like buttons

Anchors are inline elements, which means they only activate when you click the contents of the link. However, there are instances when you may want to create more of a button-like effect with a larger clickable area. You can do this by setting the `display` property of the anchor to `block` and then changing the `width`, `height`, and other properties to create the style and hit area you desire.

```
a {
    display: block;
    width: 6.6em;
    line-height: 1.4;
    text-align: center;
    text-decoration: none;
    border: 1px solid #66a300;
    background-color: #8cca12;
     color: #fff;
}
```

The resulting link should now look like Figure 5-8.

Figure 5-8. Link styled like a button

With the link now displaying as a block-level element, clicking anywhere in the block will activate the link.

If you look at the CSS, you'll see that the `width` has been explicitly set in ems. By their nature, block-level elements expand to fill the available width, so if the width of their parent elements were greater than the required width of the link, you would need to apply the desired width to the link. This would likely be the case if you wanted to use such a styled link in the main content area of your page. However, if your styled links were going in a sidebar, for example, you would probably just set the width of the sidebar and not worry about the width of the links.

You may wonder why I am using `line-height` to control the height of the button instead of `height`. Well, this is actually a handy little trick for centering the text in the button vertically. If you were to set a `height`, you would probably have to use padding to push the text down and fake vertical centering. However, text is always vertically centered in a line box, so by using `line-height` instead, the text will always sit in the middle of the box. There is one downside, though. If the text in your button wraps onto two lines, the button will be twice as tall as you want it to be.

119

The only way to avoid this is to size your buttons and text in such a way that the text won't wrap, or at least won't wrap until your text size has been increased beyond a reasonable amount.

If you choose to use this technique, make sure that you only use it on things that are actually links and don't update the server. Otherwise, you may experience some undesirable results. When Google accelerator launched, people found that content in their CMS or web application was mysteriously disappearing. Sometimes, the entire contents of a site would vanish overnight. It turns out that the authors of these tools had used anchor links rather than form elements for their delete buttons. Google accelerator would spider these links in order to cache them and inadvertently delete the content! Search engines spiders can have the same effect, recursively deleting vast swathes of data. For that reason, you should never use links to make changes on the server. Or to put it in technical terms, links should only ever be used for GET requests, and never for POST requests.

Simple rollovers

In the bad old days, people used large and overly complicated JavaScript functions to create rollover effects. Thankfully, using the :hover pseudo-class allows us to create rollover effects without the need of JavaScript. You can extend the previous example to include a very simple rollover effect simply by setting the background and text color of the link when hovered over (see Figure 5-9):

```
a:hover,
a:focus {
  background-color: #f7a300;
  border-color: #ff7400;
}
```

Figure 5-9. Hover style showing active area

Rollovers with images

Changing background colors works well for simple buttons, but for more complicated buttons, you will probably want to use background images. For the next example, I have created three button images: one for the default state, one for the hover and focus states and one for the active state (see Figure 5-10).

Figure 5-10. Images for the normal, hover, and active button states

The code for this example is very similar to the preceding example. The main difference is that background images are being used instead of borders and background colors.

```
a:link, a:visited {
    display: block;
    width: 203px;
    height: 72px;
    text-indent: -1000em;
    background: url(/img/button.png) left top no-repeat;
}


a:hover, a:focus {  background-image: url(/img/button-over.png);
}


a:active {
    background-image: url(/img/button-active.png);
}
```

This example uses fixed-width and fixed-height buttons, which is why I have set explicit pixel dimensions in the CSS. To get the exact text treatment I wanted, I have included the button text on the graphic and then hidden the anchor text off the screen with a large negative text indent. However, there is nothing to stop you from creating oversized button graphics or using a combination of background colors and images to create a fluid or an elastic button.

Pixy-style rollovers

The main drawback with the multiple image method is a slight delay as browsers load the hover image for the first time. This can cause an undesirable flickering effect and make your buttons feel a little unresponsive. It is possible to preload the hover images by applying them as a background to the parent element. However, there is another way. Instead of swapping in multiple background images, use a single image and switch its background position instead. Using a single image has the added benefit of reducing the number of server requests as well as allowing you to keep all your button states in one place. This method is known as the Pixy method after the nickname of its creator, Petr Staníček (you can find more information at his website: http://wellstyled.com/css-nopreload-rollovers.html).

Begin by creating your combined button image (see Figure 5-11). In this case, I am limiting the button to an up state, an over state, and an active state. However, you could also include a visited state if you desired.

Figure 5-11. All three button states as a single image

The code is almost identical to the previous example. However, this time, you align the background image so the normal state is in the center and then shift the background to the right or left for the hover and active states.

```
a:link, a:visited {
    display: block;
    width: 203px;
    height: 72px;
    text-indent: -1000em;
    background: url(/img/buttons.png) -203px 0 no-repeat;
}

a:hover, a:focus {
    background-position: right top;
}

a:active {
    background-position: left top;
}
```

Unfortunately, Internet Explorer still makes a round-trip to the server to request a new image, even though all you are doing is changing the alignment of the image. This causes a slight flicker, which can be a little annoying. To avoid the flicker you need to apply the rollover state to the link's parent element, for example, its containing paragraph.

```
p {
    background: url(/img/ buttons.png)↵
    no-repeat right top;
}
```

The image will still disappear for an instant while it is being reloaded. However, during this time, the same image will be revealed underneath, hiding the flicker.

An alternate way to remove the flicker is to include the following line of code in your Internet Explorer specific CSS file, which turns background caching on.

```
html {
    filter: expression(document.execCommand("BackgroundImageCache",↵
    false, true));
}
```

CSS sprites

Multiple requests to the server can have a dramatic effect on the performance of your site, so the Pixy method aims to reduce the number of requests by including all your button states in a single image. But why stop there? Why not go one step further and include all your icons or even your site navigation in a single image? That way, you could reduce the number of calls to the server from multiple figures to just two or three. This is exactly what CSS sprites are—a single image containing a multitude of different icons, buttons, or other graphics. Many large websites use this technique including the Yahoo! homepage. In fact, we use the same technique for the Clearleft site navigation (see Figure 5-12).

```
#nav li a {
    display: block;
    text-indent: -9999px;
    height: 119px;
    width: 100px;
    background-image: url('/img/nav.png');
    background-repeat: no-repeat;
}

#nav li.home a,
#nav li.home a:link,
#nav li.home a:visited {
    background-position: 0 0;
}
```

```
#nav li.home a:hover,
#nav li.home a:focus,
#nav li.home a:active {
  background-position: 0 -119px;
}


#nav li.who-we-are a,
#nav li.who-we-are a:link,
#nav li.who-we-are a:visited {
    background-position: -100px 0;
}
#nav li.who-we-are a:hover,
#nav li.who-we-are a:focus,
#nav li.who-we-are a:active {
  background-position: -100px -119px;
}
```

Figure 5-12. The CSS sprites file we use on the Clearleft site

By using this technique, you can cut down on the requests the web browser makes to your server, considerably speeding up the download times. Furthermore, using sprites keeps all your buttons, icons, and miscellaneous graphics in one location, improving maintainability. So it's a win-win situation.

Rollovers with CSS 3

CSS 3 includes a number of properties like `text-shadow`, `box-shadow`, and `border-radius` that make it possible to create heavily styled buttons that require no images whatsoever. To create such a button, I will start with the code from our first example:

```
a {
    display: block;
    width: 6.6em;
    height: 1.4em;
    line-height: 1.4;
    text-align: center;
    text-decoration: none;
    border: 1px solid #66a300;
    background-color: #8cca12;
    color: #fff;
}
```

Next, I'll add curved borders and a drop shadow. I'm also going to give the button text a subtle drop shadow (see Figure 5-13).

```
a {
    display: block;
    width: 6.6em;
    height: 1.4em;
    line-height: 1.4;
    text-align: center;
    text-decoration: none;
    border: 1px solid #66a300;
     -moz-border-radius: 6px;
     -webkit-border-radius: 6px;
     border-radius: 6px;
    background-color: #8cca12;
     color: #fff;
    text-shadow: 2px 2px 2px #66a300;
    -moz-box-shadow: 2px 2px 2px #ccc;
```

```
    -webkit-box-shadow: 2px 2px 2px #ccc;

    box-shadow: 2px 2px 2px #ccc;

}
```

Figure 5-13. A rounded corner button using only CSS

To re-create the gradient, Safari 4 beta supports a proprietary value called -webkit-gradient. While I would never normally recommend the use of proprietary code, this may provide a hint of where CSS is heading in the future. This proprietary value takes a number of different arguments including the type of gradient (liner or radial), the direction of the gradient (in this case, top-left to bottom-left), a starting color, an end color, and any stops along the way. Obviously, if you didn't want to use this proprietary code, you could simply produce your own background image gradient instead.

```
    a {
        display: block;
        width: 6.6em;
        height: 1.4em;
        line-height: 1.4;
        text-align: center;
        text-decoration: none;
        border: 1px solid #66a300;
        -moz-border-radius: 6px;
          -webkit-border-radius: 6px;
          border-radius: 6px;
        background-image: -webkit-gradient(linear, left top, left bottom, ↵
    from(#abe142), to(#67a400));
        background-color: #8cca12;
          color: #fff;
        text-shadow: 2px 2px 2px #66a300;
        -moz-box-shadow: 2px 2px 2px #ccc;
        -webkit-box-shadow: 2px 2px 2px #ccc;
```

```
box-shadow: 2px 2px 2px #ccc;
}
```

Last, Safari includes another proprietary property called box-reflect, which as the name suggests, allows you to create reflections of an object. This property contains a number of different arguments including the position and distance of the reflection along with a masking image. Interestingly, you can use the –webkit-gradient value to automatically generate this mask. In this instance, I'm positioning the reflection 2 pixels below the button and using a mask that fades to white (see Figure 5-14).

```
a {
display: block;
width: 6.6em;
  height: 1.4em;
  line-height: 1.4;
  text-align: center;
  text-decoration: none;
  border: 1px solid #66a300;
   -moz-border-radius: 6px;
   -webkit-border-radius: 6px;
   border-radius: 6px;
   background-image: -webkit-gradient(linear, left top, left bottom, ↵
from(#abe142), to(#67a400));
   background-color: #8cca12;
    color: #fff;
   text-shadow: 2px 2px 2px #66a300;
   -moz-box-shadow: 2px 2px 2px #ccc;
   -webkit-box-shadow: 2px 2px 2px #ccc;
   box-shadow: 2px 2px 2px #ccc;
   -webkit-box-reflect: below 2px -webkit-gradient↵
(linear, left top, left bottom, from(transparent),↵
color-stop(0.52, transparent), to(white));
}
```

Figure 5-14. A rounded corner button using Safari specific extensions to CSS

There is some debate around whether these types of effects should be done using CSS or not, so it's uncertain if they will ever make it into the official specification. Because of this and the lack of cross-browser support, it would be unwise to use these techniques in a production environment. However, that shouldn't stop you from playing around with them on your personal sites just as long as you realize that they're invalid CSS and may get removed or changed in future versions of the browser.

Pure CSS tooltips

Tooltips are the little yellow text boxes that pop up in some browsers when you hover over elements with title tags. Several developers have created their own custom, stylized tooltips using a combination of JavaScript and CSS. However, it is possible to create pure CSS tooltips by using CSS positioning techniques. This technique requires a modern, standards-compliant browser like Firefox to work properly. As such, it is not a technique you would add to your day-to-day arsenal. However, it does demonstrate the power of advanced CSS and gives you a hint of what will be possible when CSS is better supported.

As with all of the examples in this book, you need to start with well-structured and meaningful HTML:

```
<p>
    <a href="http://www.andybudd.com/" class="tooltip">
Andy Budd<span> (This website rocks) </span></a> is a web developer based in↵
Brighton England.
    </p>
```

I have given the link a class of `tooltip` to differentiate it from other links. Inside the link, I have added the text I wish to display as the link text, followed by the tooltip text enclosed in a span. I have wrapped my tooltip text in brackets so that the sentence still makes sense with styles turned off.

The first thing you need to do is set the `position` property of the anchor to `relative`. This allows you to position the contents of the span absolutely, relative to the position of its parent anchor.

You do not want the tooltip text to display initially, so you should set its `display` property to none:

```
a.tooltip {
  position: relative;
}


a.tooltip span {
  display: none;
}
```

When the anchor is hovered over, you want the contents of the span to appear. This is done by setting the `display` property of the span to `block`, but only when the link is hovered over. If you were to test the code now, hovering over the link would simply make the span text appear next to the link.

To position the contents of the span below and to the right of the anchor, you need to set the `position` property of the span to `absolute` and position it 1 em from the top of the anchor and 2 ems from the left.

```
a.tooltip:hover span {
  display: block;
  position: absolute;
  top: 1em;
  left: 2em;
}
```

> *Remember, an absolutely positioned element is positioned in relation to its nearest positioned ancestor or, failing that, the root element. In this example, we have positioned the anchor, so the span is positioned in relation to that.*

And that's the bulk of the technique. All that is left is to add some styling to make the span look more like a tooltip. You can do this by giving the span some padding, a border, and a background color:

```
a.tooltip:hover span, a.tooltip:focus span {
  display:block;
  position:absolute;
  top:1em;
  left:2em;
  padding: 0.2em 0.6em;
```

```
    border:1px solid #996633;

    background-color:#FFFF66;

    color:#000;

}
```

In Firefox, the applied technique should look something like Figure 5-15.

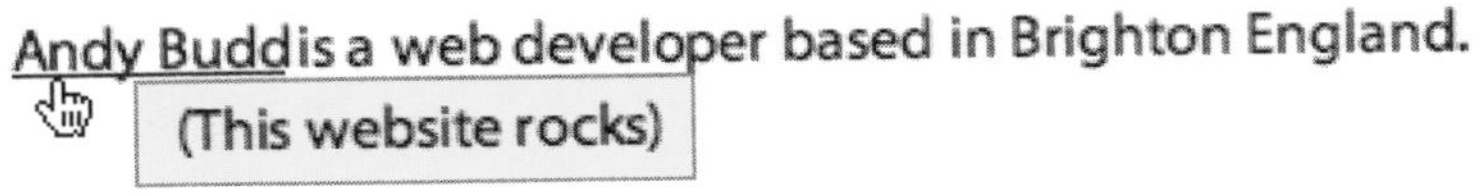

Andy Budd is a web developer based in Brighton England.
(This website rocks)

Figure 5-15. Pure CSS tooltip

Summary

In this chapter, you have learned how to style links in a variety of ways. You now know how to style links depending on the site or file they link to, and you can make links behave like buttons and create rollover effects using colors or images. You can even create advanced effects such as pure CSS tooltips.

In the next chapter, you will learn how to manipulate lists, and using the information you have learned in this chapter, create navigation lists, pure CSS image maps, and remote rollovers. Let the fun begin!

Chapter 6

Styling Lists and Creating Nav Bars

It is human nature to try to organize the world around us. Scientists create lists of animals, plants, and chemical elements. Magazines create lists of the top 10 movies, the latest fashion trends, and the worst-dressed celebrities. People write shopping lists, to-do lists, and lists to Santa. We just love making lists.

Lists provide us with a way of grouping related elements and, by doing so, we give them meaning and structure. Most web pages contain some form of list, be it a list of the latest news stories, a list of links to your favorite web pages, or a list of links to other parts of your site. Identifying these items as lists and marking them up as such can help add structure to your HTML documents, providing useful hooks with which to apply your styles.

In this chapter you will learn about

- Styling lists with CSS
- Using background images as bullets
- Creating vertical and horizontal nav bars
- Using sliding doors tabbed navigation
- Pure CSS drop-downs
- Creating CSS image maps
- Creating remote rollovers
- Using definition lists

Basic list styling

Basic list styling is very simple. Say you start with this simple to-do list:

```
<ul>
  <li>Read emails</li>
  <li>Write chapter</li>
  <li>Go shopping</li>
  <li>Cook dinner</li>
  <li>Watch Lost</li>
</ul>
```

To add a custom bullet, you could use the `list-style-image` property. However, this doesn't give you much control over the position of your bullet image. Instead, it is more common to turn list bullets off and add your custom bullet as a background image on the list element. You can then use the background image positioning properties to accurately control the alignment of your custom bullet.

Older versions of Internet Explorer and Opera control list indentation using the left margin, whereas most modern browsers, including Firefox and Safari use left padding. As such, the first thing you will want to do is remove this indentation by zeroing down the `margin` and `padding` on the list. To remove the default bullet, you simply set the list style type to `none`:

```
ul {
  margin: 0;
  padding: 0;
  list-style-type: none;
}
```

Adding a custom bullet is very straightforward. Applying padding to the left side of the list item creates the necessary space for your bullet. The bullet is then applied as a background image on the list item. If the list item is going to span multiple lines, you will probably want to position the bullet at or near the top of the list item. However, if you know the contents of the list items won't span more than one line, you can vertically center the bullet by setting the vertical position to either `middle` or `50%`:

```
li {
  background: url(/img/bullet.gif) no-repeat 0 50%;
  padding-left: 30px;
}
```

The resulting styled list can be seen in Figure 6-1.

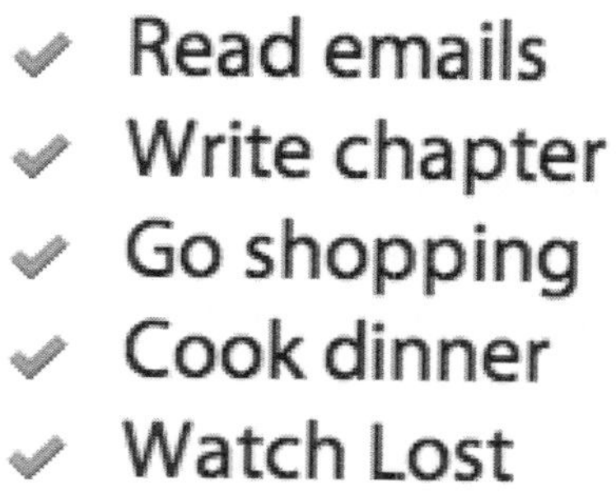

Read emails
Write chapter
Go shopping
Cook dinner
Watch Lost

Figure 6-1. Simple styled list with custom bullets

Creating a basic vertical nav bar

Combining the previous example with the link styling techniques you learned in Chapter 5, you can create graphically rich vertical navigation bars complete with CSS rollovers, like the one shown in Figure 6-2.

Home
About
Our Services
Our Work
News
Contact

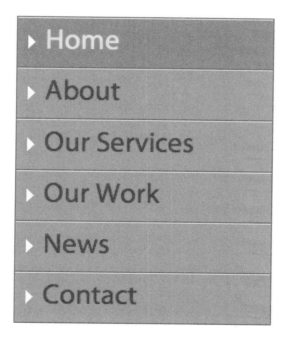

Figure 6-2. Styled vertical nav bar

As always, you need to start with good, semantic mark-up:

```
<ul class="nav">
  <li><a href="home.htm">Home</a></li>
  <li><a href="about.htm">About</a></li>
  <li><a href="services.htm">Our Services</a></li>
  <li><a href="work.htm">Our Work</a></li>
  <li><a href="news.htm">News</a></li>
  <li><a href="contact.htm">Contact</a></li>
</ul>
```

The first things you want to do are remove the default bullets and zero down the `margin` and `padding`:

```
ul.nav {
  margin: 0;
  padding: 0;
  list-style-type: none;
}
```

You can then start layering on the graphical styling. In this case, I'm giving my navigation menu a light green background and a dark green border. I'm also going to set the width of my navigate list in ems.

```
ul.nav {
  margin: 0;
  padding: 0;
  list-style-type: none;
  width: 8em;
  background-color: #8BD400;
  border: 1px solid #486B02;
}
```

Rather than style the list items, styling the enclosed anchor links provides better cross-browser compatibility. To create a button-like hit area, you simply set the `display` property of the anchors to `block`. The anchor links will then expand to take up the available space, which in this case is determined by the width of the list. You could set the width of the anchors explicitly, but I've found setting the width of the parent list makes for more maintainable code. The last couple of rules are just stylistic, setting the color of the link text and turning off the underlines.

```
ul.nav a {
   display: block;
   color: #2B3F00;
   text-decoration: none;
}
```

To create the beveled effect on the menu items, you need to set the top border to be lighter than the background color and the bottom border slightly darker. At this point, you can also drop in a background image to use as an icon.

```
ul.nav a {
   display: block;
   color: #2B3F00;
   text-decoration: none;
   border-top: 1px solid #E4FFD3;
   border-bottom: 1px solid #486B02;
   background: url(/img/arrow.gif) no-repeat 5% 50%;
   padding: 0.3em 1em;
}
```

Ideally, I would have set the positioning of my arrow to be 10 pixels from the left-hand edge of the anchor. However, the CSS specification doesn't allow the mixing of units, so I've used a percentage instead. In reality, most browsers accept mixed units, and I think this is one of several instances where the specification is wrong.

With all the borders stacked one on top of the other, you'll notice that the bottom border on the final link doubles up with the bottom border on the list. In this instance, I'm going to take the simple option and remove the bottom border from the list. However in situations where this isn't possible, the addition of a class on the first or last list item can allow you to remove the border directly. In the future, you'll also be able to use the :last-child pseudo class, but for the time being, browser support is limited.

```
ul.nav .last a {
   border-bottom: 0;
}
```

The list now looks like a stylish vertical navigation bar. To complete the effect, the last thing you need to do is apply the :hover, :focus, and :selected states. To do this, simply change the background and text colors. You could also experiment with changing the border colors to create a depressed button type effect. These styles are applied to the anchor links when the user hovers over them. They are also applied to any anchors that have a class of selected applied to their parent list item.

```
ul.nav a:hover,
ul.nav a:focus,
  ul.nav .selected a {
  color: #E4FFD3;
  background-color: #6DA203;
}
```

This technique should now work in all the major browsers except IE 6 and below for Windows. Unfortunately, IE6 inexplicably adds extra space above and below the list items. To fix this bug, you need to set the display property on the list items to inline:

```
ul.nav li {
  display: inline: /* :KLUDGE: Removes large gaps in IE/Win */
}
```

And there you have it: a styled vertical nav bar, complete with rollovers.

Highlighting the current page in a nav bar

In the previous vertical nav bar example, I used a class to indicate the current page. For small sites with the navigation embedded in the page, you can simply add the class on a page-by-page basis. For large sites, there is a good chance that the navigation is being built dynamically, in which case the class can be added on the back end. However, for medium-sized sites, where the main navigation doesn't change, it is common to include the navigation as an external file. In these situations, wouldn't it be good if there were a way to highlight the page you are on, without having to dynamically add a class to the menu? Well, with CSS there is.

This concept works by adding an ID or a class name to the body element of each page, denoting which page or section the user is in. You then add a corresponding ID or class name to each item in your navigation list. The unique combination of body ID and list ID/class can be used to highlight your current section or page in the site nav.

Take the following HTML fragment as an example. The current page is the home page, as indicated by an ID of home on the body. Each list item in the main navigation is given a class name based on the name of the page the list item relates to.

```
<body id="home">
<ul class="nav">
  <li><a href="home.htm">Home</a></li>
  <li><a href="about.htm">About</a></li>
  <li><a href="services.htm">Our Services</a></li>
  <li><a href="work.htm">Our Work</a></li>
  <li><a href="news.htm">News</a></li>
```

```
    <li><a href="contact.htm">Contact</a></li>
  </ul>
</body>
```

To highlight the current page, you simply target the following combination of IDs and class names:

```
#home .nav .home a,
#about .nav .about a ,
#news .nav .news a,
#products .nav .products a,
#services .nav .services a {
  background-position: right bottom;
  color: #fff;
  cursor: default;
}
```

When the user is on the home page, the nav item with a class of home will display the selected state, whereas on the news page, the nav item with the class of news will show the selected state. For added effect, I have changed to cursor style to show the default arrow cursor. That way, if you mouse over the selected link, your cursor will not change state and you won't be tempted to click a link to a page you are already on.

Creating a simple horizontal nav bar

Imagine you had a page of search results and you wanted to create a simple page-based navigation list like the one in Figure 6-3. To do this, you would start by creating an ordered list of your navigation options.

```
<ol class="pagination">
  <li><a href="search.htm?page=1" rel="prev">Prev</a></li>
  <li><a href="search.htm?page=1">1</a></li>
  <li class="selected">2</li>
  <li><a href="search.htm?page=3">3</a></li>
  <li><a href="search.htm?page=4">4</a></li>
  <li><a href="search.htm?page=5">5</a></li>
  <li><a href="search.htm?page=3" rel="next">Next</a></li>
</ol>
```

Figure 6-3. Horizontal search results navigation bar

You'll notice that I've used the rel attribute to denote the previous and next pages in a set of results. This is a great use of the rel attribute and will come in handy when we style these links differently later on.

As with the other list examples in this chapter, you first need to remove the default browser margin, padding, and list styles. Many developers, including myself, prefer to do this using a global reset at the start of their style sheets. So if you're using a global reset, you can skip this first step.

```
ol.pagination {
  margin: 0;
  padding: 0;
  list-style-type: none;
}
```

To make the list items line up horizontally instead of vertically you could set their display property to inline. However for more complex horizontal list styling you will gain more control if you float the items and then use margins to space the space them out instead.

```
ol.pagination li {
  float: left;
  margin-right: 0.6em;
}
```

Now the list items are all displaying horizontally you can start applying the graphical treatment. In this case, I want all the page numbers to appear in a square box with a gray background. When users hover over these links, I want their backgrounds to turn blue and the link text to turn white.

```
ol.pagination a,
 ol.pagination  li.selected {
   display: block;
   padding: 0.2em 0.5em;
   border: 1px solid #ccc;
   text-decoration: none;
}
```

```
ol.pagination a:hover,
ol.pagination a:focus,
ol.pagination li.selected {
  background-color: blue;
  color: white;
}
```

That's all very well for the page numbers, but I want to style the **prev** and **next** links slightly differently. To do this, I'm going to target their rel attributes using attribute selectors. First off, I don't want the previous and next links to have a border effect, so I'm going to turn these off.

```
ol.pagination a[rel="prev"],
ol.pagination a[rel="next"] {
  border: none;
}
```

The other thing I want to do is add a presentational arrow at the start and the end of the list. You could do this by hard-coding them into your HTML. However, you can also inject them using CSS, allowing you to change or remove them later on. To use CSS, you need to use the :before and :after pseudo-selectors in combination with the content property.

```
ol.pagination a[rel="prev"]:before {
  content: "\00AB";
  padding-right: 0.5em;
}
```

```
ol.pagination a[rel="next"]:after {
  content: "\00BB";
  padding-left: 0.5em;
}
```

The first declaration targets the anchor link at the start of the list and adds a double left arrow with the character code of "00AB" before said link. The second declaration targets the last anchor link and adds a double right arrow at the end of the link.

And there you have it, a simple, yet flexible, horizontal page navigation bar.

Creating a graphical nav bar

Simple navigation bars are great for paged content, but you'll probably want to create more graphically rich menus for your main navigation. In this example, I am going to demonstrate how to create a graphical navigation bar like the one shown in Figure 6-4.

HOME   ABOUT   NEWS   PRODUCTS   SERVICES   CLIENTS   CASE STUDIES

Figure 6-4. Horizontal nav bar

As in the previous example, you start with a simple, unordered list:

```
<ul class="nav">
    <li><a href="home.htm">Home</a></li>
    <li><a href="about.htm">About</a></li>
    <li><a href="news.htm">News</a></li>
    <li><a href="products.htm">Products</a></li>
    <li><a href="services.htm">Services</a></li>
    <li><a href="clients.htm">Clients</a></li>
    <li><a href="case-studies.htm">Case Studies</a></li>
</ul>
```

You then zero down the padding and margins, as well as remove the default bullets. For this example, I want my horizontal nav bar to be 72 ems wide and to have a repeating orange gradient as a background.

```
ul. nav {
    margin: 0;
    padding: 0;
    list-style: none;
    width: 72em;
    background: #FAA819 url(img/mainNavBg.gif) repeat-x;
}
```

The list is currently displayed vertically. To make it display horizontally, float your list items to the left.

```
ul. nav li {
    float: left;
}
```

Remember that when an element is floated, it no longer takes up any space in the flow of the document. As such, the parent list effectively has no content and collapses down, hiding the list background. As you learned in Chapter 3, there are several ways to make parent elements contain floated children. One method is to add a clearing element. Unfortunately, this adds unnecessary markup to the page so should be avoided if possible. Another other method is to float the parent element as well and clear it further down the line, say, using the site footer. The third method it to use the overflow:hidden technique, which is the method I normally use:

```
ul.nav {
  margin: 0;
  padding: 0;
  list-style: none;
  width: 72em;
  overflow: hidden;
  background: #FAA819 url(img/mainNavBg.gif) repeat-x;
}
```

As with the page navigation example, each of the links in this horizontal nav bar is made to behave like a button by setting its `display` property to `block`. If you wanted each button to be a fixed size, you could explicitly set its height and width. However, this can cause maintainability issues. Instead I'm going to let the width of each button be based on the size of the anchor text. To do this, rather than setting an explicit width, I have applied 3 ems of padding to the left and right sides of each anchor link. As in the previous example, the link text is being vertically centered using line height. After that, the link underlines are turned off, and the link color is changed to white:

```
ul.nav a {
  display: block;
  padding: 0 3em;
  line-height: 2.1em;
  text-decoration: none;
  color: #fff;
}
```

I want to create dividers between each link in the nav bar. You could do this by setting horizontal borders on the list item or anchors. However, for simplicity's sake, I'm going to apply a background image to the anchor links instead.

```
ul.nav a {
  display: block;
  padding: 0 2em;
  line-height: 2.1em;
  background: url(img/divider.gif) repeat-y left top;
  text-decoration: none;
  color: #fff;
}
```

However, the first link in the nav bar will have an unwanted divider. Adding a class to the first list item and setting the background image to none can remove this:

```
ul. nav .first a {
  background-image: none;
}
```

Alternatively, if you're not too worried about supporting IE 6, you could forego the additional class and use the :first-child pseudo class instead.

```
ul.nav li:first-child a {
  background: none;
}
```

Last, the rollover state in this example is simply a change in link color:

```
ul.nav a:hover,
ul.nav a:focus  {
  color: #333;
}
```

And there you have it: a well-styled horizontal nav bar with good, cross-browser support.

Simplified sliding door tabbed navigation

In Chapter 4, you learned about Douglas Bowman's sliding doors technique and how it could be used to create flexible, rounded-corner boxes. This technique can also be used to create flexible, expandable tabbed navigation. Using this method, tabs are created from one large image and one side image. As the text in the tabs expands, more of the large image is uncovered. The smaller image stays flush to the left, covering up the hard edge of the larger image and completing the effect (see Figure 6-5).

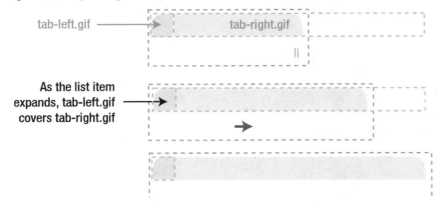

Figure 6-5. Example of the "sliding doors" technique

The images used to create the tabs in the following example can be seen in Figure 6-6. Both of these images are very large. This is to allow the font size to be increased by several hundred percent without the tabs appearing to break.

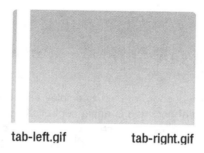

tab-left.gif   tab-right.gif

Figure 6-6. The two images that make up the tabs

The HTML for this example is exactly the same as in the previous, horizontal nav bar example:

```
<ul class="nav">
    <li><a href="home.htm">Home</a></li>
    <li><a href="about.htm">About</a></li>
    <li><a href="news.htm">News</a></li>
    <li><a href="products.htm">Products</a></li>
    <li><a href="services.htm">Services</a></li>
    <li><a href="clients.htm">Clients</a></li>
    <li><a href="case-studies.htm">Case Studies</a></li>
</ul>
```

As in the previous examples, the margin and padding are zeroed, the list bullets are removed, and a width is set for the navigation bar. An overflow of hidden is also applied to the navigation list in order to clear any enclosed floats.

```
ul.nav {
    margin: 0;
    padding: 0;
    list-style: none;
    width: 72em;
    overflow: hidden;
}
```

Like the previous example, the list elements are floated left to make them display horizontally rather than vertically. However, this time, the larger of the two images that make up the tab is applied as a background image to the list item. As this image forms the right side of the tab, it is positioned to the right

```
ul.nav li {
  float: left;
  background: url(img/tab-right.gif) no-repeat right top;
}
```

As in the previous example, the anchors are set to display as block-level elements to make the whole area clickable. The width of each tab is again controlled by the width of the contents, and setting the line height similarly controls the height. To complete the tab effect, the left part of the tab is applied as a background on the anchor and aligned left. As the tab changes size, this image will always be aligned left, sitting over the top of the larger image and covering the hard left edge. Last, to make sure this technique works in IE 5.2 on the Mac, the anchors are floated as well.

```
ul.nav li a {
  display: block;
  padding: 0 2em;
  line-height: 2.5em;
  background: url(img/tab-left.gif) no-repeat left top;
  text-decoration: none;
  color: #fff;
  float: left;
}
```

To create the rollover effect, you can simply change the link color:

```
ul.nav a:hover,
ul.nav a:focus  {
  color: #333;
}
```

The resulting tabbed navigation should look like Figure 6-7.

Figure 6-7. Sliding doors tabbed navigation at normal size

If you increase the text size in your browser, you should see that the tabs scale nicely, as illustrated in Figure 6-8.

Figure 6-8. Sliding doors tabbed navigation after the text size has been scaled several times

This method provides an easy and hassle-free way to make attractive and accessible tabbed navigation bars.

Suckerfish drop-downs

Despite some concerns about usability, drop-down menus continue to be a popular interface element on the Web. JavaScript-only solutions abound, but many of them have innate accessibility problems—namely not working in browsers where JavaScript has been disabled. Because of this, several pioneers have explored the idea of pure CSS drop-downs. One such person is Patrick Griffiths with his Suckerfish drop-downs technique (`http://www.alistapart.com/articles/dropdowns/`).

This technique is incredibly simple and works by nesting the subnavigation in an unordered list, positioning that list off screen and then repositioning it when the parent list item is hovered. You can see the final product in Figure 6-9.

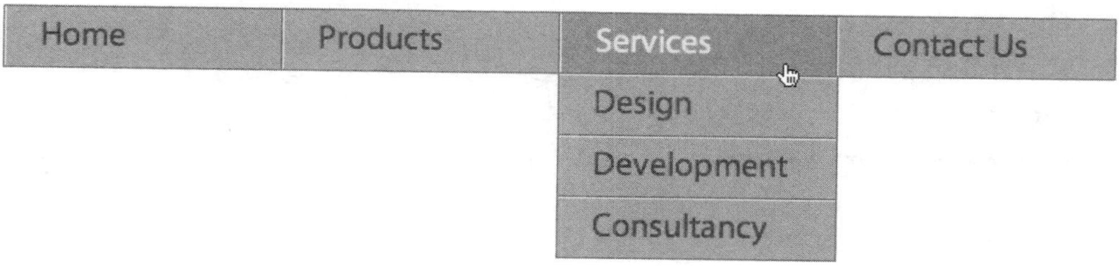

Figure 6-9. Pure CSS Suckerfish drop-downs in action

Let's start this example by marking up our multilevel navigation list.

```
<ul class="nav">
  <li><a href="/home/">Home</a></li>
  <li><a href="/products/">Products</a>
    <ul>
      <li><a href="/products/silverback/">Silverback</a></li>
      <li><a href="/products/fontdeck/">Font Deck</a></li>
    </ul>
  </li>
```

```
<li><a href="/services/">Services</a>
  <ul>
    <li><a href="/services/design/">Design</a></li>
    <li><a href="/services/development/">Development</a></li>
    <li><a href="/services/consultancy/">Consultancy</a></li>
  </ul>
</li>
<li><a href="/contact/">Contact Us</a></li>
</ul>
```

As with all the navigation examples in this chapter, you first need to zero down the margin and padding as well as remove the default bullets. As this is going to be a horizontal navigation, you then need to give your list items a width and float them all left. For stylistic reasons, I want to give my navigation lists a border and background color. However, because the enclosed list items are all floated, they take up no space, forcing the lists to collapse in on themselves. To get around this problem, I've decided to float the lists as well.

```
ul.nav, ul.nav ul {
  margin: 0;
  padding: 0;
  list-style-type: none;
  float: left;
  border: 1px solid #486B02;
  background-color: #8BD400;
}

ul.nav li {
  float: left;
  width: 8em;
  background-color: #8BD400;
}
```

To ensure the items in the drop-down menus stack up vertically, you need to set the width of the list to be the same as the width of the enclosed list items. The drop-down menu is now starting to take shape.

To hide the actual drop-downs until they are activated, we need to set their `position` to `absolute` and then hide them off the left-hand side of the screen.

```
ul.nav li ul {
    width: 8em;
    position: absolute;
    left: -999em;
}
```

Now, this is where the magic happens. By adding a hover pseudo-selector to the parent list item, we can make the drop-down list reappear by changing its position back to its regular starting position.

```
.nav li:hover ul {
    left: auto;
}
```

These last few styles set the navigation links to behave like block-level elements and then change the appearance of the list, giving the items background colors and beveled borders.

```
ul.nav a {
    display: block;
    color: #2B3F00;
    text-decoration: none;
    padding: 0.3em 1em;
    border-right: 1px solid #486B02;
    border-left: 1px solid #E4FFD3;
}

ul.nav li li a {
    border-top: 1px solid #E4FFD3;
    border-bottom: 1px solid #486B02;
    border-left: 0;
    border-right: 0;
}

/*remove unwanted borders on the end list items*/
ul.nav li:last-child a {
    border-right: 0;
    border-bottom: 0;
}
```

```
ul a:hover,
ul a:focus {
  color: #E4FFD3;
  background-color: #6DA203;
}
```

And there you have it, a simple drop-down navigation bar that uses pure CSS. This technique works in most modern browsers but fails in older version of Internet Explorer, which don't support the `:hover` pseudo-class of nonanchor elements. To get around this issue, you can use a few lines of JavaScript or a `.htc` behavior file to enable this functionality.

> *The JavaScript code for the drop-down navigation fix in Internet Explorer is beyond the scope of this book, but you can find out more details at http://htmldog.com/articles/suckerfish/dropdowns/.*

CSS image maps

Image maps allow web developers to specify regions of an image to act as hotspots. Image maps were very popular several years ago, but they are much less common these days. This is due partly to the popularity of Flash and partly to the move toward simpler and less presentational markup. While image maps are still a perfectly valid part of HTML, they do mix presentation with content. However, it is possible to create simple image maps with a combination of lists, anchors, and some advanced CSS.

For this example, I'm going to use a photograph of some members of the Clearleft team pretending to be an indie band in front of the graffiti outside our offices (see Figure 6-10). When I hover over each person, I want a rectangular box to appear. Clicking this box will take me to that person's website.

Figure 6-10. Rich, Sophie, Cath, James, and Paul posing in front of the graffiti outside our office

The first thing you need to do is add your image to the page, inside a named `div`:

```
<div class="imagemap">
  <img src="img/nerdcore.jpg" width="333" height="500"↵
  alt="Some of the Clearleft team" />
</div>
```

Then, you need to add a list of links to each person's website after the image. Each list item needs to be given a class to identify the person in that list item. You can also give each link a title attribute containing the name of the person. That way, when the link is hovered over, a tooltip showing the person's name is will be displayed on most browsers.

```
<div id="imagemap">
  <img src="img/nerdcore.jpg" width="333" height="500" ↵
  alt="Some of the Clearleft team" />
<ul>
  <li class="rich">
    <a href="http://www.clagnut.com/" title="Richard Rutter"> ↵
    Richard Rutter</a>
  </li>
  <li class="sophie">
    <a href="http://www.wellieswithwings.org/" title="Sophie Barrett">↵
    Sophie Barrett</a>
  </li>
  <li class="cath">
    <a href="http://www.electricelephant.com/" title="Cathy Jones">↵
    Cathy Jones</a>
  </li>
  <li class="james">
    <a href="http://www.jeckecko.net/blog/" title="James Box">↵
    James Box</a>
  </li>
  <li class="paul">
    <a href="http://twitter.com/nicepaul" title="Paul Annett">↵
   Paul Annett</a>
  </li>
</ul>
</div>
```

Set the width and height of the div so that it matches the dimensions of the image. Then set the position property of the div to relative. This last step is the key to this technique, as it allows the enclosed links to be positioned absolutely, in relation to the edges of the div, and hence the image.

```
.imagemap {
  width: 333px;
  height: 500px;
```

```
   position: relative; /* The key to this technique */
}
```

You won't want the list bullets to display, so remove them by setting the `list-style` property to none. For completeness, you may as well zero down the list's `margin` and `padding` as well:

```
.imagemap ul {
   margin: 0;
   padding: 0;
   list-style: none;
}
```

The next thing to do is style the links. By positioning the anchor links absolutely, they will all be moved to the top-left corner of the containing `div`. They can then be positioned individually over the correct people, forming the hotspots. However, first you will need to set their widths and heights to create your desired hit area. The link text is still displayed; therefore, it is necessary to hide it off the screen by using a large, negative text indent:

```
.imagemap a {
   position: absolute;
   display: block;
   width: 50px;
   height: 60px;
   text-indent: -1000em;
}
```

The individual links can now be positioned over the relevant people:

```
.imagemap .rich a {
   top: 50px;
   left: 80px;
}

.imagemap .sophie a {
   top: 90px;
   left: 200px;
}

.imagemap .cath a {
   top: 140px;
   left: 55px;
}
```

```
.imagemap .james a {
  top: 140px;
  left: 145px;
}

.imagemap .paul a {
  top: 165px;
  left: 245px;
}
```

Last, to create the rollover effect, a solid white border is applied to the links when they are hovered over:

```
.imagemap a:hover,
imagemap a:focus {
  border: 1px solid #fff;
}
```

And that is the basic technique finished. If you try rolling over one of the pictures, you should see something similar to Figure 6-11.

Figure 6-11. The CSS image map being rolled over

Well, that's assuming you're using a more capable browser like Safari or Firefox. If you're using Internet Explorer, you won't see anything at all! It appears that Internet Explorer doesn't like displaying links whose content has been hidden off-screen, even if you've explicitly set widths and heights. The good news is that since writing the first edition of this book, I've discovered a fix.

If you give the anchor links some kind of background, this seems to trick Internet Explorer into behaving correctly. The only problem is, we don't actually want the links to have a background, as they are supposed to be hidden! You could try setting the background to be transparent, but this doesn't seem to work. So instead, why not use a transparent image like a transparent PNG or GIF?

```
.imagemap a {
  position: absolute;
  display: block;
  background-image: url(/img/shim.gif);
  width: 60px;
  height: 80px;
  text-indent: -1000em;
}
```

Bizarrely enough, you don't actually have to point to a real image! You can simply make up a nonexistent URL and still trick IE into behaving correctly. However, linking to a nonexistent URL feels wrong, even if it is being used to fix a buggy browser, so I'd stick to using a real image, however redundant

Flickr-style image maps

If you have used the photo sharing service Flickr, you may have come across a similar technique used to annotate images (see Figure 6-12). When you roll over an annotated image, a double-bordered box will appear over the area containing each note. When you hover over one of these boxes, it will highlight and display the note. With a bit of tweaking, we can achieve the same thing using the previous technique.

Figure 6-12. Image notes on flickr

To create the double-border box, you need to add a couple of extra spans inside each anchor link. The note will also need the addition of an extra span. Once the extra spans have been added, the amended list should look like this:

```
<ul>
  <li class="rich">
    <a href="http://www.clagnut.com/">
      <span class="outer">
      <span class="inner">
```

```
    <span class="note">Richard Rutter</span>
    </span>
    </span>
  </a>
 </li>
 ...
</ul>
```

The CSS starts off identical to the previous example, setting the dimensions of the wrapper div to those of the image, and the position property to relative. The list padding and margin are again zeroed down and the bullets removed:

```
.imagemap {
  width: 333px;
  height: 500px;
  position: relative;
}


.imagemap ul {
  margin: 0;
  padding: 0;
  list-style: none;
}
```

As before, the enclosed anchor links are positioned absolutely. However this time I'm going to set the dimensions on the inner spans, and let the outer spans and anchor links take shape around them. I've given the outer span a dark border and the inner span a light border to highlight their positions on the image. Last, I don't want to hide the text inside the anchor links; I want to display it as a tool tip instead. As such, I've given this text some basic styling.

```
.imagemap a {
  position: absolute;
  display: block;
  background-image: url(/img/shim.gif);
  color: #000;
  text-decoration: none;
  border: 1px solid transparent;
}
```

```
.imagemap a .outer {
  display: block;
  border: 1px solid #000;
}


.imagemap a .inner {
  display: block;
  width: 50px;
  height: 60px;
  border: 1px solid #fff;
}
```

As before, you will need to position the anchors over each person:

```
.imagemap .rich a {
  top: 50px;
  left: 80px;
}


.imagemap .sophie a {
  top: 90px;
  left: 200px;
}


.imagemap .cath a {
  top: 140px;
  left: 55px;
}


.imagemap .james a {
  top: 140px;
  left: 145px;
}
```

```
.imagemap .paul a {
  top: 165px;
  left: 245px;
}
```

You can then apply the rollover effect to the anchor link. This is done by changing the anchor's border color from transparent to yellow, on hover and focus:

```
.imagemap a:hover,
.imagemap a:focus {
  border-color: #d4d82d;
}
```

To display the note when the hotspot is rolled over, you first need to position the contents of the note span beneath the hotspot. To do this, set the position of the note span to absolute and give it a negative bottom position. To pretty up the notes, set a width, some padding, and a background color, and then center the text:

```
.imagemap a .note {
  position: absolute;
  bottom: -3em;
  width: 7em;
  padding: 0.2em 0.5em;
  background-color:#ffc;
  text-align: center;
}
```

If you check the page in the browser, it should look something like Figure 6-13.

Figure 6-13. The Flickr style rollovers are starting to take shape

As you can see, the effect is starting to take shape. The notes look OK, but it would be nice if they were centered horizontally below the hotspot, rather than flush to the left. You can do this by positioning the left edge of the note span at the midpoint of the hotspot. Next, move the note span left, half the width of the note, using negative margins. The hotspot in this example is 50 pixels wide, so I have set the left position of the note to be 25 pixels. The notes are 8 ems wide, including the padding, so setting a negative left margin of 4 ems will horizontally center the note beneath the hotspot.

```
.imagemap a .note {
  position: absolute;
  bottom: -3em;
  width: 7em;
  padding: 0.2em 0.5em;
  background-color:#ffc;
  text-align: center;
  left: 25px;
  margin-left: -4em;
}
```

With the notes now centered, it's time to work on their interactivity. The notes should be hidden by default and only displayed when the hotspot is hovered over. To do this, you could set the `display` property to `none` and then change it to `block` when the anchor link is hovered over. However, this would prevent some screen readers from accessing the contents of the note. Instead, I am going to hide the text off the left side of the screen and reposition it on hover:

```
.imagemap a .note {
  position: absolute;
  bottom: -3em;
  width: 7em;
  padding: 0.2em 0.5em;
  background-color:#ffc;
  text-align: center;
  left: -1000em;
  margin-left: -5em;
}

.imagemap a:hover .note,
.imagemap a:focus .note {
  left: 25px;
}
```

We are almost there now. Just one more tweak is required to finish the technique. Rather than continuously display the hotspots' double borders, it would be nice if the borders only displayed when the image was rolled over. That way, people can enjoy the image normally, unfettered by the hotspots. However, when the mouse hovers over the image, the hotspots appear, letting the visitor know more information is available to be discovered. You can do this by making the borders on the outer and inner **spans** transparent by default and then setting their color when the image is hovered over:

```css
.imagemap a .outer {
  display: block;
  border: 1px solid transparent;
}

.imagemap a .inner {
  display: block;
  width: 50px;
  height: 60px;
  border: 1px solid transparent;
}

.imagemap:hover a .outer,
.imagemap:focus a .outer {
 border-color: #000;
}

.imagemap:hover a .inner,
.imagemap:focus a .inner {
 border-color: #fff;
}
```

Unfortunately, as you have already learned, IE 6 only supports hovering on anchor links. To get around this problem, it is also a good idea to display the borders when the hotspots are hovered over directly:

```css
.imagemap:hover a .outer,
.imagemap:focus a .outer,
.imagemap a:hover .outer,
.imagemap a:focus .outer {
  border: 1px solid #000;
}
```

```
.imagemap:hover a .inner,

.imagemap:focus a .inner,

.imagemap a:hover .inner,

.imagemap a:focus .inner {

  border: 1px solid #fff;

}
```

And there you have it: a Flickr-style, advanced CSS image map (see Figure 6-14).

Figure 6-14. The finished version of our Flickr-style image map

Remote rollovers

A remote rollover is a hover event that triggers a display change somewhere else on the page. This is accomplished by nesting one or more elements inside an anchor link. Then, using absolute positioning, you can position the nested elements individually. Despite being displayed in different places, they are both contained within the same parent anchor, so will both react to the same hover event. As such, when you hover over one element, it can affect the style of another element.

In this example, you are going to build on the basic CSS image map technique by placing a list of links below the image. When the links are hovered over, the image hotspots will be outlined. Conversely, when you hover over the hot areas on the picture, the text links will highlight.

The HTML for this example is similar to that of the basic CSS image map example. However, you will need two additional **spans**: one wrapped around the link text and one empty **span** to act as the hotspot. This will allow you to position the link text beneath the image and the hotspots over the respective people.

```
<div class="remote">
  <img src="img/nerdcore.jpg" width="333" height="500"↵
alt="Rich, Sophie, Cath, James and Paul" />
  <ul>


    <li class="rich">
      <a href="http://www.clagnut.com/" title="Richard Rutter">
      <span class="hotspot"></span>
      <span class="link">&raquo; Richard Rutter</span>
      </a>
    </li>


    <li class="sophie">
      <a href="http://www.wellieswithwings.org/" title="Sophie Barrett">
      <span class="hotspot"></span>
      <span class="link">&raquo; Sophie Barrett</span>
      </a>
    </li>
```

```
        <li class="cath">
          <a href="http://www.electricelephant.com/" title="Cathy Jones">
          <span class="hotspot"></span>
          <span class="link">&raquo; Cathy Jones</span>
          </a>
        </li>

        <li class="james">
          <a href="http://www.jeckecko.net/blog/" title="James Box">
          <span class="hotspot"></span>
          <span class="link">&raquo; James Box</span>
          </a>
        </li>

        <li class="paul">
          <a href="http://twitter.com/nicepaul" title="Paul Annett">
          <span class="hotspot"></span>
          <span class="link">&raquo; Paul Annett</span>
          </a>
        </li>

    </ul>
  </div>
```

The basic list styling is the same as the image map example:

```
.remote {
  width: 333px;
  height: 500px;
  position: relative;
}
```

```
.remote ul {
  margin: 0;
  padding: 0;
  list-style: none;
}
```

The first things you need to do are set the `position` property of the hotspots to `absolute` and then specify their dimensions. In this example, three of the hotspots are the same size, while two are slightly larger. As such, I've defined the default sizes first and then overridden them where necessary. Just as in the previous technique, this will position all of the anchors at the top-left corner of the image. You can then position each hotspot over the relevant person in the image, using the `top` and `left` positioning properties.

```
.remote a .hotspot {
  width: 50px;
  height: 60px;
  position: absolute;
}

.remote .rich a .hotspot {
  top: 50px;
  left: 80px;
}

.remote .sophie a .hotspot {
  top: 90px;
  left: 200px;
}

.remote .cath a .hotspot {
  top: 140px;
  left: 55px;
  width: 60px;
  height: 80px;
}
```

```
.remote .james a .hotspot {
  top: 140px;
  left: 145px;
}


.remote .paul a .hotspot {
  top: 165px;
  left: 245px;
  width: 60px;
  height: 80px;
}
```

Similarly, the spans containing the link text are also positioned absolutely and are given a width of 15 ems. They, too, are positioned in relation to the enclosing list, in this case to the right of the image using a negative right position. Last, the links are given a cursor style to make sure the correct icon is displayed in IE.

```
.remote a .link {
  position: absolute;
  display: block;
  width: 10em;
  right: -11em;
  cursor: pointer;
}


.remote .rich a .link {
  top: 0;
}


.remote .sophie a .link {
  top: 1.2em;
}


.remote .cath a .link {
  top: 2.4em;
}
```

```
.remote .james a .link {
  top: 3.6em;
}

.remote .paul a .link {
  top: 4.8em;
}
```

The hotspots should now be in the correct place, as should the text links.

To create the rollover effect on the hotspot when either the hotspot or the text is hovered over, you need to apply a border to the hotspot span, when the parent anchor is hovered over:

```
.remote a:hover .hotspot,
.remote a:focus .hotspot {
  border: 1px solid #fff;
}
```

Similarly, to change the color of the text when either the text or the hotspot span is hovered over, you need to change the style on the span when the parent anchor is hovered or otherwise gains focus:

```
.remote a:hover .link ,
.remote a:focus .link {
  color: #0066FF;
}
```

If you test this example, it works perfectly in Safari and Firefox (see Figure 6-15). If you hover over a person's name, the link text changes color, and a box appears over that person in the picture. The same happens if you hover over the person in the image.

Figure 6-15. Remote rollover demonstration. When the link text at the bottom of the image is rolled over, an outline appears over the associated person in the image.

While the styling of this example is quite simple, you are really only limited by your imagination. In fact, we use a slightly modified version of this technique on the Who we are section of the Clearleft site (`http://clearleft.com/is/`) (see Figure 6-16).

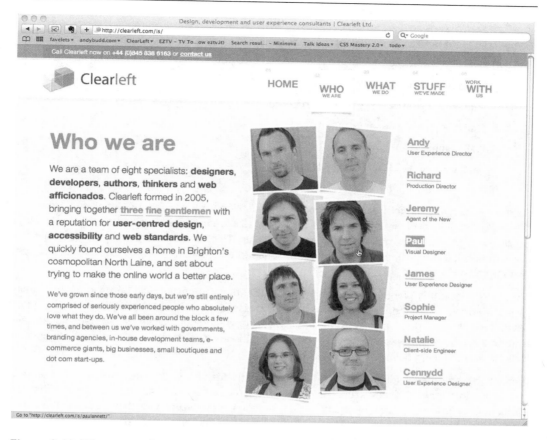

Figure 6-16. When you roll over pictures of the Clearleft team, the name of that person is highlighted in the list on the right.

A short note about definition lists

Throughout this chapter, I have discussed how unordered lists (and by extension, ordered lists) can be used to create a variety of effects. However, there is a third, often overlooked list type that has been gaining more attention of late: the definition list. A definition list consists of two core components: a definition term `<dt>` and one or more definition descriptions `<dd>`.

```
<dl>
  <dt>Apple</dt>
    <dd>Red, yellow or green fruit</dd>
    <dd>Computer company</dd>
  <dt>Bananna</dt>
    <dd>Curved yellow fruit</dd>
</dl>
```

As the name suggests, the primary purpose of a definition list is to mark up definitions. However, the HTML specification is rather vague and suggests definition lists could be used for other applications like product properties or conversations. This stretches the concept of definitions somewhat but still makes a certain amount of sense in the context of HTML's history as a simple text formatting language.

Many web standards pioneers seized on the fact that definition lists could be used to structurally group a series of related elements and started to use them to create everything from product listing and image galleries, to form and even page layouts. While these techniques are undoubtedly clever, I personally believe they stretch the implied meaning of definition lists beyond their natural breaking point.

One of the arguments for using definition lists in this fashion is that no other HTML element allows for this type of association. However, this isn't strictly true, as the purpose of the `div` element is to group a document up into logical sections. More worryingly, this is exactly the same type of argument used when justifying tables for layout. This raises concerns that definition lists are starting to be used inappropriately.

For more information on definition lists, I recommend checking out the excellent article by Mark Norman Francis at 24 Ways (`http://24ways.org/2007/my-other-christmas-present-is-a-definition-list`).

Summary

In this chapter, you have learned how flexible lists can be. You learned how to create vertical and horizontal navigation bars, including accessible tabbed navigation. Finally, you learned how to use positioning to create pure CSS image maps and remote rollovers.

In the next chapter, you will learn how to create accessible form layouts and data tables, and how to style them with CSS.

Chapter 7

Styling Forms and Data Tables

As more and more interactivity is called for on the Web, forms are becoming an increasingly important part of modern web applications. Forms allow users to interact with systems, enabling them to do everything from registering feedback to booking complicated travel itineraries. As such, forms can be as simple as an e-mail address and a message field, or they can be hugely complex, spanning multiple pages. Form layout has traditionally been done using tables; however, in this chapter, you will learn that even complicated forms can be laid out using CSS.

Tables are slowly regaining their rightful position purely as a way of displaying tabular data, rather than a means of laying out pages. As well as needing to capture user data, web applications increasingly need to display this data in a usable and an easy-to-understand format. Form and data table design have been relatively neglected in favor of higher-profile areas of design. However, good information and interaction design can make or break a modern web application.

In this chapter, you will learn about

- Creating attractive and accessible data tables

- Creating simple and complicated form layouts

- Styling various form elements

- Providing accessible form feedback

Styling data tables

Many developers realize the pitfalls of table-based design and avoid using layout tables wherever possible. A small group of individuals have gone a step further and attempted to ditch tables altogether, re-creating things like calendar layouts in pure CSS. Well-meaning as this strategy is, calendars, by their nature, are table-based content. After all, they're basically just rows of weeks and columns of days. As such, there is still a place for the use of tables on the Web.

Even relatively simple data tables can be hard to read if they contain more than a few rows and columns. Without separation between data cells, information blurs together, resulting in a jumbled and confusing layout (see Figure 7-1).

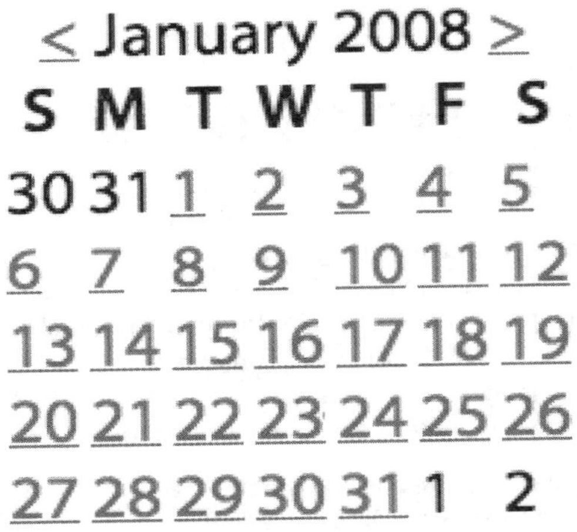

		≤ January 2008 ≥				
S	M	T	W	T	F	S
30	31	1	2	3	4	5
6	7	8	9	10	11	12
13	14	15	16	17	18	19
20	21	22	23	24	25	26
27	28	29	30	31	1	2

Figure 7-1. Compact data tables can be very confusing at first glance

Conversely, tables with a lot of whitespace can also be very difficult to read, as columns and cells start to lose their visual association with each other. This is particularly problematic when you're trying to follow rows of information on tables with very large column spacing, such as the one in Figure 7-2. If you are not careful, it is easy to accidentally stray into the wrong row when moving between columns. This is most noticeable in the middle of the table where the hard edge of the top and bottom of the table provide less of a visual anchor.

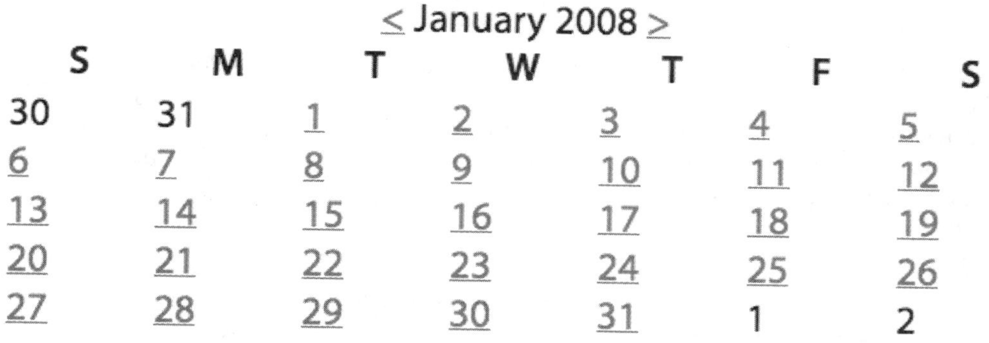

Figure 7-2. Widely spaced tables can also be difficult to immediately comprehend

By contrast, a few minutes spent designing your data tables can greatly improve their comprehension and the speed at which information can be retrieved. For instance, the dates in Figure 7-3 have been given breathing room with a small amount of vertical and horizontal padding. They have also been highlighted with a subtle beveled effect, making them look clickable. The main column headings have been distinguished from the data through subtly different background colors, the use of a bottom border, and typographic treatment. The result is an easy-to-use calendar widget.

Figure 7-3. Stylized data table

Table-specific elements

If data tables can be difficult for sighted users, imagine how complicated and frustrating they must be for people using assistive technologies such as screen readers. Fortunately, the HTML specification includes a number of elements and attributes intended to increase the accessibility of data tables for these devices. Not all of these elements are currently supported by screen readers, but it is definitely good practice to use them where possible.

Summary and caption

The first of these elements is a table `caption`, which basically acts as a heading for the table. Although this is not a required element, it is always a good idea to use a caption wherever possible. In this example, I'm using the caption to show users which month they are looking at. Another useful addition is a table `summary`. The `summary` attribute can be applied to the `table` tag and is used to describe the content of the table. Much like an image's `alt` text, the summary should effectively summarize the data in the table, and a well-written summary may alleviate the need to read the contents of the table.

```
<table class="cal" summary="A calendar style date picker">
  <caption>
    <a href="cal.php?month=dec08" rel="prev">&lt;</a> January 2008 ↵
    <a href="cal.php?month=feb09" rel="next">&gt;</a>
  </caption>
</table>
```

thead, tbody, and tfoot

Using `thead`, `tfoot`, and `tbody` allows you to break tables up into logical sections. For instance, you can place all of your column headings inside the `thead` element, providing you with a means of separately styling that particular area. If you choose to use a `thead` or `tfoot` element, you must use at least one `tbody` element. You can only use one `thead` and `tfoot` element in a table, but you can use multiple `tbody` elements to help break complicated tables into more manageable chunks.

Row and column headings should be marked up as `th` rather than `td`, although if something is both a heading and data it should be left as a `td`. Table headings can be given a `scope` attribute of `row` or `col` to define whether they are row or column headings. They can also be given a value of `rowgroup` or `colgroup` if they relate to more than one row or column.

```
<thead>
  <tr>
    <th scope="col">Sun</th>
```

```
        <th scope="col">Mon</th>
        <th scope="col">Tue</th>
        <th scope="col">Wed</th>
        <th scope="col">Tur</th>
        <th scope="col">Fri</th>
        <th scope="col">Sat</th>
    </tr>
  </thead>
```

col and colgroups

While the `tr` element allows developers to apply styles to whole rows, it is much more difficult to apply a style to an entire column. To get around this problem, the W3C introduced the `colgroup` and `col` elements. A `Colgroup` is used to define and group one or more columns using the `col` element. Unfortunately, not many browsers support the styling of `col` and `colgroup` elements.

```
  <colgroup>
    <col id="sun" />
    <col id="mon" />
    <col id="tue" />
    <col id="wed" />
    <col id="thur" />
    <col id="fri" />
    <col id="sat" />
  </colgroup>
```

Data table markup

Putting all of these HTML elements and attributes together, you can create the basic outline for the calendar table shown in Figure 7-3.

```
<table class="cal" summary="A calendar style date picker">
  <caption>
    <a href="#" rel="prev">&lt;</a> January 2008 <a href="#"
rel="next">&gt;</a>
</caption>
    <colgroup>
      <col id="sun" />
      <col id="mon" />
      <col id="tue" />
      <col id="wed" />
      <col id="thur" />
      <col id="fri" />
      <col id="sat" />
    </colgroup>

<thead>
  <tr>
    <th scope="col">Sun</th>
    <th scope="col">Mon</th>
    <th scope="col">Tue</th>
    <th scope="col">Wed</th>
    <th scope="col">Tur</th>
    <th scope="col">Fri</th>
    <th scope="col">Sat</th>
  </tr>
</thead>

<tbody>
  <tr>
    <td class="null">30</td>
    < td class="null">31</td>
    <td><a href="#">1</a></td>
    <td><a href="#">2</a></td>
    <td><a href="#">3</a></td>
    <td><a href="#">4</a></td>
```

```
    <td><a href="#">5</a></td>
  </tr>
  <tr>
    <td><a href="#">6</a></td>
    <td><a href="#">7</a></td>
    <td class="selected"><a href="#">8</a></td>
    <td><a href="#">9</a></td>
    <td><a href="#">10</a></td>
    <td><a href="#">11</a></td>
    <td><a href="#">12</a></td>
  </tr>
...
</tbody>
</table>
```

Styling the table

The CSS specification has two table border models: separate and collapsed. In the separate model, borders are placed around individual cells, whereas in the collapsed model, cells share borders. Most browsers default to the separate model, but the collapsed model is usually of more use. As such, one of the first things you would normally do is set the `border-collapse` property of your table to `collapse`. However, for the purposes of this demonstration, I want to keep the double borders in order to create a beveled effect. As such, I start by setting the `border-collapse` property to `separate`. Then, for stylistic reasons, I'm going to center all the text in the table and remove the default padding and margin.

```
table.cal {
  border-collapse: seperate;
  border-spacing: 0;
  text-align: center;
  color: #333;
}

.cal th, .cal td {
  margin: 0;
  padding: 0;
}
```

CSS has a `border-spacing` property that allows you to control the spacing between cells. Unfortunately, IE 7 and below do not understand this property, so you need to fall back on the old but reliable `cellspacing` attribute. This attribute is, strictly speaking, presentational in nature. However, it is still valid HTML and is the only means of controlling cell spacing in IE 6 and 7.

```
<table cellspacing="0" class="cal" summary="A calendar style date picker">
```

Adding the visual style

The groundwork has been set, so it is now time to start adding the visual style. To make the table caption look a little more like a regular heading, you can increase the font size and make it bold. You can also give the caption some breathing room by applying vertical padding.

```
.cal caption {
  font-size:1.25em;
  padding-top: 0.692em;
  padding-bottom: 0.692em;
  background-color: #d4dde6;
}
```

To position the previous and next links on either side of the current month, give them some horizontal margin and then float them left and right respectively. You can then give them a more prominent hit area by applying some padding. To style these links, I've decided to use the attribute selector to target their `rel` attributes. However, if you wanted to support older browsers, you could add a class to each link instead. Once you've positioned these links, you can style them any way you like. In this example, I'm simply going to change the links' background color when a user hovers over them.

```
.cal caption [rel="prev"] {
  float: left;
  margin-left: 0.2em;
}

.cal caption [rel="next"] {
  float: right;
  margin-right: 0.2em;
}
```

```
.cal caption a:link,
.cal caption a:visited {
  text-decoration: none;
  color: #333;
  padding: 0 0.2em;
}


.cal caption a:hover,
.cal caption a:active,
.cal caption a:focus {
  background-color: #6d8ab7;
}
```

To distinguish the initial row of table headings, I'm going to give them a slightly lighter background than the rest of the table, along with a subtle underline. I'm also going to make the text slightly smaller than the rest of the form.

```
.cal thead th {
  background-color: #d4dde6;
  border-bottom: 1px solid #a9bacb;
  font-size:0.875em;
}
```

By default, I want the text in the body of the table to be grayed out, indicating that it can't be selected. You'll notice that I've also given the text a subtle text shadow.

```
.cal tbody {
  color: #a4a4a4;
  text-shadow: 1px 1px 1px white;
  background-color: #d0d9e2;
}
```

To give the table cells a beveled effect, you need to set slightly different colors on each side; lighter colors on the top and left, darker ones on the bottom and right. You then need to style the anchor links. In this case, I'm setting them all to block and applying padding to create a button like hit area. I'm also going to embolden the fonts and give them a slightly darker background.

```
.cal tbody td {
  border-top: 1px solid #e0e0e1;
  border-right: 1px solid #9f9fa1;
  border-bottom: 1px solid #acacad;
  border-left: 1px solid #dfdfe0;
}

.cal tbody a {
  display: block;
  text-decoration: none;
  color: #333;
  background-color: #c0c8d2;
  font-weight: bold;
  padding: 0.385em 0.692em 0.308em 0.692em;
}
```

Last, I'm going to set a hover state for the anchor links. Previously selected dates will also inherit this style through the inclusion of a selected class. In this case, I'm going to make the links turn white on a blue background and give them a subtle text shadow.

```
.cal tbody a:hover,
.cal tbody a:focus,
.cal tbody a:active,
.cal tbody .selected a:link,
.cal tbody .selected a:visited,
.cal tbody .selected a:hover,
.cal tbody .selected a:focus,
.cal tbody .selected a:active {
  background-color: #6d8ab7;
  color: white;
  text-shadow: 1px 1px 2px #22456b;
}
```

You'll notice that the dates still retain their beveled appearance when hovered over. If you want give the appearance that the dates have been depressed, change the color of the cell borders so the top and left borders are darker, while the bottom and right borders are lighter. Be aware that, because this style is using a hover pseudo selector on a nonanchor element, it won't display in IE 6. If you need this technique to work in IE 6, you'll want to add borders to the links instead.

```
.cal tbody td:hover,
.cal tbody td.selected {
  border-top: 1px solid #2a3647;
  border-right: 1px solid #465977;
  border-bottom: 1px solid #576e92;
  border-left: 1px solid #466080;
}
```

And there you have it, a beautifully styled calendar picker similar to the one in Figure 7-3.

Simple form layout

Short and relatively simple forms are easiest to fill in when the form labels appear vertically above their associated form elements. Users can simply move down the form step by step, reading each label and completing the following form element. This method works best on short forms collecting relatively simple and predictable information such as contact details (see Figure 7-4).

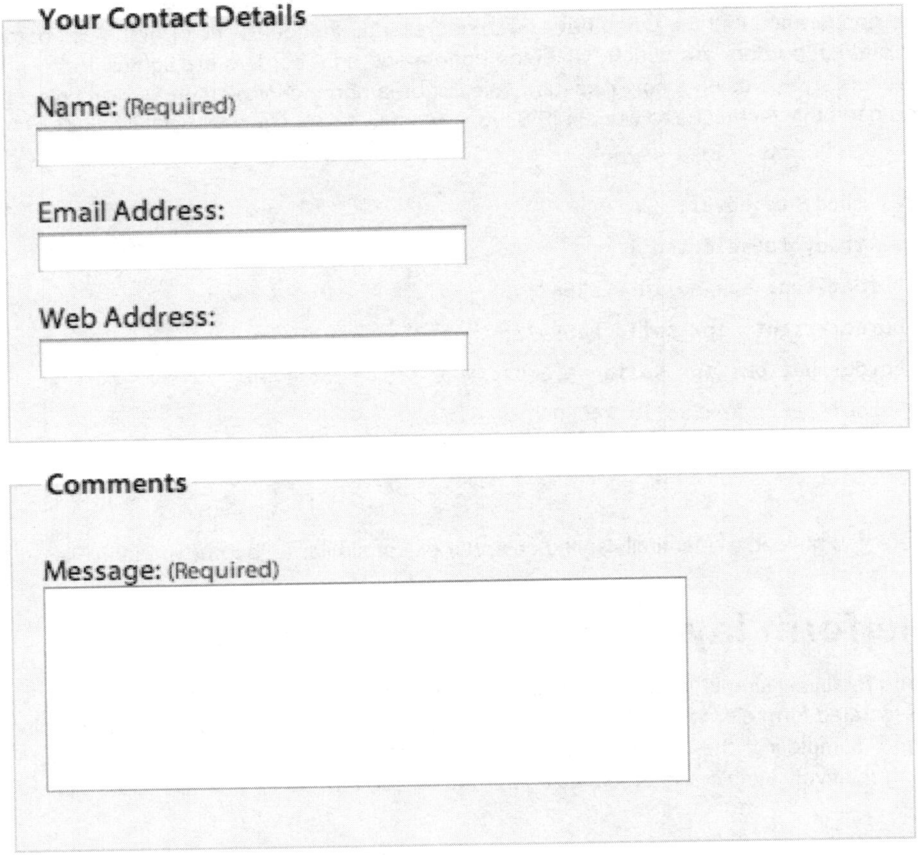

Your Contact Details

Name: (Required)

Email Address:

Web Address:

Comments

Message: (Required)

Figure 7-4. Simple form layout

Useful form elements

HTML provides a number of useful elements that can help add structure and meaning to a form. The first one of these is the `fieldset` element. A `Fieldset` is used for grouping related blocks of information. In Figure 7-4, two `fieldsets` are being used: one for the contact details and one for the comments. Most user agents apply a thin border around `fieldsets`, which can be turned off by setting the `border` property to `none`.

To identify the purpose of each `fieldset`, you can use a `legend` element. Legends act a little like a `fieldset`'s heading, usually appearing vertically centered with the top of the `fieldset` and indented a little to the right. Unfortunately, legends are notoriously difficult to style because of the inconsistent way browsers place them. Some browsers, like Firefox and Safari, use padding to create a small indent. However, other browsers, such as Opera and IE, have large default indents that are not controllable using padding, margins, or even positioning. As such, if you choose to use legends, you will have to accept a certain amount of variation between browsers.

Form labels

The `label` element is an extremely important one, as it can help add structure and increase the usability and accessibility of your forms. As the name suggests, this element is used to add a meaningful and descriptive label to each form element. In many browsers, clicking the `label` element will cause the associated form element to gain focus. The real benefit of using labels is to increase form usability for people using assistive devices. If a form uses labels, screen readers will correctly associate a form element with its label. Without labels, the screen reader will have to "guess" which text relates to which form element, sometimes getting it wrong. Screen reader users can also bring up a list of all the labels in a form, allowing users to audibly scan through the form in much the same way as you would visually scan through them.

Associating a label with a form control is very easy and can be done in one of two ways: either implicitly by nesting the form element inside the `label` element:

```
<label>email <input name="email" type="text"/><label>
```

or explicitly by setting the `for` attribute of the `label` equal to the `id` name of the associated form element:

```
<label for="email">email<label>
<input name="email" id="email" type="text"/>
```

You will notice that this input, and all the form controls in this chapter, contain both a `name` and an `id` attribute. The `id` attribute is required to create the association between the form input and the label, while the `name` is required so that the form data can be sent back to the server. The `id` and `name` don't have to be the same, although I prefer to keep them identical when possible, for the sake of consistency.

Labels associated with form controls using the `for` attribute don't need to be near those controls in the source code; they could be in a completely different part of the document. However, from a structural point of view, separating form controls from their labels isn't wise and should be avoided wherever possible.

The basic layout

Using these three structural elements, you can start laying out your form by marking up the contents of the first `fieldset`. The unstyled form is shown in Figure 7-5.

```
<fieldset>
  <legend>Your Contact Details</legend>
  <div>
    <label for="author">Name:</label>
    <input name="author" id="author" type="text" />
  </div>
  <div>
    <label for="email">Email Address:</label>
    <input name="email" id="email" type="text" />
  </div>
  <div>
    <label for="url">Web Address:</label>
    <input name="url" id="url" type="text" />
  </div>
</fieldset>
```

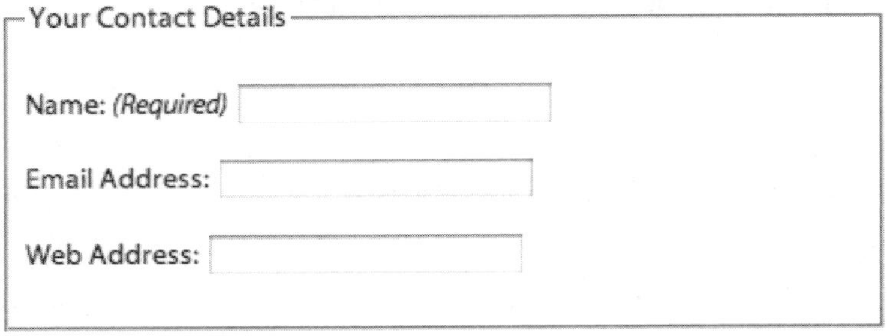

Figure 7-5. Unstyled form

First, you will need to set the general styles for the fieldset and legend elements. The fieldsets must be vertically separated using margins, and the contents can be given breathing space using padding. To highlight the fieldsets, you can give them a light background with a slightly darker, 1-pixel border. Try not to make the background too dark, though, as this can add too much visual weight to the form, making it more difficult to comprehend. Making the legends bold can also help break up the information and make it easier to digest.

```
fieldset {
  margin: 1em 0;
  padding: 1em;
```

```
    border : 1px solid #ccc;
    background: #f8f8f8;
  }


  legend {
    font-weight: bold;
  }
```

Positioning the labels so they appear vertically above the form elements is actually very simple. A `label` is an inline element by default. However, setting its `display` property to `block` will cause it to generate its own block box, forcing the input elements onto the line below. The width of text input boxes varies from browser to browser, so for consistency, you should explicitly set the width of your text input boxes. In this example, I am using ems to create a more scalable form layout.

```
  label {
    display: block;
    cursor: pointer;
  }


  input {
    width: 20em;
  }
```

Changing the cursor style of the label to `pointer` is a good idea here, as it shows that the `labels` can be interacted with.

Other elements

This layout works equally well for other form elements such as text areas:

```
  <fieldset>
    <legend>Comments</legend>
    <div>
    <label for="text">Message: </label>
    <textarea name="text" id="text">
    </textarea>
```

```
    </div>
  </fieldset>
```

The dimensions of text areas also vary across browsers, so it is a good idea to explicitly set their width and height as well. In this instance, I'm setting a width of 100 percent so it is effectively defined by its parent element. Setting widths in this way is a good idea, as it makes your layouts more flexible and independent.

```
textarea {
  width: 100%;
  height: 10em;
}
```

Unlike text areas and text inputs, radio buttons and check boxes need to be handled differently. Rather than having their labels above them, these elements usually have their labels to the right of them. When stacked vertically, all the elements are left aligned, creating a nice solid vertical and making them easier to select (see Figure 7-6).

Figure 7-6. Radio button layout

Earlier in this example, the width of the text boxes was defined by applying a width to the input element. However, the input element covers other form widgets such as check boxes, radio buttons, and submit buttons, as well as the more common text input box. As such, by setting the input element to be 20 ems wide, all of the input elements will be 20 ems.

One way around this problem is to use the attribute selector to target particular types of form element. So instead of setting all the inputs to 20 ems, you could specifically target text inputs:

```
input[type="text"] {
  width: 20em;
}
```

Unfortunately, the attribute selector is only supported on more modern browsers and does not work in IE 6 and below. Until the attribute selector is more widely supported, the best way to distinguish between input elements is to give them a class.

For instance, you could give radio buttons a class name of `radio`:

```
<fieldset>
  <legend>Remember Me</legend>
  <div>
    <label for="remember-yes"><input id="remember-yes" class="radio"↵
name="remember" type="radio" value="yes" />Yes</label>
  </div>


  <div>
    <label for="remember-no"><input id="remember-no" class="radio"↵
name="remember" type="radio" value="no" checked="checked" />No</label>
  </div>
</fieldset>
```

You could then override the previously set input width by setting the width of radio buttons to auto. The same can be done for check boxes and submit buttons:

```
input.radio, input.checkbox, input.submit {
  width: auto;
}
```

Notice how I've wrapped the labels around the form elements on this occasion. If you remember, I previously set all the labels in this form to behave as block level elements, forcing their associated form controls onto a separate line. Obviously, I don't want this to happen with radio button labels, so wrapping the labels around the form controls prevents this.

The last thing you need to do is add a little bit of right margin to the radio buttons, in order to provide so spacing between the labels.

```
#remember-me .radio {
  margin-right: 1em;
}
```

Embellishments

The layout is now complete, but you can incorporate a few nice additions for more advanced browsers. For instance, you could help users easily anchor themselves to the form field they are filling in by changing the element's background color when it receives focus:

```
Input[type="text"]:focus, textarea:focus {
   background: #ffc;
}
```

You can also harmonize the look of the text field and text area elements by giving them custom borders. This is particularly useful for Firefox, which renders the bottom and right borders on these elements as white, causing them to lose definition when on a white background (see Figure 7-7).

Figure 7-7. The bottom and right borders of text inputs and text areas in Firefox are white, causing them to lose definition on white backgrounds

In this example, an attribute selector is used to target the text inputs as this style is mostly for the benefit of Firefox, which understands this selector.

```
input[type="text"], textarea {
  border-top: 2px solid #999;
  border-left: 2px solid #999;
  border-bottom: 1px solid #ccc;
  border-right: 1px solid #ccc;
}
```

In this example, we're not using any password fields. However, if you were creating a generic form style for your entire site, you would need to include [type="password"] in the previous two examples as well.

Required fields

Many forms contain fields that must be filled in. You can indicate these required fields by placing styled text, or an asterisk, next to them. Because this information is emphasizing the field's required status, the most appropriate element for this information is an em or **strong** element:

```
<div>
<label for="author">Name:<em class="required">(required)</em>/label>
<input name="author" id="author" type="text" />
</div>
```

You can then style this information however you want. In this example I'm reducing the font size and making the text red:

```
.required {
  font-size: 0.75em;
  color:#760000;
}
```

And there you have it: a simple yet attractive-looking form layout using pure CSS.

Complicated form layout

For longer and more complicated forms, vertical space starts to become an issue, as does the ease of scanning. To improve scanning and reduce the amount of vertical space used, it makes sense to position the labels and form elements horizontally, rather than vertically above one

193

another. Creating a form such as the one in Figure 7-8 is actually very simple and uses almost exactly the same code as the previous example.

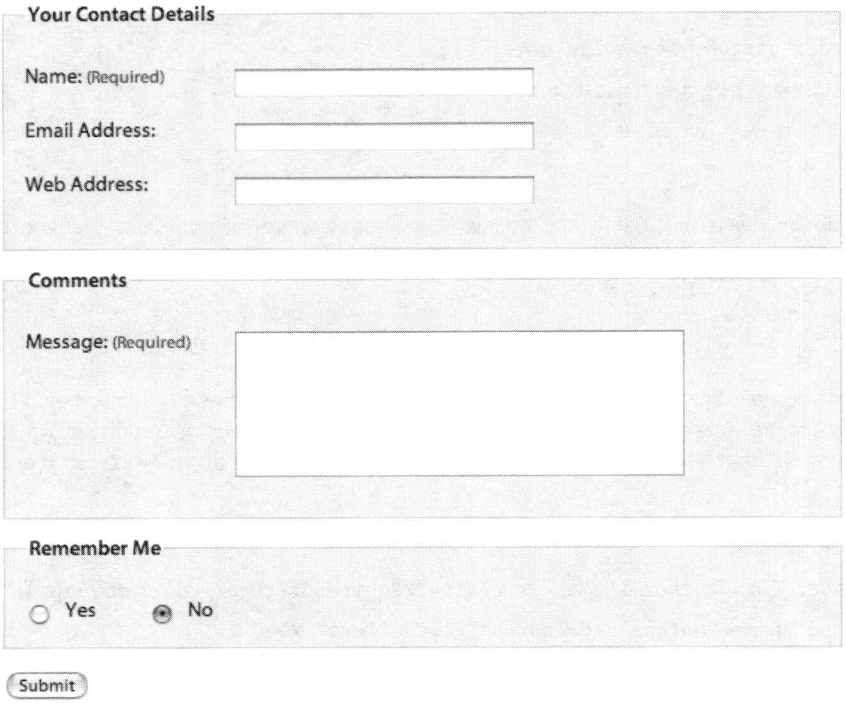

Figure 7-8. Horizontal form alignment

The only difference between this and the previous example is that, instead of setting the label to be a block-level element, you float the labels left instead. You also need to give the label a width so that all of the form elements line up nicely:

```
label {
    float: left;
    width: 10em;
    cursor: pointer;
}
```

If the form labels are likely to wrap onto multiple lines, it would be a sensible idea to clear the container divs as well. This will prevent them from interfering with the next set of labels and ruining your carefully crafted layout.

```
form div {
  clear: left;
}
```

Forms are rarely as simple as the one in Figure 7-8, and you will often need to create exceptions to your basic form styling rules to handle things such as multiple form widgets on a single line or columns of check boxes or radio buttons (see Figure 7-9). The next couple of sections will explain how to handle these types of exceptions.

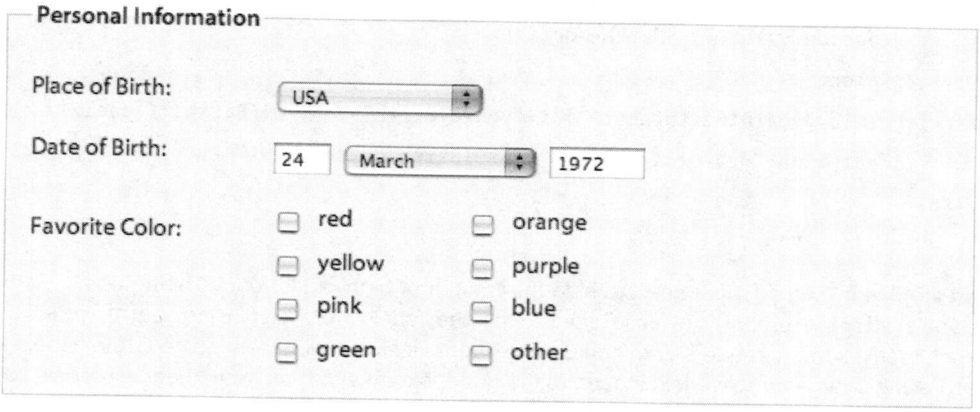

Figure 7-9. More complicated form layouts

Accessible date input

As you learned in the previous examples, form labels are important for the accessibility of your forms. However, there are situations when you may not want to display a label for every element. For instance, in Figure 7-9 you can see a group of form elements for collecting date information. In this situation, visually displaying each label would be overkill, as it would split the date of birth up into three separate entities rather than being perceived as a single entity. However, while you may not want to display the labels, it is still important that the labels appear in the source code and are available to screen readers.

```
<div>
  <label for="dateOfBirth">Date of Birth:</label>
    <input name="dateOfBirth" id="dateOfBirth" type="text" />
  <label id="monthOfBirthLabel" for="monthOfBirth">↵
Month of Birth:</label>
    <select name="monthOfBirth" id="monthOfBirth">
      <option value="1">January</option>
      <option value="2">February</option>
      <option value="3">March</option>
    </select>
  <label id="yearOfBirthLabel" for="yearOfBirth">Year of Birth:</label>
    <input name="yearOfBirth" id="yearOfBirth" type="text" />
</div>
```

To create this layout, you first need to hide the "month of birth" and "year of birth" labels. Setting the labels' display property to none would stop the labels from displaying, but it would also prevent many screen readers from accessing them. Instead, you can position the labels off screen using a large negative text indent. In the generic form style we created earlier, labels have been given a set width. To prevent the labels from affecting the layout, the width needs to be zeroed down for these labels as well:

```
#monthOfBirthLabel, #yearOfBirthLabel {
  text-indent: -1000em;
  width: 0;
}
```

The various form controls can then be sized individually and given margins to control their horizontal spacing:

```
input#dateOfBirth {
  width: 3em;
  margin-right: 0.5em;
}
```

```
select#monthOfBirth {
  width: 10em;
  margin-right: 0.5em;
}


input#yearOfBirth {
  width: 5em;
}
```

Multicolumn check boxes

Creating a two-column layout for large groups of check boxes or radio buttons is a little more involved. Labels only work for individual elements, not groups of elements. Ideally, we would wrap the whole group in a `fieldset` and use the legend to act like a label for the group. Unfortunately, due to the inconsistent way browsers handle the positioning of legends, this is not currently a practical solution. So until the browsers offer more consistent support, the best option is to use a heading element instead.

To create the column effect, the check boxes are split into two sets, and each set is wrapped in a `div` with a class of col. These elements are then grouped together by wrapping them in a `fieldset` with a descriptive ID:

```
<fieldset id="favoriteColor">
  <h2>Favorite Color:</h2>
    <div class="col">
      <div>
        <label><input class="checkbox" id="red" name="red" type="checkbox"↵
value="red" />red</label>
        ...
      </div>
    </div>


    <div class="col">
      <div>
        <label><input class="checkbox" id="orange" name="orange"↵
type="checkbox" value="orange" />orange</label>
      </div>
      ...
    </div>
</fieldset>
```

Because a generic `fieldset` style has already been created, the first thing you need to do is override those styles, zeroing down the `padding` and `margin`, removing the borders and setting the background color to be transparent:

```
fieldset#favoriteColor {
    margin: 0;
    padding: 0;
    border: none;
    background: transparent;
}
```

The heading is going to act like a label, so it needs to be floated left and given a width of 10 ems like the other labels. The headline also needs to look like a label, so the font weight needs to be set to normal, and the font size needs to be reduced.

```
#favoriteColor h2 {
    width: 10em;
    float: left;
    font-size: 1em;
    font-weight: normal;
}
```

The two-column layout can then be created by giving the `divs` a width and floating them left. However, as all of the `divs` in this form have been cleared by default, we need to override that declaration by using `clear:none`.

```
#favoriteColor .col {
    width: 8em;
    float: left;
clear: none;
}
```

All the labels in this form have been floated left and set to be 10 ems wide. However, the labels for the check boxes do not need to be floated, so we should override that declaration here.

```
#favoriteColor label {
float: none;
}
```

And there you have a relatively complex form layout. The basic form style takes care of the general layout, and exceptions can be handled on an individual basis by overriding these styles.

Submit buttons

Forms are a great way of adding interactivity to your site and for posting data back to the server. In order to activate the form, you therefore need some kind of button control. Normally, people use an input element with the type value set to submit. Input buttons are the most common way of submitting data to the server, but they are not without problems, not least the fact that you can't target them with just an element selector. You could target them with an attribute selector, but this isn't supported by older version of Internet Explorer, so your only option is to target them directly with an ID or class selector. So instead of using an input element, why not use the button element?

The button element has been gaining in popularity of late but is still relatively unknown and underutilized. This is a shame as button elements give you a great deal of flexibility. For a start, you can wrap button tags around an image and that image becomes your control (see Figure 7-10).

```
<div>
<button type="submit">
<img src="/img/button.png" alt="Book Now" />
</button>
</div>
```

Figure 7-10. Button element using a button image

As buttons have some default styling, you will want to turn this off.

```css
button {
  border: none;
  background: none;
  cursor: pointer;
}
```

Many operating systems, like OS X, prevent authors from changing the style of their input buttons, preferring to keep consistency throughout the operating system. However, the button element doesn't suffer from these constraints. As such, it is possible to create fairly advanced button styles purely using CSS. For instance, say you started with this simple submit button.

```html
<p>
<button type="submit">Book Now »</button>
</p>
```

You could start by giving the button some explicit dimensions and a colored border. You could then round the corners off using border-radius and apply a nice text shadow. Last, you could apply a gradient background, either by using an image or possibly even using Webkit-specific gradients. The result would look something like Figure 7-11.

```css
button.two {
  width: 200px;
  height: 50px;
  border: 1px solid #989898;
   -moz-border-radius: 6px;
   -webkit-border-radius: 6px;
   border-radius: 6px;
   background: url(/img/button-bg.png) #c5e063 bottom left repeat-x;
  -moz-box-shadow: 2px 2px 2px #ccc;
  -webkit-box-shadow: 2px 2px 2px #ccc;
  box-shadow: 2px 2px 2px #ccc;
   color: #fff;
   font-size: 26px;
```

```
    font-weight: bold;
    text-shadow: 1px 1px 1px #666;
}
```

Figure 7-11. Button element using pure CSS

The main limitation with button elements is the way IE 6 and, to a lesser extent, IE 7 handle their submission. Rather than submitting the contents of the `value` attribute, as other browsers do, IE 6 and IE 7 submit the contents of the element. Furthermore, if you have multiple buttons on a page, IE 6 will submit the contents of all the buttons, rather than just the one that was clicked. As such, if you wanted to use more than one button per page, you need to make sure that they all have the same function, as you won't be able to tell which one had been activated in older version of Internet Explorer.

Form feedback

Forms will usually require some type of feedback message to highlight fields that have been missed or incorrectly filled in. This is usually done by adding an error message next to the appropriate field (see Figure 7-12).

Your Contact Details

Name: (Required) [   ]

Email Address: [   ]   ⚠ Incorrect email address.
Please try again.

Web Address: [   ]

Figure 7-12. Example of form feedback

To produce this effect, you could wrap your feedback text in a em and place it after the text input in the source code. However, for everything to line up correctly, both the em and the preceding `input` would need to be floated. This will have an effect on the behavior of the enclosing paragraph, which in turn will have an effect on the whole layout. Furthermore, many screen readers will ignore text between form elements, unless they are enclosed in a label. To avoid

201

these problems, the best approach is to include the error message text inside the form `label`, and then position it using CSS:

```
<div>
  <label for="email">Email Address:
  <em class="feedback">Incorrect email address. Please try again. ⏎
  </em>
  </label>
  <input name="email" id="email" type="text" />
</div>
```

To position the feedback em, you first need to set the `position` of all of the paragraphs in the form to `relative`, thereby setting up a new positioning context. You can then position the feedback em absolutely, so it appears to the right of the text input. We know that the labels are 10 ems wide and the text boxes are 20 ems wide, so we can set the left position of the feedback span to be 30 ems.

```
form div {
  position: relative;
}

form .feedback {
  position: absolute;
left: 30em;
  right :0;
  top: 0.5em;
}
```

Rather annoyingly, IE 6 and below incorrectly set the width of the feedback em to be the minimum width possible. To get around this problem, you need to set an explicit width for this browser. One way to use conditional comments as detailed in Chapter 8:

```
form .feedback{
  width: 10em;
}
```

You can then apply whatever styling you want to your feedback messages. In this case, I have made the text bold red and have applied a warning image to the left side of the message:

```
form div {
  position: relative;
}

.feedback {
  position: absolute;
left: 30em;
  right :0;
  top: 0.5em;
  font-weight: bold;
  color: #760000;
  padding-left: 18px;
  background: url(/img/error.png) no-repeat left top;
}
```

You could also use this technique to provide positive feedback or advice on how to fill out particular parts of the form.

Summary

In this chapter, you have learned how different form layouts can work in different situations. You can now lay out complicated forms using CSS, without harming a single table in the process. You have learned how tables should be used—for data rather than layout—and have learned that data table design can be fun.

In the next chapter, you will use everything you have learned so far to start building CSS-based layouts.

Chapter 8

Layout

One of the major benefits of CSS is the ability to control page layout without needing to use presentational markup. However, CSS layout has gained an undeserved reputation for being difficult, particularly among those new to the language. This is partly due to browser inconsistencies, but mostly due to a proliferation of different layout techniques available on the Web. It seems that each CSS author has their own preferred way of creating multicolumn layouts, and new CSS developers will often use a technique without really understanding how it works. This situation has been exacerbated by the rise of so-called CSS frameworks, which aim to make CSS layout easier by creating a strong coupling between markup and presentation—the very reason we ditched table-based layout in the first place. This black box approach to CSS may get quick results but ultimately stunts the developer's understanding of the language and ability to implement changes.

All these CSS layout techniques rely on three basic concepts: positioning, floating, and margin manipulation. The different techniques really aren't that different, and if you understand the core concepts, it is relatively easy to create your own layouts with little or no hassle. In fact, layout is generally the easiest part of CSS; it's all the tweaking that takes time.

In this chapter, you will learn about

- Horizontally centering a design on a page

- Creating two- and three-column float-based layouts

- Creating fixed-width, liquid, and elastic layouts

- Creating equal height columns

- CSS frameworks versus CSS systems

Planning your layout

When it's time to start turning your designs into fully functional templates, it is very tempting to jump straight in and start marking up your page or slicing up your images. However, you can find that you've painted yourself into a corner very quickly. Instead, a small amount of planning can save a lot of hassle further down the line. Or, as the saying goes, "Measure twice; cut once."

The first step in creating a scalable and easy to maintain CSS system is to review your designs, looking for repeating patterns. These could be patterns in the structure of the page or the way certain elements are repeated across the site. You shouldn't be too concerned with the visual representation at this stage. Instead, look at the structure and meaning. I like to do this by printing out each design, spotting the patterns and then scribbling mark-up notes on each page (see Figure 8-1). However, I've seen people do this by annotating their Photoshop files or grey-box designs.

Figure 8-1. Markup guides

Begin by breaking your pages into major the structural areas like the wrapper, header, content area, and footer. These areas tend to be consistent across the whole site and rarely change. To use an architectural analogy, you could think of these as the external walls of the building.

Then, turn your attention to the content area itself, and start building out your grid structure. How many different content areas does the design have, and how do they differ? Are the content areas actually that different, or can they be treated the same from a layout perspective? Most designs will have only a couple of unique content areas, so look for shared characteristics rather than the visual representation. You could consider these content areas as the internal load-bearing walls of your construction.

Finally, we need to start looking at the different layout constructs that appear in the various content areas. Do you need to present certain types of information in two, three, or four columns? Unlike the previous step, these layout constructs tend to be very flexible and change from page to page. So you could think of them like the dry wall partitions in your building. Combined with the previous step, these construct help form the floor plan of each of your pages. At this point, reach for the graph paper and colored pencils, and start mapping the structure and dimensions in more detail (see Figure 8-2).

Figure 8-2. Working out dimensions on graph paper

With the structure in place, you can now turn your attention to the different kinds of content. Is this is a news story, an article, or a press release? Give each block a meaningful name and then see how they relate to each other. It may turn out that there's actually very little difference between your news stories and press releases, in which case, combining them into a single content type would make sense.

Look at how each content block is structured, and see if you can see patterns emerging across different types. For instance, you may notice that both your articles and news stories have a prominent header and footer, so identify them as such. It really doesn't matter if the headers and footers look different, as you can style them later based on context. The same is true of things like error messages, search boxes, and menu items. Try to keep the class names as generic as possible, and style them based on context.

Once I've got patterns and naming conventions sorted, I find it useful to start defining the elements I'm going to use. For example, a list of links might be an unordered list, while a story might to be a `div` with an `h2`, a paragraph, and an anchor element. It's much easier to do this up front, with a few of your colleagues, than on the fly. I also find it useful to jot down color codes, dimensions, and anything else that will help during production. Again, you can make these annotations on a printout of the designs for quick reference, as shown in Figure 8-3.

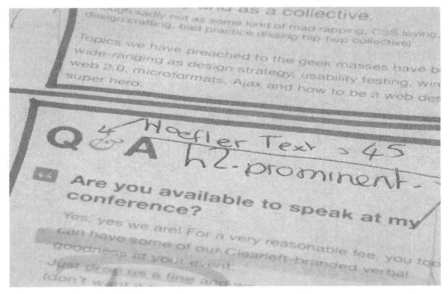

Figure 8-3. Working out the details of the different content types

Setting the foundations

Let's assume that we're going to be building a classic three-column blog template, like the one shown in Figure 8-4.

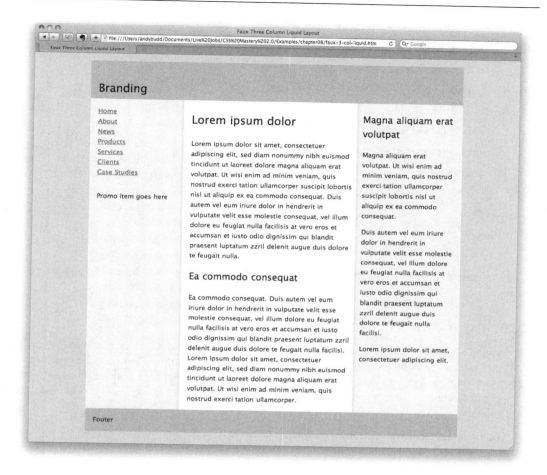

Figure 8-4. Classic, three-column layout

By analyzing the design, it's clear that we're going to need a wrapper element to center the design, along with a header, content area, and footer. The markup would, therefore, look something like this:

```
<body>
  <div class="wrapper">


    <div class="header">
      <!--Your header content goes here-->
    </div>
```

209

```
<div class="content>
  <!--Your page content goes here-->
</div>

<div class="footer">
  <!--Your footer content goes here-->
</div>

    </div>
  </body>
```

As these last three areas are enclosed inside the wrapper, let's start by styling the wrapper element.

Centering a design using margins

Long lines of text can be difficult and unpleasant to read. As modern monitors continue to grow in size, the issue of screen readability is becoming increasingly important. One way designers have attempted to tackle this problem is by centering their designs. Rather than spanning the full width of the screen, centered designs span only a portion of the screen, creating shorter and easier-to-read line lengths.

Say you have a typical layout where you wish to center a wrapper `div` horizontally on the screen:

```
<body>
  <div class="wrapper">
  </div>
</body>
```

To do this, you simply define the width of your wrapper `div` and set the horizontal margins to auto:

```
.wrapper {
  width: 920px;
  margin: 0 auto;
}
```

In this example, I have decided to fix the width of my wrapper `div` in pixels, so that it fits nicely on an 1024×768–resolution screen. However, you could just as easily set the width as a percentage of the body or relative to the size of the text using ems.

This works on all modern browsers. However, IE 5.*x* and IE 6 in quirks mode don't honor the `margin:auto` declaration. Luckily, IE misunderstands `text-align: center`, centering everything instead of just the text. You can use this to your advantage by centering everything in the `body` tag, including the wrapper `div`, and realigning the contents of the wrapper back to the left:

```
body {
  text-align: center;
}


.wrapper {
  width: 920px;
  margin: 0 auto;
  text-align: left;
}
```

Using the `text-align` property in this way is a hack—but a fairly innocuous hack that has no adverse effect on your site. The wrapper now appears centered in older versions of IE as well as more standards-compliant browsers (see Figure 8-5).

Figure 8-5. Centering a design using margin:auto

Float-based layouts

There are a few different ways of doing CSS-based layout, including absolute positioning and using negative margins. I find float-based layouts the easiest and most reliable method to use. As the name suggests, in a float-based layout, you simply set the width of the elements you want to position and then float them left or right.

Because floated elements don't take up any space in the flow of the document, they no longer appear to exert any influence on the surrounding block boxes. To get around this, you will need to clear the floats at various points throughout the layout. Rather than continuously floating and clearing elements, it is quite common to float nearly everything and then clear once or twice at strategic points throughout the document, such as the page footer. Alternatively, you could use the overflow method to clear the contents of particular elements. This is my current preferred method, so it's the one I'll be using throughout the rest of these examples.

Two-column floated layout

To create a two-column layout inside our content area, we first need to create our basic HTML structure.

```
<div class="content">


<div class="primary">
  <!-- main content goes here -->
</div>


<div class="secondary">
  <!--navigation and secondary content goes here -->
</div>


</div>
```

The secondary content area for this design—including the site navigation—will be on the left side of the page, while the primary content will be on the right. However, I have chosen to put the primary content area above the secondary content area in the source order for usability and accessibility reasons. First, the primary content is the most important thing on the page and so should come first in the document. Second, there is no point forcing screen reader users to trawl through navigation links and less important content like site promotions before they get to the primary content if they don't have to.

Normally, when people create float-based layouts, they float both columns left and then create a gutter between the columns using margin or padding. When using this approach, the columns are packed tightly into the available space with no room to breathe. Although this wouldn't be a problem if browsers behaved themselves, buggy browsers can cause tightly packed layouts to break, forcing columns to drop below each other.

This can happen on IE because it honors the size of an element's content, rather than the size of the element itself. In standards-compliant browsers, if the content of an element gets too large, it will simply flow out of the box. However, on IE, if the content of an element becomes too big, the whole element expands. This can be triggered by the smallest things, such as some of your text being set in italic. If this happens in very tightly packed layouts, there is no longer enough room for the elements to sit next to each other, and one of the floats will drop. Other IE bugs, such as the 3-pixel text jog bug and the double-margin float bug (see Chapter 9), along with various browser-rounding errors can also cause float dropping.

To prevent your layouts from breaking, you need to avoid cramming floated layouts into their containing elements. Rather than using horizontal margin or padding to create gutters, you can create a virtual gutter by floating one element left and one element right (see Figure 8-6). If one element inadvertently increases in size by a few pixels, rather than immediately running out of horizontal space and dropping down, it will simply grow into the virtual gutter.

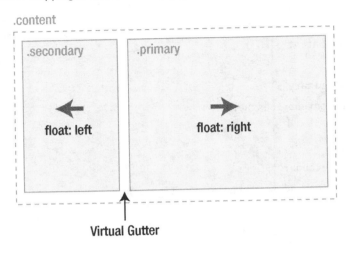

Figure 8-6. Creating a two-column layout using floats

The CSS for achieving this layout is very straightforward. You simply set the desired width of each column and then float the secondary content left and the primary content right. You also need to add a small amount of padding to the primary content to prevent the enclosed text being flush to the right hand edge of the element. You'll notice that I've also added `display:inline` to all the floated items. This is a defensive measure to prevent the double margin float bug in IE (more on that in the next chapter).

```
.content .primary {
  width: 650px;
  padding-right: 20px;
  float: right;
  display: inline;
}

.content .secondary {
  width: 230px;
  float: left;
  display: inline;
}
```

As the total width available is 920 pixels, these dimensions leave a 20-pixel wide virtual gutter between each floated element. As mentioned previously, doing this protects the layout from float drops due to accidental content expansion.

Because these elements are floated, they no longer take up any space in the flow of the document, causing the footer to rise up. In order to prevent this, you need to clear the floated items by applying the overflow method to their parent element, in this case the content `div`.

```
.content {
  overflow: hidden;
}
```

And there you have it: a simple two-column CSS layout (see Figure 8-7).

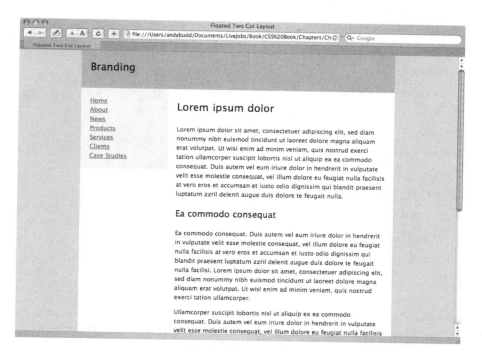

Figure 8-7. Floated two-column layout

You'll notice that rather than creating two separate elements called `primary-content` and `secondary-content`, I've simply used the terms `primary` and `secondary`. I've then used the fact that these two elements are nested within the `content` element to create the association. This has a couple of benefits. First off, it means that you don't have to keep creating new class names for every element you want to style. Instead, you can use the cascade to help you out. Secondly, and arguably more importantly, you can use the same primary and secondary classes more than once, creating a very flexible naming system. For instance, say we wanted to create a three-column layout instead of just a two-column one.

Three-column floated layout

The HTML needed to create a three-column layout is very similar to that used by the two-column layout, the only difference being the addition of two new divs inside the primary content div: one for the main content and one for the secondary content. Therefore, we can reuse our flexible primary and secondary class names again.

```
<div class="content">

  <div class="primary">
    <div class="primary">
      <-- your primary primary content goes here -->
    </div>
    <div class="secondary">
      <-- your secondary primary content goes here -->
    </div>
  </div>

  <div class="secondary">
    <!--navigation and secondary content goes here -->
  </div>

</div>
```

Using the same CSS as the two-column technique, you can float the secondary content left and the primary content right. Then, inside the primary content div, you can float the primary div left and the secondary div right (see Figure 8-8). This essentially divides the primary content area in two, creating a three-column effect.

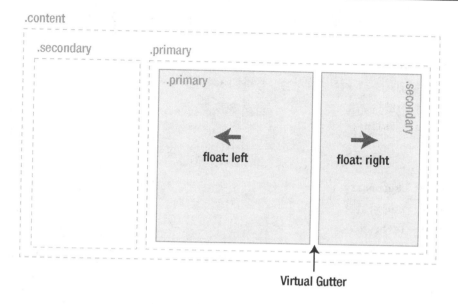

Virtual Gutter

Figure 8-8. Creating a three-column layout by dividing the content column into two columns

As before, the CSS for this is very simple. You just set your desired widths and then float the primary `div` left and the secondary `div` right, creating a 20-pixel gap in the middle:

```
.content .primary .primary {
  width: 400px;
  float: left;
  display: inline;
}

.content .primary .secondary {
  width: 230px;
  float: right;
  display: inline;
}
```

One thing you'll notice is that the right-hand padding we gave to the primary `div` in the in the first example is now being applied to our new primary `div` in the second example. As such, we need to remove the pading from the more general style and apply it to the more specific style.

```
.content .primary {
  width: 670px; /* width increased and padding removed*/
  float: right;
  display: inline;
}

.content .secondary {
  width: 230px;
  float: left;
  display: inline;
}



.content .primary .primary {
  width: 400px;
  float: left;
  display: inline;
}

.content .primary .secondary {
  width: 230px;
  padding-right: 20px; /*  padding applied here instead*/
  float: right;
  display: inline;
}
```

This leaves you with a nice and solid three-column layout (see Figure 8-9).

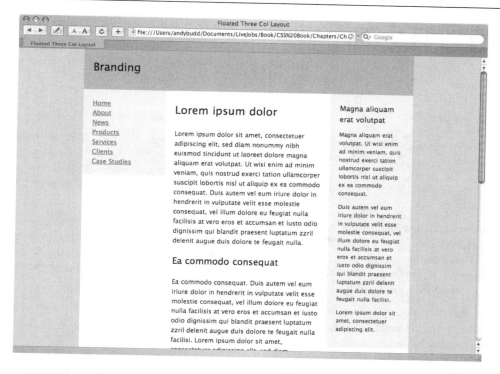

Figure 8-9. Three-column layout using floats

Fixed-width, liquid, and elastic layout

So far, all the examples have used widths defined in pixels. This type of layout is known as fixed-width layout. Fixed-width layouts are very common, as they give the developer more control over layout and positioning. If you set the width of your design to be 960 pixels wide, it will always be 960 pixels. If you then want a branding image spanning the top of your design, you know it needs to be 960 pixels wide to fit. Knowing the exact width of each element allows you to lay them out precisely and know where everything will be. This makes fixed-width layout the easiest and therefore most common approach.

However, fixed-width designs have their downsides. First, because they are fixed, they are always the same size no matter what your window size. As such, they don't make good use of the available space. On large screen resolutions, designs created for 1024×760 can appear tiny and lost in the middle of the screen. Conversely, a design created for a 1024×760 screen will cause horizontal scrolling (or crawling) on smaller screen resolutions. With an increasingly diverse range of screen sizes to contend with, fixed-width designs don't adapt well to the flexible nature of the Web. As such, they often feel like a poor compromise.

Another issue with fixed-width design revolves around line lengths and text legibility. Fixed-width layouts usually work well with the browser default text size. However, you only have to increase the text size a couple of steps before sidebars start running out of space and the line lengths get too short to comfortably read.

To work around these issues, you could choose to use liquid or elastic layout instead of fixed-width layout.

Liquid layouts

With liquid layouts, dimensions are set using percentages instead of pixels. This allows liquid layouts to scale in relation to the browser window. As the browser window gets bigger, the columns get wider. Conversely, as the window gets smaller, the columns will reduce in width. Liquid layouts make for very efficient use of space, and the best liquid layouts aren't even noticeable.

However, liquid layouts are not without their own problems. At small window widths, line lengths can get incredibly narrow and difficult to read. This is especially true in multicolumn layouts. As such, it may be worth adding a min-width in pixels or ems to prevent the layout from becoming too narrow. However, set the min-width too large and your liquid designs inherit the same constraints as their fixed-width cousins.

Conversely, if the design spans the entire width of the browser window, line lengths can become long and difficult to read. You can do a couple of things to help avoid this problem. First, rather than spanning the whole width, you could make the wrapper span just a percentage—say, 85 percent. You could also consider setting the internal padding and margins as percentages as well. That way, the padding and margins will increase in width in relation to the window size, stopping the columns from getting too wide, too quickly. Last, you should add a maximum width on the wrapper to prevent the content from getting ridiculously wide on oversized monitors.

You can use these techniques to turn the previous fixed-width, three-column layout into a fluid, three-column layout. Start by setting the width of the wrapper as a percentage of the overall width of the window. Most people will pick an arbitrary size based on what looks good on their screens, and that's perfectly fine. However if you want to be more precise, take a look at your browser stats to calculate the most common window size and then pick a wrapper percentage that matches how the fixed width version would look at that size. A good tool for this is Liquid Fold (http://liquidfold.net/). For example, if your designer used a width of 960 pixels and the majority of your users have their browser windows set to 1250 pixels, the percentage to use would be $(960 \div 1250) \times 100 = 76.8$ percent.

Next, set the width of the primary and secondary content areas as a percentage of the wrapper width. In the previous example, the width of our primary content div was 670 pixels. As the total width was 920 pixels, this works out as 72.82 percent. Similarly, the width of the secondary content div works out at exactly 25 percent. This leaves a 2.18 percent virtual gutter between the navigation and the wrapper to deal with any rounding errors and width irregularities that may occur:

```
.wrapper {
  width: 76.8%;
  margin: 0 auto;
  text-align: left;
}


.content .primary {
  width: 72.82%;
  float: right;
  display: inline;
}
.content .secondary {
  width: 25%;
  float: left;
  display: inline;
}
```

You then need to set the widths of the columns inside the primary content area. This gets a bit trickier, because the widths of the content divs are based on the width of the primary content element and not the overall wrapper. So this time, the width of the primary div is 400 pixels, which works out to be 59.7 percent of the parent element. Similarly, the width of the secondary div works out to be 34.33 percent. Finally, we still need a 20-pixel gutter, which works out at 2.63 percent of the parent element.

```
.content .primary .primary {
  width: 59.7%;
  float: left;
  display: inline;
}
```

```
.content .primary .secondary {
  width: 34.33%;
  padding-right: 2.63%;
  float: right;
  display: inline;
}
```

This produces a liquid layout that is optimal at window size of 1250 pixels but is comfortable to read at both larger and smaller screen resolutions (see Figure 8-10).

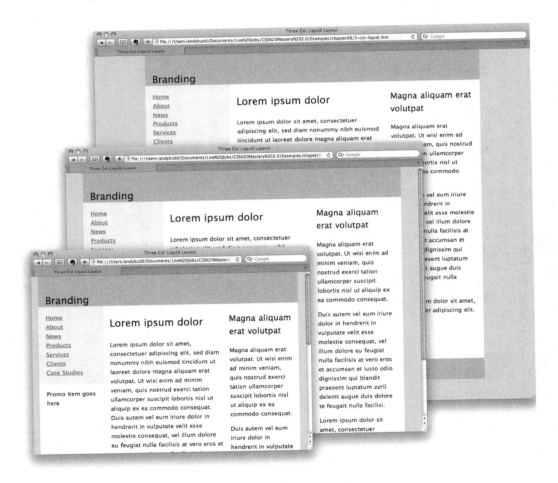

Figure 8-10. Three-column liquid layout at 800×600, 1024×768, and 1250×900

Because this layout scales so nicely, there isn't any need to add a `max-width` property. However, to ensure the lines of text remain a readable length, it's always a good idea to add a `max-width` in ems. The layout does start to get a little cramped at smaller window sizes, so I'm going also to add a min-width in ems as well.

```
.wrapper {
  width: 76.8%;
  margin: 0 auto;
  text-align: left;
  max-width: 125em;
  min-width: 62em;
}
```

And there you have it, a nice, flexible, liquid layout.

Elastic layouts

While liquid layouts are useful for making the most of the available space, line lengths can still get uncomfortably long on high-resolution monitors. Conversely, lines can become very short and fragmented in narrow windows or when the text size is increased a couple of steps. If these limitations are of concern, elastic layouts may be your solution.

Elastic layouts work by setting the width of elements relative to the size of the font instead of the width of the browser. By setting widths in ems, you ensure that when the font size is increased the whole layout scales. This allows you to keep line lengths to a readable size and is particularly useful for people with reduced vision or cognitive disorders.

Like other layout techniques, elastic layouts are not without their issues. Elastic layouts share some of the problems with fixed-width layouts, such as not making the most use of the available space. Also, because the whole layout increases when the text size is increased, elastic layouts can become much wider than the browser window, forcing the appearance of horizontal scroll bars. To combat this, it may be worth adding a `max-width` of 100% to the wrapper `div`; `max-width` wasn't supported by IE6 and below, but it is supported by newer versions. If you need to support `max-width` in IE 6, you can use JavaScript as well.

Elastic layouts are much easier to create than liquid layouts as all of the HTML elements essentially stay in the same place relative to each other; they just all increase in size. Turning a fixed-width layout into an elastic layout is a relatively simple task. The trick is to set the base font size so that 1 em roughly equals 10 pixels.

The default font size on most browsers is 16 pixels. Ten pixels works out at 62.5 percent of 16 pixels, so setting the font size on the body to 62.5% does the trick:

```css
body {
    font-size: 62.5%;
    text-align: center;
}
```

Because 1 em now equals 10 pixels at the default font size, we can convert our fixed-width layout into an elastic layout relatively easily. In previous editions of this book, I recommended setting all the widths in ems. However, my esteemed colleague and technical reviewer Natalie Downe suggested keeping the internal widths as percentages and only setting the wrapper width in ems. That way, the internal widths will still size themselves relative to the font size. This allows you to change the overall size of the layout without having to change the width on each individual element, making for a more flexible and maintainable solution.

```css
.wrapper {
    width: 92em;
    max-width: 95%;
    margin: 0 auto;
    text-align: left;
}

.content .primary {
    width: 72.82%;
    float: right;
    display: inline;
}

.content .secondary {
    width: 25%;
    float: left;
    display: inline;
}
```

```
.content .primary .primary {
  width: 59.7%;
  float: left;
  display: inline;
}


.content .primary .secondary {
  width: 34.33%;
  padding-right: 2em;
  float: right;
  display: inline;
}
```

This produces a layout that looks identical to the fixed-width layout at regular text sizes (see Figure 8-11), but scales beautifully as the text size is increased (see Figure 8-12).

Figure 8-11. Elastic layout at the default text size

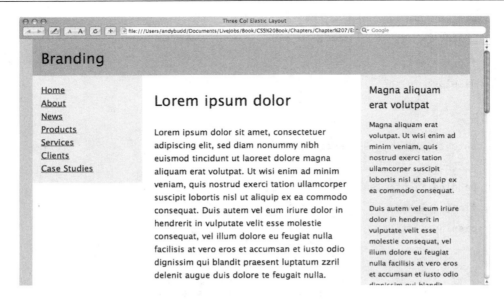

Figure 8-12. Elastic layout after the text size has been increased a few times

With the increasing prevalence of page zooming in modern browsers, some people have begun to question the need for elastic layouts. However, until all browsers support page zooming by default, you may still want to consider elastic layouts for older browsers.

Liquid and elastic images

If you choose to use a liquid or an elastic layout, fixed-width images can have a drastic effect on your design. When the width of the layout is reduced, images will shift in relation to it and may interact negatively with each other. Images will create natural minimum widths, preventing some elements from reducing in size. Other images will break out of their containing elements, wreaking havoc on finely tuned designs. Increasing the width of the layout can also have dramatic consequences, creating unwanted gaps and unbalancing designs. But never fear—there are a few ways to avoid such problems.

For images that need to span a wide area, such as those found in the site header or branding areas, consider using a background image rather than an image element. As the `branding` element scales, more or less of the background image will be revealed:

```
#branding {
  height: 171px;
  background: url(/img/branding.png) no-repeat left top;
}

<div id="branding"></div>
```

If the image needs to be on the page as an image element, try setting the `width` of the container element to `100%` and the `overflow` property to `hidden`. The image will be clipped on the right-hand side so that it fits inside the `branding` element but will scale as the layout scales:

```
#branding {
  width: 100%;
  overflow: hidden;
}
```

```
<div id="branding">
  <img src="/img/branding.png" width="1600" height="171" />
</div>
```

For regular content images, you will probably want them to scale vertically as well as horizontally to avoid clipping. You can do this by adding an image element to the page without any stated dimensions. You then set the percentage width of the image, and add a `max-width` the same size as the image to prevent pixelization.

For example, say you wanted to create a news story style with a narrow image column on the left and a larger text column on the right. The image needs to be roughly a quarter of the width of the containing box, with the text taking up the rest of the space. You can do this by simply setting the `width` of the image to `25%` and then setting the `max-width` to be the size of the image, in this case 200 pixels wide:

```
.news img {
  width: 25%;
  max-width: 200px;
  float: left;
  display: inline;
  padding: 2%;
}
```

```
.news p {
  width: 68%;
  float: right;
  display: inline;
  padding: 2% 2% 2% 0;
}
```

As the news element expands or contracts, the image and paragraphs will also expand or contract, maintaining their visual balance (see Figure 8-13). However, on standards-compliant browsers, the image will never get larger than its actual size.

Figure 8-13. Giving images a percentage width allows them to scale nicely in relation to their surroundings

Faux columns

You may have noticed that the navigation and secondary content areas on all these layouts have been given a light gray background. Ideally, the background would stretch the full height of the layout, creating a column effect. However, because the navigation and secondary content areas don't span the full height, neither do their backgrounds.

To create the column effect, you can make fake columns by applying a repeating background image to an element that does span the full height of the layout, such as a wrapper div. Dan Cederholm coined the term "faux column" to describe this technique.

Starting with the fixed-width, two-column layout, you can simply apply a vertically repeating background image, the same width as the navigation area, to the wrapper element (see Figure 8-14):

```
#wrapper {
  background: #fff url(/img/nav-bg-fixed.gif) repeat-y left top;
}
```

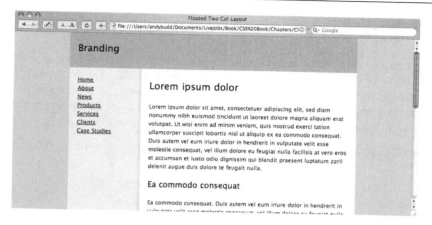

Figure 8-14. Faux fixed-width column

For the three-column fixed width layout, you can use a similar approach. This time, however, your repeating background image needs to span the whole width of the wrapper and include both columns (see Figure 8-15). Applying this image in the same way as before creates a lovely faux two-column effect (see Figure 8-16).

Figure 8-15. Background image used to create the faux three-column effect

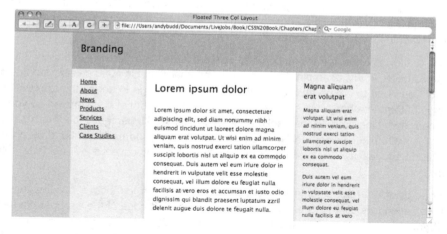

Figure 8-16. Faux three-column effect

Creating faux columns for fixed-width designs is relatively easy, as you always know the sizes of the columns and their positions. Creating faux columns for fluid layouts is a little more complicated; the columns change shape and position as the browser window is scaled. The trick to fluid faux columns lies in the use of percentages to position the background image.

If you set a background position using pixels, the top-left corner of the image is positioned from the top-left corner of the element by the specified number of pixels. With percentage positioning, it is the corresponding point on the image that gets positioned. So if you set a vertical and horizontal position of 20 percent, you are actually positioning a point 20 percent from the top left of the image, 20 percent from the top left of the parent element (see Figure 8-17).

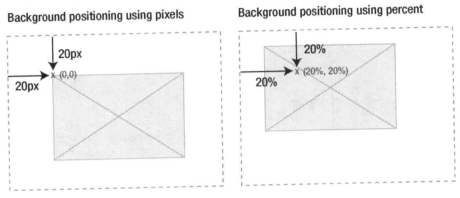

Figure 8-17. When positioning using percentages, the corresponding position on the image is used

Positioning background images using percentages can be very useful, as it allows you to create background images with the same horizontal proportions as your layout and then position them where you want the columns to appear.

To create a faux column for the secondary content area, you start by creating a very wide background image. In this example, I have created an image that is 4000 pixels wide and 5 pixels high. Next, you need to create an area on the background image to act as the faux column. The secondary content area has been set to be 25 percent of the width of the wrapper, so you need to create a corresponding area on the background image that is 25 percent wide. For a background image that is 4000 pixels wide, the faux column part of the image needs to be 1000 pixels wide. Output this image as a GIF, making sure that the area not covered by the faux column is transparent.

The right edge of the faux column is now 25 percent from the left side of the image. The right edge of the secondary content area is 25 percent from the left edge of the wrapper element. That means if you apply the image as a background to the wrapper element, and set the horizontal position to be 25 percent, the right edge of the faux column will line up perfectly with the right edge of the navigation element.

```
.wrapper {
  background: #fff url(/img/secondary-faux-column.gif) repeat-y 25% 0;
}
```

You can create the background for the primary content area using a similar method. The left edge of this faux column should start 72.82 percent from the left edge of the image, matching the position of the primary content element relative to the wrapper. Because the wrapper element already has a background image applied to it, you will need to add a second wrapper element inside the first. You can then apply your second faux column background image to this new wrapper element.

```
.inner-wrapper {
  background: url(/img/primary-faux-column.gif) repeat-y 72.82% 0;
}
```

If you have worked out your proportions correctly, you should be left with a beautiful three-column liquid layout with columns that stretch the height of the wrapper (see Figure 8-18).

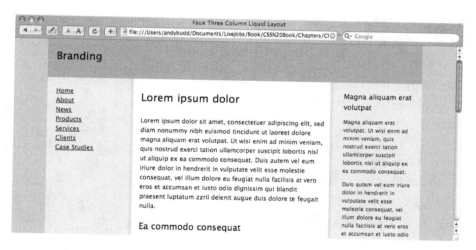

Figure 8-18. Faux three-column layout

Equal-height columns

As well as creating columns as part of your main layout, you may want to create equal-height columns elsewhere in your design, like the ones in Figure 8-19. While this is easy to accomplish using tables, it's a little trickier in CSS.

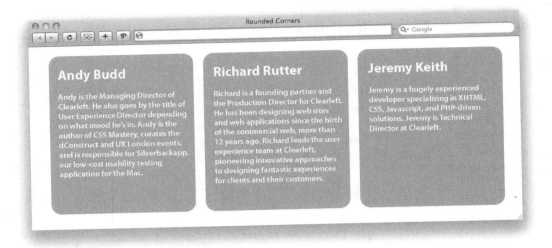

Figure 8-19. Three, equal-height columns

Let's start with the mark-up.

```
<div class="wrapper">
  <div class="box">
    <h1>Andy Budd</h1>
      <p>...</p>
    <div class="bottom"></div>
  </div>

  <div class="box">
    <h1>Richard Rutter</h1>
      <p>...</p>
    <div class="bottom"></div>
  </div>
```

```
<div class="box">
  <h1>Jeremy Keith</h1>
    <p>...</p>
  <div class="bottom"></div>
  </div>
</div>
```

For this example, you are going to need three divs, one for each of the three columns. Inside each div, you'll need a heading, some copy, and an empty div to use as a hook for the bottom corners. All three divs are then enclosed in a wrapper div, which we will use to constrain the height. We can now start styling our boxes.

```
.wrapper {
  width: 100%;
}

.box {
  width: 250px;
  margin-left: 20px;
  float: left;
  display: inline;
  padding: 20px;
  background: #89ac10  url(/img/top.gif) no-repeat left top;
}
```

You will see from Figure 8-20 that this leaves us with three, uneven columns.

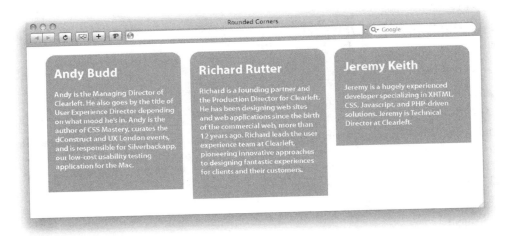

Figure 8-20. The three columns before the main technique being applied

The trick to this technique is to give each box a large amount of bottom padding and then remove this height with a similar amount of negative margin. This causes each column to overflow the wrapper element (see Figure 8-21). If you then set the `overflow` property of the wrapper to `hidden`, the columns get clipped at their tallest point. In this example, I'm giving each element a bottom padding of 520 pixels and a bottom margin of 500 pixels. The 20 pixels difference forms the visible padding at the bottom of each box.

```css
.wrapper {
  width: 100%;
  overflow: hidden;
}

.box {
  width: 250px;
  padding-left: 20px;
  padding-right: 20px;
  padding-top: 20px;
  padding-bottom: 520px;
  margin-bottom: 500px;
  margin-left: 20px;
  float: left;
  display: inline;
  background: url(/img/top.gif) #89ac10 top left no-repeat;
}
```

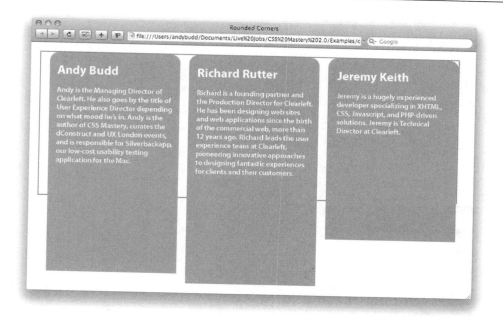

Figure 8-21. The red border shows the bounds of the wrapper div, so you can see how the three colums flow out of this element

To position the bottom of the columns in the right place, you need to align them with the bottom of the wrapper element. To do this, you first need to set the positioning context by giving the wrapper a position of relative. You can then set to position of the empty divs to be absolute and set their bottom properties to be zero. Now, all you need to do is give the elements the correct width and height and apply the bottom image as a background.

```
.wrapper {
  width: 100%;
  overflow: hidden;
  position: relative;
}

.box {
  width: 250px;
  padding-left: 20px;
  padding-right: 20px;
  padding-top: 20px;
```

```
    padding-bottom: 520px;
    margin-bottom: 500px;
    margin-left: 20px;
    float: left;
    display: inline;
    padding: 20px;
    background: url(/img/top.gif) #89ac10 top left no-repeat;
}

.bottom {
    position: absolute;
    bottom: 0;
    height: 20px;
    width: 290px;
    background: url(/img/bottom.gif) #89ac10 bottom left no-repeat;
    margin-left: -20px;
}
```

The result is a three-column layout that retains the height of the longest column, as shown in Figure 8-19. Neat, huh?

CSS 3 columns

CSS 3 also gives us the ability to create equal-height text columns, as shown in Figure 8-22. This is achieved through the `column-count` ,`column-width` and `column-gap` properties.

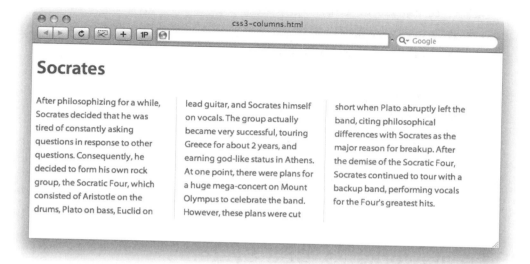

Figure 8-22. Text columns using the CSS 3 column properties

Say you start with the following markup:

```
<h1>Socrates</h1>
<div class="col">
  <p>After philosophizing for a while...</p>
</div>
```

Applying these rules will create a three-column layout where each column is 14 ems wide and has a 2-em gap between it and the next columns. One of the nice features of CSS columns is what happens if the available space becomes smaller than the width of the defined columns. Rather than the columns wrapping, as you'd get if you were using floats, the column count simply reduces. So if there weren't enough space for three columns, you would reduce down to two.

```
.col {
  -moz-column-count: 3;
  -moz-column-width: 14em;
  -moz-column-gap: 2em;
  -moz-column-rule: 1px solid #ccc;
  -webkit-column-count: 3;
```

```
    -webkit-column-width: 14em;

    -webkit-column-gap: 2em;

    -webkit-column-rule: 1px solid #ccc;

    column-count: 3;

    column-width: 14em;

    column-gap: 2em;

    column-rule: 1px solid #ccc;

}
```

As you can probably see from the preceding code, CSS columns aren't widely supported yet. As such, you need to back up the regular code with the use of browser-specific extensions.

CSS Frameworks vs. CSS Systems

In the programming world, frameworks like Rails or Django take common patterns in web development, such as adding records to a database, and abstract them into a simple set of reusable components. This abstraction allows developers to build fairly sophisticated applications without needing to engineer these functions from scratch. Unlike a library of stand-alone functions, frameworks tend to be highly integrated. As such, frameworks are abstracted to such a degree that it's possible, although not desirable, to build entire applications without needing to understand the parent language.

Over the last couple of years, we've slowly seen the rise of so-called CSS frameworks. These frameworks aim to take some of the drudgery out CSS and help users create a variety of common layouts without needing to edit the underlying CSS. Instead, these frameworks encourage developers to use a series of markup patterns and naming conventions and then manage the layout behind the scenes. The three most popular frameworks are YUI Grids, Blueprint, and 960 (see Figure 8-23), although there are several others to choose from.

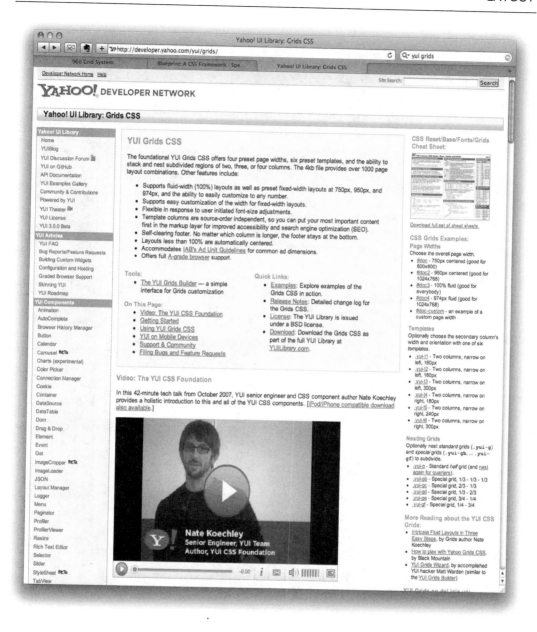

Figure 8-23. The YUI, Blueprint, and 960 web sites

These frameworks offer a number of useful productivity benefits including global style resets, sitewide typographical handling, and consistent form treatment—things you will need on the majority of your projects. However, frameworks also change the way you write your markup, losing the important separation of presentation from meaning. For instance, the markup used in the Blueprint framework is clearly presentational in nature, talking, as it does, in terms of columns and column spans.

```
<div class="column span-24">
<!-- header -->
</div>
<div class="column span-4">
<!-- left sidebar -->
</div>
<div class="column span-16">
<!-- main content -->
</div>
<div class="column span-4 last">
<!-- right sidebar -->
</div>
```

By using frameworks to control layout, developers are forced to use a presentational style of markup that more closely resembles table-based design. In fact, you could argue that tables are better than CSS frameworks, because tables have the same ridged, presentational mark-up without the extra CSS to download. Frameworks also force the developer to learn not only the underlying language but the framework as well. Often this doesn't happen, and the developer is left with a partial understanding of both.

Frameworks have another disadvantaged in the fact that they enforce a specific grid structure on your designs. This is fine if your designs happen to fit the widths and margins defined by the framework. However, just as it's unacceptable for your programming framework to dictate the user experience of your website, it's unacceptable for your CSS framework to dictate the design of your site. By selecting a specific framework, the danger is that you'll end up using it for every project and thus painting yourself into a corner. Or, as the saying goes, if you only have a hammer, everything looks like a nail.

These problems become evident when you understand where frameworks came from. Rather than being designed from scratch as a flexible layout system for any possible design, most were created for the use on specific sites like Yahoo or the *Laurence Kansas Journal*. These sites already had well-defined grid structures and style guides, so the developers knew that every new page would follow the same pattern. Over time, the developers found other uses for these systems, so they abstracted them and released them to the general public. However, the focus of these frameworks on their original sites is still evident in their design.

So how do we get the productivity benefits from CSS frameworks without the obvious disadvantages? This is where the concept of CSS systems comes in. A CSS system is essentially a toolbox of reusable styles and markup patterns that can be used to develop site-specific frameworks. This toolbox could include your global resets, typographic styles, and form treatments, along with markup patterns for common HTML widgets such as sign-up forms, calendar tables, and navigation lists. You can then use the techniques you've learned in this book to develop a system for your clients that acts like a customized framework, complete with all the different layout options they will need. This process initially involves a little more work on the your part, but it provides all the benefits of a CSS framework without the pitfalls.

Summary

In this chapter, you learned how to create simple two- and three-column fixed-width layouts using floats. You then learned how these layouts could be converted into liquid and elastic layouts with relative ease, as well as exploring some of the problems associated with these layouts and how setting maximum widths in ems or pixels can offer solutions. You also saw how to create full height column effects on both fixed-width and flexible layouts, using vertically repeating background images. This chapter also touched on some of the techniques used to create CSS-based layouts. However, there are a lot of techniques out there, enough to fill a whole book of their own. Last, you learned some of the dangers inherent in CSS frameworks and the importance of developing your own CSS system instead.

One of the big problems developers face with CSS layouts is that of browser inconsistency. To get around browser-rendering issues, you need to have a good understanding of the various bugs and how to fix them. In the next chapter, you will learn about some of the better-known browser bugs along with the fundamentals of CSS debugging.

Chapter 9

Bugs and Bug Fixing

Compared to many programming languages, CSS is a relatively simple language to learn. The syntax is straightforward, and due to its presentational nature, there is no complicated logic to grapple with. The difficulties start when it comes time to test your code on different browsers. Browser bugs and inconsistent rendering are major stumbling blocks for most CSS developers. Your designs look fine on one browser, but your layout inexplicably breaks on another.

The misconception that CSS is difficult comes not from the language itself, but the hoops you need to jump through to get your sites working in older browsers. Bugs are difficult to find information on, poorly documented, and often misunderstood. Hacks are seen by many as magic bullets—arcane sigils with exotic names that, when applied to your code, will magically fix your broken layouts. Hacks are definitely potent tools in your armory, but they need to be applied with care and generally as a last resort. A much more important skill is the ability to track, isolate, and identify bugs. Only once you know what a bug is can you look for ways to squash it.

In this chapter, you will learn about

- How to track down CSS bugs

- The mysterious hasLayout property

- Hacks and filters

- The most common browser bugs and their fixes

- Graded browser support

Bug hunting

We all know that browsers are buggy, some of them more than others. When a CSS developer comes across a problem with code, there is the immediate temptation to mark it as a browser bug and look for a hack or workaround. However, browser bugs aren't as common as everybody likes to think. The most common CSS problems arise not from the browser bugs but from an incomplete understanding of the CSS specification. To avoid these problems, it is always best to approach a CSS bug assuming that you have done something wrong. Only once you are sure that there are no errors on your part should you consider the problem to be the result of a browser bug.

Common CSS problems

Some of the simplest CSS problems are caused by typographical and syntactical errors in your code. Things like forgetting to end your declarations with a semi-colon or typing `font-face` when you meant `font-family`. A simple way to get round this problem is to choose a CSS editor like SKEdit or CSS Edit that includes syntax highlighting and code completing. These features will help prevent basic errors but are no substitute for proper validation. Running your code through a service like the CSS Validator (`http://jigsaw.w3.org/css-validator/`) will highlight any grammatical errors, showing you the lines the issues are on and a brief description of each error (see Figure 9-1).

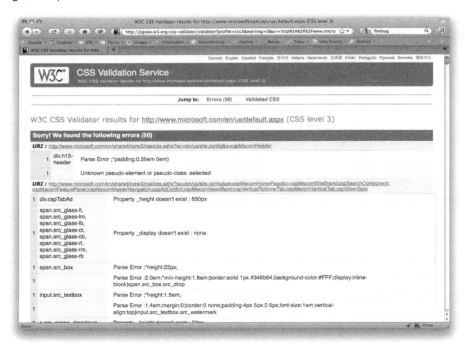

Figure 9-1. The Microsoft website as seen through the eyes of the CSS Validator

The Firefox Web Developer Toolbar extension (`https://addons.mozilla.org/en-US/firefox/addon/60`) includes shortcuts to the online versions of both the HTML and CSS validators. There is also the popular HTML Validator for Firefox (`http://users.skynet.be/mgueury/mozilla/`)

When validating your HTML and CSS, you may be greeted with a page full of errors. This can be quite intimidating at first, but don't worry. Most of these errors will be the result of one or two actual errors. If you fix the first error mentioned and revalidate, you will see many of the original errors disappear. Do this a couple of times, and your code should quickly become error free.

Remember that the validator is only an automated tool and is not infallible. There are a growing number of reported bugs with the validator, so if you think something is right but the validator is saying something different, always check against the latest CSS specification. For instance, at the time of this writing, the CSS validator was still throwing up errors for vendor-specific extensions like -moz-border-radius, even though these are allowed in the CSS specification. If in doubt, validate your code using the CSS 3 profile and then check the specification if you're unsure of anything.

Problems with specificity and sort order

As well as syntactic errors, one of the more common problems revolves around specificity and sort order. Specificity problems usually manifest themselves when you apply a rule to an element, only to find it not having any effect. You can apply other rules and they work fine, but certain rules just don't seem to work. In these situations, the problem is usually that you have already defined rules for this element elsewhere in your document using a more specific selector.

In the following example, CSS developers have set the background color of all the paragraphs in the content area to be white. However, they want the introductory paragraph to be orange and so have applied that rule directly to the paragraph:

```
.content p {
  background-color: white;
}


.intro {
  background-color: orange;
}
```

If you test this code in a browser, you will see that the introductory paragraph is still white. This is because the selector targeting all the paragraphs in the content area is more specific than the selector targeting the introductory paragraph. To achieve the desired result, you need to make the selector targeting the introductory paragraph more specific. In this case, the best way to achieve this is to add the class for the content element to the start of the intro paragraph selector:

247

```
.content p {
  background-color: white;
}


.content .intro {
  background-color: orange;
}
```

Try not to add more-specific selectors without thinking, as you may cause specificity issues is other parts of your code. Instead, it is often better to remove extraneous selectors, making them as generic as possible, and only add more specific selectors when you need fine-grain control.

As mentioned in Chapter 1, the Firebug add-on for Firefox (`https://addons.mozilla.org/en-US/firefox/addon/1843`) is an invaluable tool for debugging your CSS. One of its many useful features is the ability to inspect an element to see which CSS styles are being overridden. It does this by crossing out any styles that are being overridden elsewhere in the style sheet, as shown in Figure 9-2.

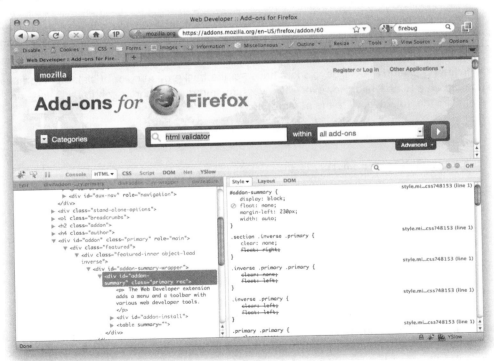

Figure 9-2. Styles appear crossed out when they are overriden in other parts of the stylesheet

Problems with margin collapsing

Margin collapsing (see Chapter 3) is another CSS feature that, if misunderstood, can cause a lot of gray hairs. Take the simple example of a paragraph nested inside a `div` element:

```
<div id="box">
    <p>This paragraph has a 20px margin.</p>
</div>
```

The box `div` is given a 10-pixel margin and the paragraph is given a 20-pixel margin:

```
#box {
    margin: 10px;
    background-color:#d5d5d5;
}


p {
    margin: 20px;
    background-color:#6699FF;
}
```

You would naturally expect the resulting style to look like Figure 9-3, with a 20-pixel margin between the paragraph and the `div`, and a 10-pixel margin around the outside of the `div`.

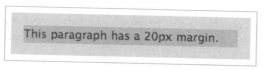

Figure 9-3. This is how you would expect the preceding style to look

However, the resulting style actually looks like Figure 9-4.

Figure 9-4. This is how the style actually looks

Two things are going on here. First, the paragraph's 20-pixel top and bottom margins collapse with the 10-pixel margin on the `div`, forming a single 20-pixel vertical margin. Second, rather than being enclosed by the `div`, the margins appear to protrude from the top and bottom of the `div`. This happens because of the way elements with block-level children have their height calculated.

If an element has no vertical border or padding, its height is calculated as the distance between the top and bottom border edges of its contained children. Because of this, the top and bottom margins of the contained children appear to protrude from the containing element. However, there is a simple fix. By adding a vertical border or padding, the margins no longer collapse and the height of the element is calculated as the distance between the top and bottom margin edges of its contained children instead.

To get the preceding example looking like Figure 9-3, you simply need to add padding or a border around the div:

```css
#box {
   margin: 10px;
   padding: 1px;
   background-color:#d5d5d5;
}

p {
   margin: 20px;
   background-color:#6699FF;
}
```

Most problems with margin collapsing can be fixed by adding a small amount of padding or a thin border with the same color as the background of the element in question.

A great tool for visualizing how elements interact with each other is the topographic view in the Web Developer Toolbar. Enabling this option gives each element a colored background based on its position in the document. This makes it easy to see how elements are positioned relative to each other in the document (see Figure 9-5).

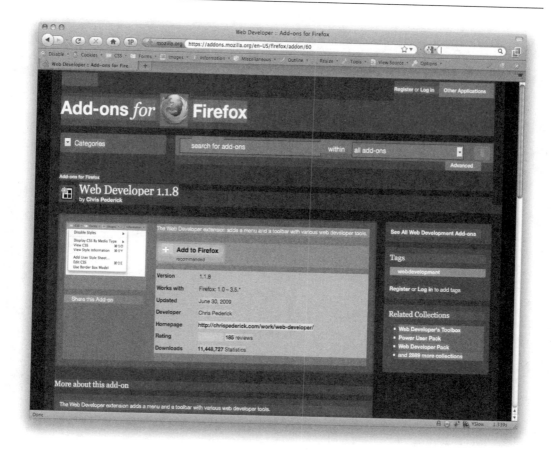

Figure 9-5. A topographic view of the Mozilla Add-ons site

Another useful tool is the layout view in Firebug (see Figure 9-6), which shows you the various dimensions of the element being inspected.

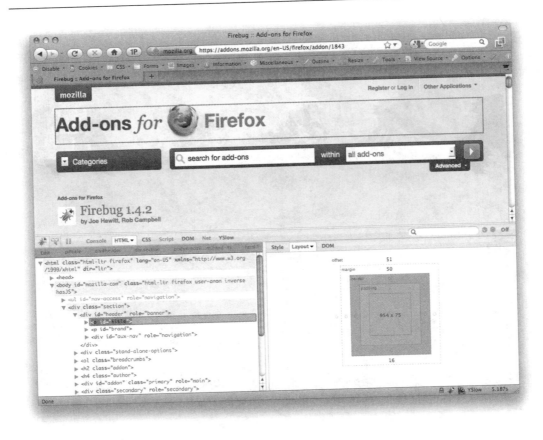

Figure 9-6. The layout view of the header from the Mozilla Add-ons site

Bug hunting basics

The first step in tracking down a bug is to validate your HTML and CSS to check for typographical or syntactic errors. Some display errors are caused by browsers rendering pages in quirks mode. As such, it is a good idea to check that you are using the correct DOCTYPE for your markup language in order for your pages to render in standards mode (see Chapter 1). You can tell the mode your page is rendering in by checking it in the Firefox developer's toolbar. If your page is rendering in quirks mode, the checkmark at the top right of the toolbar will be gray. If your page is rendering in standards mode, the checkmark will turn green. Clicking this checkmark will provide more information about the page, as well as explicitly define the rendering mode (see Figure 9-7).

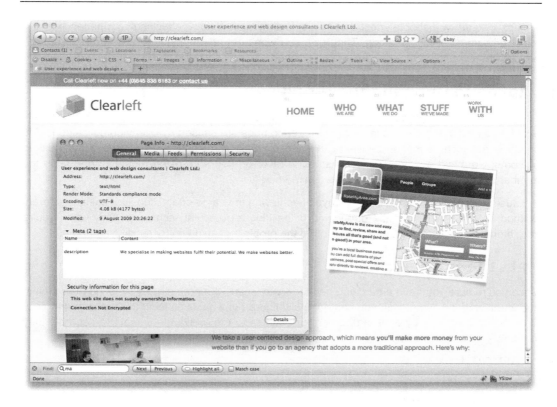

Figure 9-7. The Firefox web developer's toolbar shows if your page is displaying in standards or quirks mode

Many Windows developers used to develop their pages primarily using Internet Explorer, so each time they made a change, they previewed the page in IE to see if it was working correctly. Once the pages were almost ready, they would test in a variety of browsers and try to fix any inconsistencies that appeared. However, this is a very dangerous approach that can cause many long-term problems.

IE 6 is a notoriously buggy browser with several important CSS flaws. By using IE as their primary development browser, some developers mistakenly interpret IE's behavior as the correct behavior and wonder why more modern browsers "break" their carefully crafted CSS layouts. In reality, the pages are actually "broken" in IE and are displaying as written in the more standards-compliant browsers.

A much safer approach is to use a more standards-compliant browser, such as Firefox or Safari, as your primary development browser. If your layout works in one of these browsers, it will most likely work correctly in all standards-compliant browsers and is a sign that you're doing things correctly. You can then test your pages on less-capable browsers and devise workarounds for any display problems you find. Just remember not to leave browser testing until the end of the project. Instead, you should adopt a continual testing methodology, checking your pages in all the major browsers as you go along. That way, you won't get any nasty surprises at the end of the project when you thought you were almost finished.

Try to avoid bugs in the first place

This advice may sound obvious, but one of the best ways of becoming bug free is to actually avoid problems in the first place. A lot of rendering bugs are caused by overly complicated HTML or CSS. As such, it makes sense to use the simplest code possible to achieve the desired outcome. So avoid overly clever techniques in favor of tried and tested methods, and keep the number of hacks you use to an absolute minimum.

Because there are so many different ways of achieving the same effect, consider using a different method before spending hours debugging or hacking a particular technique. Only when you're sure there's not a simple way to route around the problem should you try tackling it head on.

Isolate the problem

Once you're sure you have a bug, you need to try to isolate the problem. By isolating the problem and identifying the symptoms, you can hopefully figure out what is causing the problem and fix it. One way to do this is by applying borders or outlines to the relevant elements to see how they interact:

```
.promo1 {
  float: left;
  margin-lrft: 5px;
  border: 1px solid red;
}


.promo2 {
  float: left;
  border: 1px solid green;
}
```

I tend to add borders directly to my code, although you could use the outline option in the web developer's toolbar, or one of many bookmarklets for outlining different elements. Sometimes just the act of adding borders will fix the problem, usually indicating a margin collapsing issue.

Try changing a few properties to see if they affect the bug, and if so, in what way. It may be useful to attempt to exaggerate a bug. For instance, if the gap between these two boxes is bigger than you expected in IE, try upping the margin to see what happens. If the space between the boxes in IE has doubled, you have probably fallen foul of IE's double-margin float bug.

```
.promo1 {
  float: left;
  margin-left: 40px;
  border: 1px solid red;
}

.promo2 {
  float: left;
  border: 1px solid green;
}
```

Try some common fixes. For instance, many IE bugs are fixed by setting the `position` property to `relative`, by setting the `display` property to `inline` (on floated elements), or by setting a dimension such as `width`. You will learn more about these common fixes and why they work later in this chapter.

Many CSS problems can be found and fixed quickly, with a minimum of effort. If the problem starts to drag on, you should consider creating a minimal test case.

Creating minimal test cases

A minimal test case is simply the smallest amount of HTML and CSS required to replicate the bug. By creating a minimal test case, you help cut out some of the variables and make the problem as simple as possible.

To create a minimal test case, you should first duplicate the problem files. Start by removing extraneous HTML until you are left with just the basics. Then start commenting out style sheets to work out which style sheets are causing the problem. Go into those style sheets and start deleting or commenting out blocks of code. If the bug suddenly stops, you know that the last block of code you commented out is contributing to the problem. Keep going until you are left only with the code that is causing the problems.

From here, you can start investigating the bug in more detail. Delete or comment out declarations and see what happens. How does that change the bug? Change property values and see if the problem goes away. Add common fixes to see if they have any effect. Edit the HTML to see if that has any effect. Use different combinations of HTML elements. Some browsers have strange whitespace bugs, so try removing whitespace from your HTML. The list of potential areas for exploration are almost endless.

Fixing the problem, not the symptoms

Once you know the root of the problem, you are in a much better position to implement the correct solution. Because there are many ways to skin a CSS site, the easiest solution is simply to avoid the problem in the first place. If margins are causing you problems, think about using padding instead. If one combination of HTML elements is causing problems, try changing the combination.

Many CSS bugs have very descriptive names. This makes searching for answers on the Web fairly easy. So if you have noticed that IE is doubling the margins on all floated elements, search for "Internet Explorer Double Margin Float Bug" and you are bound to find a solution.

If you find that you cannot avoid the bug, you may have to simply treat the symptoms. This usually involves filtering the rule off into a separate style sheet and applying a fix just for that browser.

Asking for help

If you have created a minimal test case, tried common solutions, searched for possible fixes, and still cannot find a solution, ask for help. You'll find lots of active CSS communities out there, such as CSS-Discuss (`www.css-discuss.org/`), the Web Standards Group (`http://webstandardsgroup.org/`), and Stackoverflow (`http://stackoverflow.com`). These communities are full of people who have been developing CSS sites for many years, so there is a good chance somebody will have experienced your bug before and know how to fix it. If you have a new or particularly intriguing bug, people may be willing to pitch in with suggestions and even help you work out a fix.

The thing to remember when asking for help is that most web developers are extremely busy people. If you haven't validated your code or have simply posted a link to your full site expecting them to trawl through hundreds of lines of HTML/CSS, don't expect a flood of help. The best way to ask for help on a mailing list or forum is to use a title that accurately describes the problem, write a succinct summary of the problem, and then either paste in your minimal test case or, if it is more than a few lines of code, link to the test case on your site. Annotated screenshots are also useful, as it's not always obvious from a written description what the problem is, especially if it only affects specific browser versions.

Having layout

We all know that browsers can be buggy, and Internet Explorer 6 seems buggier than most. One of the reasons IE behaves differently from other browsers is because the rendering engine uses an internal concept called layout. Because layout is a concept particular to the internal working of the rendering engine, it is not something you would normally need to know about. However, layout problems are the root of many IE rendering bugs, so it is useful to understand the concept and how it affects your CSS.

What is layout?

Internet Explorer on Windows uses the layout concept to control the size and positioning of elements. Elements that are said to "have layout" are responsible for sizing and positioning themselves and their children. If an element "does not have layout," its size and position are controlled by the nearest ancestor with layout.

The layout concept is a hack used by Internet Explorer's rendering engine to reduce its processing overhead. Ideally, all elements would be in control of their own size and positioning. However, this causes huge performance problems in IE. As such, the Internet Explorer team decided that by applying layout only to those elements that actually needed it, they could reduce the performance overhead substantially.

Elements that have layout by default include

- body
- html (in standards mode)
- table
- tr and td
- img
- hr
- input, select, textarea, and button
- iframe, embed, object, and applet
- marquee

The concept of layout is specific to Internet Explorer on Windows, and is not a CSS property. Layout cannot be explicitly set in the CSS, although setting certain CSS properties will give an element layout. It is possible to see if an element has layout by using the JavaScript function, hasLayout. This will return true if the element has layout and false if it doesn't. hasLayout is a read-only property and so cannot be set using JavaScript.

Setting the following CSS properties will automatically give that element layout:

- float: left or right
- display: inline-block
- width: any value
- height: any value
- zoom: any value (Microsoft property—doesn't validate)
- writing-mode: tb-rl (Microsoft property—doesn't validate)

As of IE 7, the following properties also became layout triggers:

- `overflow`: `hidden`, `scroll`, or `auto`

- `min-width`: any value

- `max-width`: any value except `none`

What effect does layout have?

Layout is the cause of many Internet Explorer rendering bugs. For instance, if you have a paragraph of text next to a floated element, the text is supposed to flow around the element. However, in IE 6 and below, if the paragraph has layout—because you've set the height, for example—it is constrained to a rectangular shape, stopping the text from flowing around the float (see Figure 9-8).

Text flows around floats

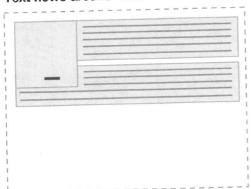

But not in IE 6 and below

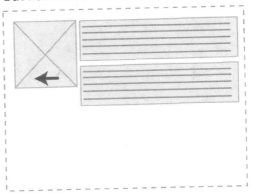

Figure 9-8. Text is supposed to flow around adjacent floated elements. However, in IE on Windows, if the text element has layout, this doesn't happen

The difference in rendering between browsers can cause all kinds of problems with floated layouts. Worse still, many people who use IE as their main browser mistakenly assume this is the correct behavior and get confused when other browsers treat floats differently. Furthermore, giving something layout appears to clear any floats contained therein, much like setting `overflow:hidden`.

Another problem revolves around how elements with layout size themselves. If the content of an element becomes larger than the element itself, the content is supposed to flow out of the element. However, in IE 6 and below, elements with layout incorrectly grow to fit the size of their contents (see Figure 9-9).

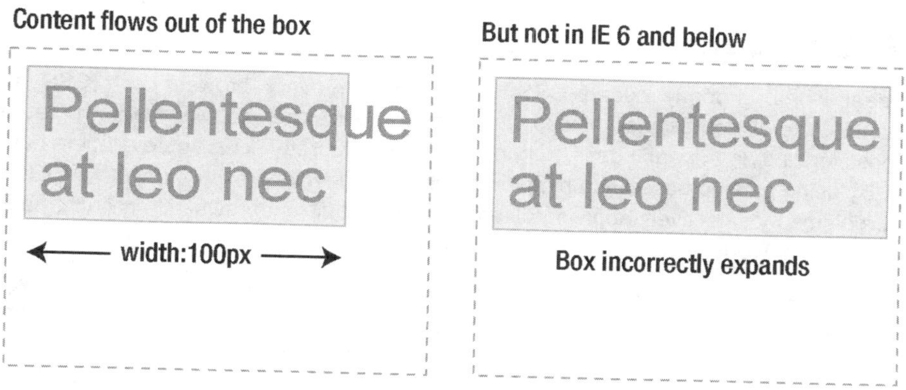

Content flows out of the box

But not in IE 6 and below

Pellentesque
at leo nec

←——— width:100px ———→

Pellentesque
at leo nec

Box incorrectly expands

Figure 9-9. Elements with layout incorrectly grow to fit their contents

This rendering error means that width in IE on Windows actually acts more like min-width. This behavior is also the cause of many broken floated layouts in IE. When the content of a floated box incorrectly forces the width of the box to grow, the box becomes too big for the available space and drops below the other floated elements.

Other problems related to layout include

- Elements with layout not shrinking to fit

- Floats being auto-cleared by layout elements

- Relatively positioned elements not gaining layout

- Margins not collapsing between elements with layout

- The hit area of block-level links without layout only covering the text

- Background images on list items intermittently appearing and disappearing on scroll

You will notice that many of the IE fixes covered later in this chapter involve setting properties that force the element to have layout. In fact, if you come across an IE bug, one of the first things you can do is try applying rules that force layout to see if that fixes the problem.

If you would like to learn more about IE's internal hasLayout property, I recommend reading "On Having Layout" at http://www.satzansatz.de/cssd/onhavinglayout.html.

Thankfully, the IE team fixed most of the layout related problems in IE 7. However, the team did this by spotting common rendering bugs and creating exceptions in the code to handle them, rather than fixing the underlying causes. As such, there may still be a few obscure layout bugs kicking around that have not yet been discovered. IE 8 uses a completely new rendering engine that purportedly ditches the use of the hasLayout property and therefore fixes the cause of these problems.

Workarounds

In an ideal world, properly coded CSS would work in every browser with CSS support. Unfortunately, like all complicated pieces of software, browsers come with their own set of bugs and inconsistencies. In the early days, support for CSS was pretty poor, so developers had to get creative. By using parsing bugs and unimplemented CSS, developers were able to work their way around problems by selectively applying different rules to different browsers. As such, hacks and filters became a powerful weapon in a CSS developer's arsenal.

Thankfully, modern browsers have much better support than their predecessors, so we don't need to worry about hacks any more. However until older browsers disappear for good, you may find yourself maintaining legacy code. Therefore, it's a good idea to familiarize yourself with some of the more popular hacks and filters, if only so you can banish them from your code. Before we do this though, let's take a quick look at conditional comments.

Internet Explorer conditional comments

Conditional comments are a proprietary, and thus nonstandard, Microsoft extension of regular HTML comments. As the name suggests, conditional comments allow you to show blocks of code depending on a condition, such as a browser version. Despite being nonstandard, conditional comments appear to all other browsers as regular comments, so they are essentially harmless. Because of this, conditional comments are generally regarded as the best way to deal with IE-specific bugs. Conditional comments first appeared in IE 5 on Windows and are supported by all subsequent versions of the Windows browser.

To deliver a specific style sheet to all versions of IE 5 and above, you could place the following code in the head of your HTML document:

```
<!-- [if IE]
    <link rel="stylesheet" type="text/css" href="/css/ie.css" />
-->
```

Versions of IE 5 and above on Windows would receive the stylesheet `ie.css`, while all other browsers would simply see some commented-out text. This is interesting but not particularly useful, as it's rare to find a bug that all versions of Internet Explorer exhibit. Instead, you will probably want to target a specific version or range of versions.

With conditional comments you could target a particular browser such as IE 6.0 using the following code:

```
<!-- [if IE 6]
    <link rel="stylesheet" type="text/css" href="/css/ie6.css" />
-->
```

You could also target sets of browsers such as IE 5 and IE 5.5:

```
<!-- [if lt IE 6]
    <link rel="stylesheet" type="text/css" href="/css/ie5x.css" />
-->
```

As well as using conditional comments to present style sheets to Internet Explorer, you can also use them to hide specific style sheets. Called downlevel-revealed conditional comments, the following syntax will hide more advanced styles from all versions of IE:

```
<!--[if !IE]>-->
    <link rel="stylesheet" type="text/css" href="/css/advanced.css" />
<!--<![endif]-->
```

And this code effectively hides your styles from Internet Explorer 5.x:

```
<!--[if gte IE 6]><!-->
    <link rel="stylesheet" type="text/css" href="/css/modern.css" />
<!--<![endif]-->
```

Conditional comments work extremely well and are relatively simple to remember. The main downside is that these comments need to live in your HTML, not your CSS. If a new version of Internet Explorer comes out you may be forced to update the conditional comments on each page of your site. However as long as you remember to do this, you should be fairly safe.

A warning about hacks and filters

As a language, CSS was designed to be very forward compatible. If a browser doesn't understand a particular selector, it will ignore the whole rule. Likewise, if it doesn't understand a particular property or value, it will ignore the whole declaration. This feature means that the addition of new selectors, properties, and values should have no adverse effect on older browsers.

You can use this feature to supply rules and declarations to more advanced browsers, safe in the knowledge that older browsers will degrade gracefully. When a new version of the browser is launched, if it now supports the CSS you were using as a filter, it should work as expected. If you are using the more-advanced CSS to circumvent a problem in the older browsers, hopefully this problem will have been solved in the newer version. Because of this behavior, the use of unsupported CSS as a filtering mechanism is a relatively safe option. I say *relatively* because there is always a chance that the browser will support your new CSS but still exhibit the bug you were trying to fix.

Using filters that rely on parsing bugs is a slightly more dangerous route, because you are relying on a bug, not a feature. Similar to the previous method, if the parsing bug gets fixed but the bug you are trying to fix hasn't been addressed, you could end up with problems. However, more of a concern is that parsing bugs could find their way into newer versions of browsers. Say, for instance, a new version of Firefox has a particular parsing bug. If that bug is being used as a filter to supply IE with different width values to account for its proprietary box model, all of a sudden Firefox would inherit that width, potentially breaking a lot of sites. It is also worth bearing in mind that these kinds of hacks and filters will often invalidate your code. So as a general rule, it is probably safer to use filters that rely on unsupported CSS, rather than ones that use some kind of browser bug. Or better yet, avoid them all together.

Using hacks and filters sensibly

There is a rather unfortunate overreliance on hacks and filters, especially among those new to CSS. When something does not work in a particular browser, some CSS developers will immediately employ a hack, seeing it as some kind of magic bullet. In fact, a few developers seem to measure their expertise by the number of obscure hacks and filters they know.

If you have done your homework and realize that the only option is to employ some form of hack or filter, you need to do so in a sensible and controlled manner. If your CSS files are small and simple, and you need to employ only a couple of hacks, it is probably safe to place these hacks in your main CSS files with comments indicating that is the case. However, hacks are usually fairly complicated and can make your code more difficult to read. If your CSS files are long and complicated, or you need to use more than a couple of hacks, you may be best separating them into their own style sheets. As well as making your code easier to read, separating out hacks means that if a hack starts causing problems in a future browser, you will know exactly where it is. Similarly, if you decide to drop support for a particular browser, removing the associated hacks is as simple as removing the CSS file.

Applying the IE for Mac band pass filter

Tantek Çelik created a series of filters (http://tantek.com/CSS/Examples/) based on browser parsing errors that allow you to supply stylesheets to selected browsers using the @import rule The filters used to be the recommended way of filtering out various versions of Internet Explorer until conditional comments became commonplace. However, you may still find these filters handy if, for instance, you need to explicitly target is IE 5.2 on the Mac. You can do this using Tantek's IE 5 for Mac band pass filter, which exploits an escaping bug within CSS comments:

```
/*\*//*/
    @import "ie5mac.css";
/**/
```

IE 5 for Mac incorrectly escapes the second asterisk, causing the @import rule to be applied. As such, IE 5 for Mac sees something like this:

```
/* blah */
    @import "ie5mac.css";
/**/
```

All other browsers correctly ignore the escaping element, as it is enclosed within a comment, and the @import rule is commented out. Essentially, all other browsers see a rule that looks like this:

```
/* blah *//*
    blah
*/
```

As with the other band pass filters, it is not necessary to understand how this filter works in order to use it. The beauty of these filters is they specifically target bugs in older, out-of-date browsers. Therefore, you should be able to use these filters safe in the knowledge that they shouldn't cause problems in newer browsers.

Applying the star HTML hack

One of the best-known and possibly most useful inline CSS filters is known as the star HTML hack. This filter is incredibly easy to remember and targets IE 6 and below. As you are aware, the HTML element is supposed to be the first, or root, element on a web page. However older versions of IE have an anonymous root element wrapping around the HTML element. By using the universal selector, you can target an HTML element enclosed inside another element. Because this only happens in IE 6 and below, you can apply specific rules to these browsers:

```
* html {
  width: 1px;
}
```

As this bug was fixed in IE 7, it is a relatively safe way of targeting older versions of IE.

This hack forms part of the modified simplified box model hack (MSBMH), which used to be a popular way of managing Internet Explorer's propriety box model in older browsers.

```
#content {
  width: 80px;
  padding: 10px;
}

* html #content {
  width: 100px;
  w\idth: 80px;
}
```

While I wouldn't recommend using this technique now, it is useful to know what it looks like as you may come across it in legacy code.

Applying the child selector hack

Instead of explicitly targeting older versions of Internet Explorer, say that you wanted to create a rule that these browsers will ignore. You can do this by using the child selector hack, though this technique isn't really a hack, as it simply uses a selector that older versions of IE don't understand but more modern browsers do.

In this example, the child selector hack is being used to hide a transparent background PNG image from IE 5-6 on Windows:

```
html>body {
    background-image: url(bg.png);
}
```

This rule will be hidden from older versions of Internet Explorer. However, IE 7 supports both the child selector and native PNG transparency, so it will interpret the code correctly.

Common bugs and their fixes

One of the greatest skills any CSS developer can have is the ability to spot common browsers bugs. By knowing the various elements that conspire to cause these bugs, you can spot and fix them before they ever become a problem.

Double-margin float bug

One of the most common and easy-to-spot bugs is the double-margin float bug in IE 6 and below. As the name suggests, this Windows bug doubles the margins on any floated elements (see Figure 9-10).

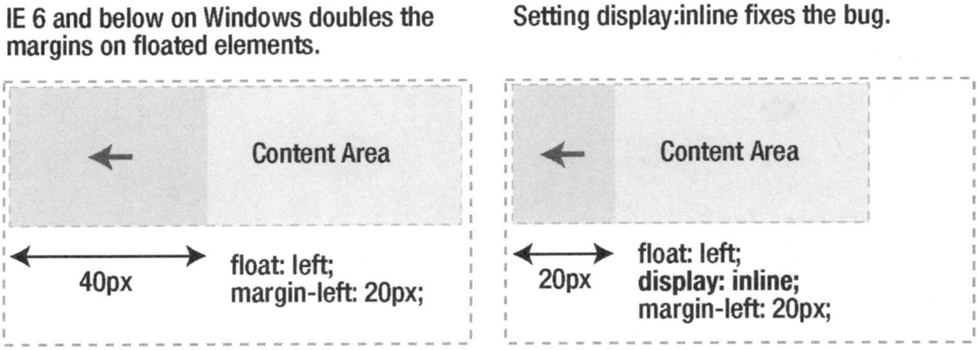

Figure 9-10. Demonstration of IE on Windows's double-margin float bug

This bug is easily fixed by setting the `display` property of the element to `inline`. As the element is floated, setting the `display` property to `inline` won't actually affect the display characteristics. However, it does seem to stop IE 6 and below on Windows from doubling all of the margins. This is such a simple bug to spot and fix: every time you float an element with horizontal margins, you should automatically set the `display` property to `inline`, just in case margin gets added in the future.

Three-pixel text jog bug

Another bug very common in IE 5 and 6 on Windows is the three-pixel text jog bug. This bug manifests itself when you have text adjacent to a floated element. For instance, say you had an element floated left, and you don't want the text in the adjacent paragraph to wrap around the float. You would do this by applying a left margin to the paragraph, the same width as the image:

```
.myFloat {
  float: left;
  width: 200px;
}


p {
  margin-left: 200px;
}
```

When you do this, a mysterious 3-pixel gap appears between the text and the floated element. As soon as the floated element stops, the 3-pixel gap disappears (see Figure 9-11).

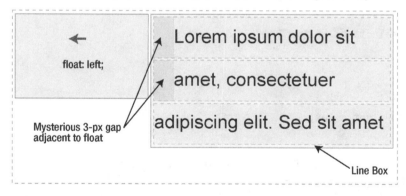

Figure 9-11. Demonstration of the IE 5 and 6 three-pixel text jog bug

Fixing this bug requires a two-pronged attack. First, the element containing the text is given an arbitrary height. This forces the element to have layout, which seemingly removes the text jog. Because IE 6 and below on Windows treat `height` like `min-height`, setting a tiny height has no effect on the actual dimensions of the element in that browser. However, it will affect other browsers, so you need to hide this rule from everything other than IE 6 and below on Windows. The best way to do this is to move these styles into a separate CSS file using conditional comments.

```
p {
  height: 1%;
}
```

Unfortunately, this technique causes another problem. As you learned earlier, elements with layout are constrained to a rectangular shape and appear next to floated elements rather than underneath them. The addition of 200 pixels of padding actually creates a 200-pixel gap between the floated element and the paragraph in IE 5 and 6 on Windows. To avoid this gap, you need to reset the margin on IE 5-6/Win back to zero:

```
p {
  height: 1%;
  margin-left: 0;
}
```

The text jog is fixed, but another 3-pixel gap has now appeared, this time on the floated image. To remove this gap, you need to set a negative 3-pixel right margin on the float:

```
p {
  height: 1%;
  margin-left: 0;
}

.myFloat {
  margin-right: -3px;
}
```

This will fix the problem if the floated element is anything other than an image. However, if the floated element is an image, there is one last problem to solve. IE 5.x on Windows adds a 3-pixel gap to both the left and the right of the image, whereas IE 6 leaves the image's margins untouched. As such, if you need to support IE 5.x, you will want to have one style sheet for those browsers:

```
p {
  height: 1%;
  margin-left: 0;
}


img.myFloat {
  margin: 0 -3px;
}
```

and another for IE 6:

```
p {
  height: 1%;
  margin-left: 0;
}


img.myFloat {
  margin: 0;
}
```

IE 6 duplicate character bug

Another curious bug involving floats is IE 6's duplicate character bug. Under certain conditions, the last few characters in the last of a series of floats will be duplicated beneath the float, as shown in Figure 9-12.

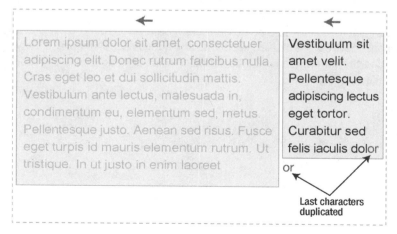

Figure 9-12. Demonstration of IE 6's duplicate character bug

This bug manifests itself when you have multiple comments in between the first and last of a series of floated elements. The first two comments have no effect, but each subsequent comment causes two characters to be duplicated. So three comments would result in two duplicate characters; four comments would result in four duplicate characters; and five comments would result in six duplicate characters.

```
<div id="content">
  <!-- mainContent -->
<div id="mainContent">
...
</div><!-- end mainContent -->
  <!-- secondaryContent -->
<div id="secondaryContent">
...
</div>
```

Strangely, this bug seems related to the three-pixel text jog bug you saw previously. To fix the bug, you can remove 3 pixels from the final float by setting a negative right margin or make the container 3 pixels wider. However, both these methods are likely to cause problems in IE 7, which isn't expected to exhibit this bug. Because of this, the easiest and safest way to avoid this bug is to remove the comments from your HTML code.

IE 6 peek-a-boo bug

Another strange and infuriating bug is IE 6's peek-a-boo bug, so called because under certain conditions text will seem to disappear, only to reappear when the page is reloaded. This happens when there is a floated element followed by some nonfloated elements and then a clearing element, all contained within a parent element that has a background color or image set. If the clearing element touches the floated element, the nonfloated elements in between seem to disappear behind the parent element's background color or image, only to reappear when the page is refreshed (see Figure 9-13).

Content is next to a floated element
and followed by a cleared element.

The content disappears in IE 6, but
reappears if the page is refreshed.

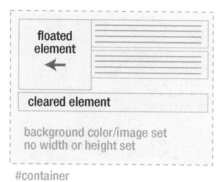
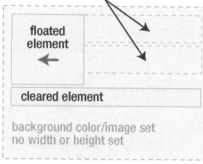

Figure 9-13. Demonstration of IE 6's peek-a-boo bug

Luckily, there are a number of ways you can combat this bug. The easiest way is probably to remove the background color or image on the parent element. However, this is often not practical. Another way is to stop the clearing element from touching the floated element. The bug doesn't seem to manifest itself if the container element has specific dimensions applied. The bug also doesn't manifest itself if the container is given a line height. Last, setting the position property of the float and the container to relative also seems to alleviate the problem.

Absolute positioning in a relative container

The last major browser bug I am going to cover involves absolutely positioned elements within a relatively positioned container. You learned in earlier chapters how useful nesting an absolutely positioned element in a relative container can be. However, IE 6 and below have a number of bugs when you use this technique.

These bugs arise from the fact that relatively positioned elements don't gain IE on Windows's internal hasLayout property. As such, they don't create a new positioning context, and all of the positioned elements get positioned relative to the viewport instead (see Figure 9-14).

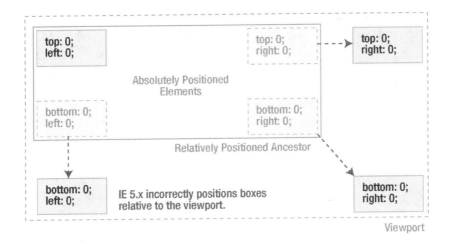

Figure 9-14. Demonstration showing how IE 5.x incorrectly positions absolutely positioned elements within a relative container

To get IE 6 and below on Windows to behave correctly, you need to force the relatively positioned container to have layout. One way to do this is to explicitly set a width and height on the container. However, you will often want to use this technique when you don't know the width and height of the container, or when you want one or both of these properties to be flexible.

Instead, you can use conditional comments to filter out IE 5 and 6 and then give the container layout by applying an arbitrary dimension. Because elements in IE 6 and below incorrectly expand to fit their contents, the actual height won't be affected.

```
.container {
  height: 1%;
}
```

Stop picking on Internet Explorer

Internet Explorer isn't the only buggy browser around, so you may wonder why I have been focusing my attentions on IE bugs. Don't worry; it's not another case of Microsoft bashing; there are good reasons for this focus.

First, IE still has a significant market share so bugs tend to get found and documented pretty quickly. However, the pace of development is much slower in IE than other browsers. So, while Firefox and Safari are releasing new builds every few months, it can take years to see a new version of IE. As such, IE bugs tend to stick around longer.

The speed at which bugs are found and fixed in Firefox and Safari is excellent, but it does have its own problems. Rather than having two or three versions of a browser to deal with, you may have 10 or 20. You can never be sure if your users have the latest version, and this makes testing extremely difficult. IE, on the other hand, didn't see a major revision for about five years. As such, there has been much more time for bugs to surface and much more impetus to find a fix.

Luckily, IE 8 is a much more standards-compliant browser than previous versions. Many of the better-known IE bugs have been addressed, along with increased support for advanced CSS 2.1. As with all browsers, new bugs will surface, and IE 8 is far from perfect. However, the faster people can be convinced to upgrade to modern browsers such as IE 8 and Firefox, the quicker older browsers such as IE 6 can be retired.

Graded browser support

No discussion about bugs would be complete without mentioning browser support. Each time a new version of Internet Explorer comes out, the release sparks a big discussion about when it is going to be safe to stop supporting the previous versions. After all, if Microsoft no longer officially supports IE6, why should we bother? Unfortunately, there is no clear solution to the problem of browser support, and the honest answer is that it depends on the individual site.

If you are hosting a site for web developers, you probably have a large Firefox and Mac user-base, in which case IE 6 usage may be so low as to deem it not worth worrying about. However, even a couple of percent on a site that receives a million visitors a month could equate to tens of thousands of unhappy customers. For business or consumer sites, the number of IE 6 users is likely to be much higher. You may even find that on specific sites IE 6 usage outstrips that of IE 7. This is because many corporate IT departments lock their users into specific browser versions, while many home users only update their browsers when they get a new machine. So instead of talking about dropping support for a certain browser, we need to grade on the curve and decide what support actually means on a site-by-site basis. This is where the idea of graded browser support comes in.

Large organizations like Yahoo and the BBC realize that not all browsers are created equal and that ensuring your site looks and behaves exactly the same in all browsers will increase maintenance costs while hampering innovation. In order to avoid having to design for the lowest common denominator in browser terms, these companies have started to adopt graded support charts (see Figures 9-15 and 9-16). Rather than seeing browser support as a binary supported/unsupported option, these charts offer a variety of different support levels, from rendering the full design for modern browsers, down to just the content for older versions. While each organization frames the problem differently, the steps are pretty much the same.

First, you need to identify the browsers for which you want to ensure render consistently across your site and then test on all of these browsers. This group will usually contain the latest and most popular browsers used by your audience. So the latest versions of Firefox, Safari, and Opera, as well as IE 7 and 8 will probably fall into this category. With these browsers, you want the sites to look largely the same, although for practical reasons a couple of pixels here or there won't make much difference.

	Win 2000	Win XP	Win Vista	Mac 10.4.+	Mac 10.5.+
Firefox 3.0.+		A-grade	A-grade		A-grade
Firefox 2.0.+		A-grade			A-grade
IE 8.0		A-grade	A-grade		
IE 7.0		A-grade	A-grade		
IE 6.0	A-grade	A-grade			
Opera 9.6+		A-grade			A-grade
Safari 3.2+				A-grade	A-grade

Figure 9-15. Yahoo's graded browser support chart for A-grade browsers

Browser	IE	Mozilla	Opera	Safari	Konqueror	IE	NS 4-
Platform	Windows	All	All	Mac	Linux	Mac	All
Level 1	6, 7	FF 1.5.x/ 2.0.x	9	1.3+, 2.x, 3.x			
Level 2	5, 5.5	FF 1.0.x	8	1.0, 1.1, 1.2	3+		
Level 3	1, 2, 3, 4		7-		2-	5-	1, 2, 3, 4
Must test	6, 7	FF 2.0.x	9	2.0			
Should test	5.5	FF 1.5	8	1.3, 3.x			
Notes		#1	#1	#1	#2		
Engine	Trident (4-7), Ohare (1-3)	Gecko	Presto	Webcore	KHTML	Tasman	Mariner

Figure 9-16. Graded browser support table at the BBC

Next, you identify a set of aging but still important browsers. This could include older versions of Firefox and Safari along with IE 6. You'll test on a random sampling of these browsers and attempt to fix any problems you find. However, you'll accept that rendering may not be perfect and may differ from browser to browser, just as long as the content is accessible.

Last, you'll identify a set of obscure or out-of-date browsers that you don't officially support. This would be browsers like IE 4, Netscape Navigator 4, or Opera 7. With these browsers, you still want to make the content and functionality available, but you're not worried about the presentation. As such, you are happy to accept fairly major design variations. Even better would be to remove the styling from these browsers altogether.

A graded support philosophy gives you a much more flexible way of dealing with the volume of browsers and other user agents out there. The charts from the BBC are a good starting point, but as every site is unique, I strongly recommend that you create your own on a project-by-project basis.

Summary

In this chapter, you have learned some important techniques for tracking down and squashing CSS bugs. You have learned about IE on Windows internal hasLayout property and how this is the root of many IE on Windows browser bugs. You also learned about some of the most common browser bugs and how to fix them. Finally, you've learnt how to deal with a plethora of different browsers through the use of graded support charts.

Next, you will see how all of this information can be put together, through two stunning case studies created by two of the best CSS designers and developers of our time.

Chapter 10

Case Study: Roma Italia

Annotated and worn, my first-edition copy of this book still sits proudly on my bookshelf. I've referenced it often during the three years since its publication. Much has changed in our industry during this period, most notably the release of Internet Explorer 7 (and later, 8) yielding a bevy of new CSS 2 and CSS 3 features now supported among the major browsers. We'll cover several of these in this case study.

Yet, much has remained the same. Markup is still markup. Standards are still standards. And the need for talented individuals such as yourself who know how to produce beautiful, usable experiences with HTML, CSS, and JavaScript remains not only imperative but even more important, if anything.

Chances are you, the reader, are more knowledgeable and experienced since publication of the first edition. As such, I hope the case study I've crafted will challenge you even more than the previous one. In this case study you will learn about

- The 1080 layout and grid
- Advanced CSS2 and CSS3 features
- Font linking and better web typography
- Adding interactivity with Ajax and jQuery

View the case study online here: `roma.cssmastery.com`. The source files are also available from `www.friendsofed.com`.

About this case study

Roma Italia is a fictitious website created expressly for this case study (Figure 10-1 shows the home page). The CSS techniques employed in this case study, however, are anything but artificial. Each technique was carefully selected with the intent of providing you with a solid selection of advanced CSS techniques, many of which are applicable in real-world environments. Other experimental techniques with less consistent support among current browsers are meant to demonstrate what's coming in the near future.

This case study site, which purports to be a guide to Rome, Italy, consists of two pages: the home page and the video page. Some of the links on the home page link out to real resources, and the rest are dead links only for demonstration purposes. All photography, video, and content for *Roma Italia* are material from a trip my wife and I recently took to Rome, Italy. For all intents and purposes, this fictitious site could very well be a real site if all of the links actually went somewhere.

Special thanks to Aaron Barker (`aaronbarker.net`) who assisted with several of the jQuery and AJAX examples in this case study, and my wife Suzanne for some of the photos featured on the site.

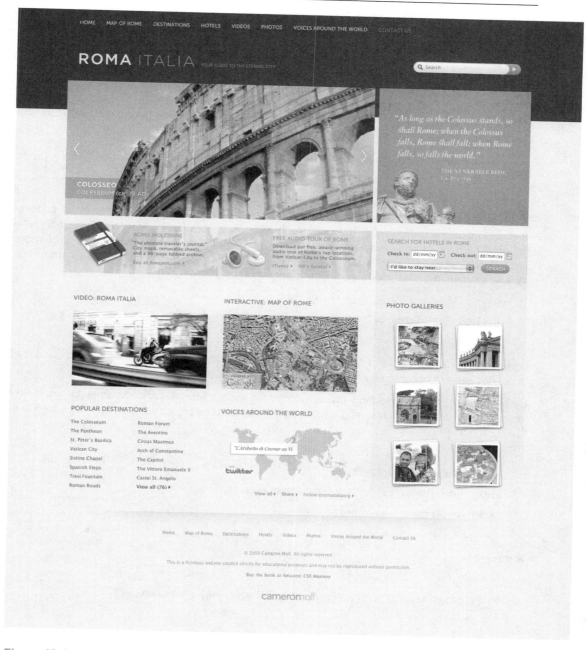

Figure 10-1. Roma Italia home page

The foundation

When drafting markup, the factors I consider most important are that it be as meaningful and as lightweight as possible. By *meaningful*, I mean the HTML elements and selector names we choose appropriately represent the content in such a way that if we were to experience the web with all styling removed, the hierarchy and structure of the content would still make sense. Long gone are the days of spacer GIFs and repeated `br` elements. These have been replaced with elements that logically, or semantically, represent the content:

- An ordered list of top-selling items (`ol`)
- The principal heading on a page (`h1`)
- A quotation from a happy customer (`blockquote` and `cite`)

This approach requires that we remove presentational information from our thinking, a concept described comprehensively by Andy Clarke in his remarkable book, *Transcending CSS* (New Riders, 2006). I still vividly recall my early experiences with CSS as we coded a rather large-scale web application, thinking we were cleverly creating a series of presentational class names that allowed us to mark up content with elegant clarity such as this:

```
<p class="arial red 10">
```

only to endure a painful day of reckoning when the application required a redesign, and dozens of templates were to become anything but red Arial 10-pixel type.

By *lightweight*, I mean marking up our content with the fewest parts possible for all things markup—elements, attributes, and values for HTML; selectors, properties, and values for CSS. For example,

```
background-color: #c27e28;
background-image: url(../img/feature-orange.jpg);
background-repeat: no-repeat;
```

is minimized as

```
background: #c27e28 url(../img/feature-orange.jpg) no-repeat;
```

You'll see numerous examples of meaningful and lightweight markup throughout this case study, some of which I'll describe here and the large majority of which you'll be able to discover on your own.

An eye toward HTML 5

On the topic of meaningful and lightweight markup, I've chosen to go with HTML 4.01 Strict as the DOCTYPE, favoring it above XHTML 1.0 Strict and HTML 5. I'll briefly explain my reasoning.

XHTML 1.0 Strict: This is what many of us in the industry, including myself, have been using for the past few years. However, Dave Shea offers a compelling argument to drop XHTML with an eye towards HTML 5:

> "Six years ago, many of us thought XHTML would be the future of the Web, and we'd be living in an XML world by now. But in the intervening time, it's become fairly apparent to myself and others that XHTML2 really isn't going anywhere, at least not in the realm that we care about. . .I'm not ready to start working through the contortions needed to make my sites work with an HTML5 DOCTYPE yet, which leaves me with the most recent implemented version of the language. . .[U]ntil I get a better sense that HTML5 has arrived, 4.01 will do me just fine for the next four or five years" ("Switched," `http://mezzoblue.com/archives/2009/04/20/switched/`).

HTML 5: In a nutshell, HTML 5 is the next major version of the hypertext markup language. The good news is meaningless `div` and `span` elements will be replaced by more meaningful elements such as `nav`, `header`, and `video`.

This means instead of marking up something such as

```
<div class="header">
  <h1>Page Title</h1>
</div>
```

or

```
<object><param/><embed src="http://vimeo.com/3956190"></embed></object>
```

we'll be able to mark up the same HTML like this:

```
<header>
  <h1>Page Title</h1>
</header>
```

and this:

```
<video src="http://vimeo.com/3956190">
```

The bad news is as of the publication of this case study, HTML 5 is not supported adequately by major browsers (notably Internet Explorer). Estimates range from months to years before HTML 5 is fully supported and therefore a viable option for all of us creating websites.

An alternate approach is to maintain that same watchful eye towards HTML 5 by writing markup using current DOCTYPEs but with semantic, HTML 5-like class names. Jon Tan covers this approach beautifully in "Preparing for HTML 5 with Semantic Class Names" (http://jontangerine.com/log/2008/03/preparing-for-html5-with-semantic-class-names).

For example, using the nav element, HTML 5 markup would be

```
<nav>
  <ul>
    <li><a href="">Menu item 1</a></li>
    ...
  </ul>
</nav>
```

while our semantic, HTML 5–like markup using HTML 4 or XHTML 1 would be

```
<div class="nav">
  <ul>
    <li><a href="">Menu item 1</a></li>
    ...
  </ul>
</div>
```

However, the drawback to this approach is you potentially end up with a lot of extra divs. If our goal is meaningful and lightweight markup, the most optimal markup *right now* would instead be the following:

```
<ul class="nav">
  <li><a href="">Menu item 1</a></li>
  ...
</ul>
```

So, my opinion about HTML 5? We'll all adapt just fine when it's ready for prime-time and fully supported. The mental shift will be minimal. Until then, I'll keep coding the way we've always done it.

For additional resources on the topic of HTML 5, visit the following:

- 12 Resources for Getting a Jump on HTML 5:
  http://cameronmoll.com/archives/2009/01/12_resources_for_html5/
- **Coding a HTML 5 Layout from Scratch**:
  http://smashingmagazine.com/2009/08/04/designing-a-html-5-layout-from-scratch/
- **Wikipedia article on HTML 5**: http://en.wikipedia.org/wiki/HTML_5
- **The Rise of HTML 5**: http://adactio.com/journal/1540
- **Google Bets Big on HTML 5**:
  http://radar.oreilly.com/2009/05/google-bets-big-on-html-5.html

reset.css

When I first began coding CSS-styled sites several years ago, it was common to declare a few "global" styles at the top of the master style sheet: body, a img, h1, h2, h3, and so on. What was done back then as a means of overriding the default styles of any given browser eventually evolved into today's practice of using a "reset" style sheet, typically named reset.css.

As stated by the team at Yahoo, a reset style sheet "removes and neutralizes the inconsistent default styling of HTML elements, creating a level playing field across A-grade browsers. . ." (http://developer.yahoo.com/yui/reset/). I personally prefer Eric Meyer's Reset CSS, which is used in this case study. You can download this style sheet here: http://meyerweb.com/eric/tools/css/reset/.

I use a single style sheet, master.css, to import any number of style sheets for a site. I declare the reset style sheet first, thereby allowing any style sheets that come after to override the reset styles as needed:

```
@import url("reset.css");
@import url("screen.css");
@import ...
```

All styles for screen display are listed in screen.css. In the case study site, three additional style sheets are used:

- autocomplete.css contains styling for the live search feature.
- datepicker.css contains styling for the calendar date picker.
- ie.css, which is referenced using conditional comments (see next section), contains styling specific to Internet Explorer.

We could have easily inserted the styles from `autocomplete.css` and `datepicker.css` into `screen.css`, but for the purposes of walking you through this case study, they remain separate.

The 1080 layout and grid

In 2006, I posted a quandary about the optimal width for monitors with a resolution of 1024 × 768 or greater (see `http://www.cameronmoll.com/archives/001220.html`). It was around this time that many of us who had been developing websites optimized for 800 × 600 for quite some time were beginning to explore widths optimized for a 1024-pixel resolution.

In the same article, I proposed 960 pixels as the ideal width for moving beyond 800 × 600. It accounted for browser chrome as well as for the fact that many users don't browse full-screen. More importantly, 960 is a rather magical number: it's divisible by 2, 3, 4, 5, 6, 8, 10, 12, 15, and 16. Imagine the grid possibilities (we'll get to grids in a minute).

Following publication of the article, 960 nearly became the de facto standard for fixed-width designs on the web. A number of Photoshop, browser, and operating system plug-ins default to it. There's even an entire CSS framework built on a 960 grid, aptly named `960.gs` (`http://960.gs/`). More than three years later, a new question arises: is it time to move beyond 960? I'm uncertain of the answer, but this case study provides the perfect opportunity to explore one.

Before the flak begins flying from fixed-width naysayers, allow me to inform you that I'm a *huge* fan of fluid designs with min-width and max-width limits, as evidenced by my Extensible CSS series (`http://cameronmoll.com/archives/2008/02/the_highly_extensible_css_interface_the_series/`) and case study design for the first edition of this book (`http://tuscany.cssmastery.com/`). In fact, there are some fascinating things we can do with fluid layouts using resources such as Cameron Adams' excellent resolution dependent layout method (`http://themaninblue.com/writing/perspective/2006/01/19/`) and Ethan Marcotte's fluid images technique (`http://unstoppablerobotninja.com/entry/fluid-images/`). But I believe there will always be a need for fixed width, and frankly in many ways, it's more practical than fluid width.

So, assuming we agree it's time to at least engage in a discussion about moving beyond 960, what is the ideal width? Here are a few options:

- **1020** is divisible by 2, 3, 4, 5, 6, 10, 12, 15 but not 8 and 16. It's not much wider than 960.
- **1040** is divisible by 2, 4, 5, 8, 10, 16 but not 3, 12, or 15. Yet it has a reasonable width that sits somewhere between the lower end of 960 and higher end of users browsing full screen (many don't, as I already mentioned).
- **1080** is divisible 2, 3, 4, 5, 6, 8, 10, 12, 15 but oddly enough, not 16. It pushes the upper end of the width spectrum, and measure (line length) could become an issue if not dealt with appropriately.

It's worth noting that integer divisions are not the only possibility for grid divisions, or even the most optimal in some cases. Ratio divisions such as the golden ratio (http://en.wikipedia.org/wiki/Golden_ratio) can also be considered. But as Jason Santa Maria points out, ratio divisions may not be practical on the web as they rely on the horizontal and vertical divisions being viewable concurrently, the latter of which often is not (see http://jasonsantamaria.com/articles/whats-golden/).

Conclusively, if we move beyond 960, I'm not certain we'll settle on a clear winner this time around as we did before. None of the widths listed here seem as extensible as 960, at least mathematically. But for this case study, I've chosen 1080. It provides ample options for grids, and it's sufficiently beyond 960 to make the exploration worthwhile.

Using grids in web design

Grids have been in use in graphic design for several decades, but only in the last few years have they really found favor in the minds and voices of web designers—and with good reason at last. Wikipedia offers a succinct description of the grid and its merits, "A typographic grid is a two-dimensional structure made up of a series of intersecting vertical and horizontal axes used to structure content. The grid serves as an armature on which a designer can organize text and images in a rational, easy to absorb manner" (http://en.wikipedia.org/wiki/Grid_(page_layout)).

Grids are comprised of things such as columns, rows, margins, gutters (the space between columns and rows), flow lines (horizontal divisions), and other components. In a medium such as print design, the width and height for each of these components are bound to the finished size of the material; their dimensions are easily calculated by the designer. In web design, however, width dimensions are often much more calculable than height dimensions. This is because of the potentially endless height of a scrollable page.

Accordingly, the armature for the *Roma Italia* focuses on vertical divisions. Figure 10-2 shows the grid for the site.

Figure 10-2. The 12-division grid used to design the site

You can toggle this grid on and off by uncommenting the following markup:

```
<div id="grid"><img src="img/grid.png" alt="" width="1090" height="1380"></div>
```

This is even easier to do if you have a browser plug-in such as Firebug for Firefox (`http://getfirebug.com/`) that allows you to temporarily alter a document's markup within the browser. With Firebug open, double-click the **body** tag to reveal the comment and then edit the HTML right there in Firebug.

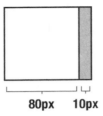

80px   10px

Figure 10-3. Each column is 80 pixels wide with a 10-inch gutter to the right

As you can see, the grid is divided into 12 columns. Each column is 80 pixels wide with a 10-pixel gutter to the right of each column (as shown in Figure 10-3), which produces a layout 1080-pixel wide. An offset of 10 pixels—essentially an extra gutter—is added to the left margin to balance the grid. However, this offset as well as the gutter alongside the last column to the right are invisible to the viewer. You could argue the grid is actually 1070 pixels wide with these invisible components removed, or conversely, 1090 pixels with the same components made visible. Regardless, our grid is based on an overall measure of 1080.

For the most part, text and images align with columns and gutters. Of course, that's the point of using a grid. Yet you'll notice I haven't aligned every element perfectly. What's important to note here is that a grid doesn't necessarily *dictate* the exact placement of items. Rather, it *facilitates* the general positioning of elements, leaving precise positioning to the good judgment of the designer. In *Making and Breaking the Grid* (Rockport Publishers, 2005), Timothy Samara describes this concept perhaps better than I:

> It's important to understand that the grid, although a precise guide, should never subordinate the elements within it. Its job is to provide overall unity without snuffing out the vitality of the composition. In most circumstances, the variety of solutions for laying out a page within a given grid are inexhaustible, but even then it's wise to violate the grid on occasion. A designer shouldn't be afraid of his or her grid, but push against it to test its limits. A really well-planned grid creates endless opportunities for exploration.

But the real power of a grid is found not just in a single page but in the composition as a whole. For example, in a printed brochure, a grid serves to unify the placement of elements throughout the brochure. Similarly, if *Roma Italia* were a real site, all of its pages—not just the two you see here—would leverage the same grid, yielding visual continuity for the user and limitless layout options for the designer.

I've offered only a cursory discussion of grids in this section. You can find many more resources at The Grid System (`http://www.thegridsystem.org/`) and in *Smashing* magazine's "Designing with Grid-Based Approach" (http://www.smashingmagazine.com/2007/04/14/designing-with-grid-based-approach/).

Advanced CSS 2 and CSS 3 features

It wasn't until Internet Explorer 7 was released in October 2006 that instructions like that of this section became both rational and technically feasible. At last IE7 yielded access to many of the exciting features found in the CSS2 and CSS3 specs that had already been supported by Firefox, Safari, and other browsers. Among the most notable were min-width and max-width, attribute selector, adjacent sibling selector, child selector, and alpha-transparency in PNG images.

These well-supported features combined with other features not yet well-supported allows us to do some rather fascinating stuff. An extreme example of this is John Allsopp's recreation of Apple's navigation bar using only CSS, no images (see http://westciv.com/style_master/blog/apples-navigation-bar-using-only-css). Less extreme examples—though I hope still fascinating—are found in this section.

The following advanced CSS2 and CSS3 features are used in *Roma Italia*:

- Adjacent selector
- Attribute selector
- box-shadow
- opacity
- RGBa
- content
- Multicolumn
- text-overflow
- Multiple backgrounds
- @font-face
- min-/max-width, min-/max-height
- Alpha transparency in PNG images

Of this list, we'll cover the following features throughout this case study: attribute selector, box-shadow, RGBa text-overflow, multicolumn, multiple backgrounds, and @font-face. For those features that are not covered, I've tried to add comments in the markup to assist you in learning on your own time. You may also find it helpful to have this CSS cheat sheet handy in soft copy or printed format: http://cameronmoll.com/articles/widget/cheatsheet.pdf.

Dowebsitesneedtolookexactlythesameineverybrowser.com?

Type this heading into your browser's address bar and you'll discover the answer. This simple site, developed by Dan Cederholm, circled the web in 2008 as virtual propaganda discrediting the myth that websites must look exactly the same in any and all browsers. It was a wake-up call to the web development community to become a little more progressive in its approach to markup, rather than being enslaved by absolute uniformity. In a single word, Dan's site denounced the labeling of visual inconsistency as the red-headed stepchild.

In *Roma Italia*, the most obvious visual inconsistency deals with the multiple background feature. This feature will allow for several background images per a single element, whereas currently only one image per element is allowed. Rounded corner aficionados rejoice.

As of this writing, Safari is the only major browser to support multiple backgrounds. (Interestingly enough, Safari has supported the feature since version 1.3, dating all the way back to 2005!) This means that in browsers such as Firefox and Internet Explorer, the site will look slightly different. Not only is this intentional for the purpose of this case study, but it's also to demonstrate that it's perfectly legitimate to deliver a slightly different experience to different browsers with no negative effect on the overall user experience.

Multiple backgrounds, which are sure to be a boon to web professionals once fully supported, are easy to style. Simply separate each image and its values with a comma:

```
background: url(image1.png) no-repeat top left,
    url(image2.png) no-repeat top right,
    url(image3.png) no-repeat bottom left;
```

Alternatively, properties and values can be defined separately:

```
background-color: #000;
background-image: url(image1.png), url(image2.png), url(image3.png);
background-repeat: no-repeat;
background-position: top left, top right, bottom left;
```

Multiple backgrounds are used in our case study site in a couple places, as shown in Figure 10-4. Notice the differences between Safari and Firefox and Internet Explorer.

Multiple backgrounds rendered by Safari

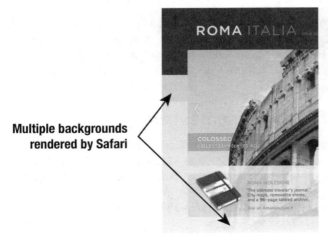

Figure 10-4. Differences in the background images between Safari (left) and Firefox and Internet Explorer (right)

Two background images are used in the body to give the site its background texture: the large dark brown image and light brown stripe with a subtle gradient, respectively named bg-dark.jpg and bg-light.jpg. The CSS looks like this:

```
body {
   background: url(../img/bg-dark.jpg) repeat-x top center,
   url(../img/bg-light.jpg) repeat-x 239px left;
   background-color: #f1efe8;
   }
```

Because Firefox and Internet Explorer don't yet support multiple backgrounds, and if we leave the CSS as shown, neither image will show up. This will leave the background completely empty, which isn't desirable. So, as a means of at least displaying the dark image, we insert the following duplicate property above the first:

```
   background: #f1efe8 url(../img/bg-dark.jpg) repeat-x;
```

Firefox reads this property and ignores the other. We repeat the same property in ie.css as Internet Explorer isn't fond of this little hack we've thrown together. The final CSS found in screen.css is as follows:

```
body {
   background: #f1efe8 url(../img/bg-dark.jpg) repeat-x;
   background: url(../img/bg-dark.jpg) repeat-x top center,
      url(../img/bg-light.jpg) repeat-x 239px left;
   background-color: #f1efe8;
   }
```

Let's be clear: This isn't the most efficient way to accomplish what we've shown here. First, we could have used a single image that combined the dark and light designs, eliminating the need for multiple background images. Second, we're adding duplicate markup to force Firefox and Internet Explorer to display at least one image. However, the point of these inefficiencies is solely to defend insignificant visual inconsistencies from browser to browser and to demonstrate what's around the corner with multiple backgrounds. For the sake of the collective industry, let's keep our hopes up that the corner is closer than expected.

Attribute selector

The attribute selector eliminates the need to add a `class` or ID to an element by referencing any attribute or attribute value contained in the element. It can be used on virtually any element with inherent attributes. For example, `img[alt]` targets an *attribute* while `img[src="small.gif"]` targets an *attribute value*. Further, similar attribute values can be targeted using syntax strings such as `img[src^="sm"]` which will target any value beginning with the prefix "sm" (e.g., "*sm*all"). See "CSS3: Attribute selectors" (`http://www.css3.info/preview/attribute-selectors/`) for additional examples.

Attribute selectors come in handy in a variety of situations, but probably the most useful is with forms. If elements are styled with a generic hook of `input { }`, all `input` elements within the form will be styled. This means that if you're hoping to target text fields only or the submit button only, you're relegated to adding superfluous `classes` and IDs to do so. The attribute selector, therefore, is a clean way to target specific elements.

Figure 10-5. This search field uses two input elements, each targeted by an attribute selector

The search field near the top of the site serves as our attribute selector example (see Figure 10-5). The HTML is as follows:

```
<form action="#" method="get" accept-charset="utf-8">
  <fieldset>
    <legend></legend>
    <label for="search-input">Search</label>
    <input type="text" id="search input" name="search" value="" title="Search">
    <input type="image" name="" src="img/search-go.gif">
  </fieldset>
</form>
```

Here, we'd like to style the text field with several properties and float `search-go.gif` to the left. In bold are the two input elements we'll target with an attribute selector. Notice the absence of a `class` or ID selector within each input element. This is because we can target each using the `type` attribute, and we do so like this:

```
#header form input[type="text"] {
display: block;
...
background: url(../img/search-bg.gif) no-repeat;
}


#header form input[type="image"] {
float: left;
}
```

Any input element containing the attribute type="image" will be floated left, while any input element containing the attribute type="text" will be styled as we've indicated. Additionally, this same syntax is used in jquery.plugins.js to add jQuery and AJAX functionality:

```
$('#header form input[type="text"]').searchField();
```

Both jQuery and AJAX will be treated in a later section.

Box-shadow, RGBa, and text-overflow

In the center of the *Roma Italia* site, toward the bottom of the page, you'll see a Voices Around the World featurette. If this featurette were real, Twitter updates (tweets) from any users who include the hash tag #romaitalia in their tweet would appear randomly on the map based on the Twitter user's geographical location. Visitors to the site could click these randomized quotes and be taken to page with the full tweet, the author's user name, and tweets from other *Roma Italia* fans as a means of learning about Rome real-time via Twitter updates. The tweets displayed in the case study are fictitious, but you may follow @roma_italia, a real Twitter account I've set up for this case study.

Figure 10-6. Map markers that fade in and out with additional text revealed on hover

The markers that fade in and out every couple of seconds are rather complex codewise (see Figure 10-6), and we'll use the markup for these to demonstrate the CSS 3 features box-shadow, RGBa, and text-overflow.

Each marker is composed of three parts: the tweet text, a white background with a drop shadow, and a dot image for the map marker. The marker is wrapped in a list item (li), which is housed in an unordered list (ul) containing the world map background image:

```
<ul>
  <li class="l1" id="map2" style="top: 61px; left: 53px;"><a href="#">
  <em>"Absolutely divine. Don't skip the Il Vittoriano. Its size alone is
  impressive. There's a stunning view from the top."</em></a></li>
  <li>...</li>
</ul>
```

We style the ul with the following properties:

```
#voices ul {
  position: relative;
  width: 310px;
  height: 178px;
  background: url(../img/bg-map.gif) no-repeat;
}
```

Notice we've set the position to relative. This allows us to absolutely position each list item relative to the ul. Otherwise, the list item would position relative to another parent element, most likely the body. (See chapter 3 for a refresher on absolute positioning.)

Each map marker li is styled accordingly:

```
#voices ul li.l1 {
  position: absolute;
  padding-top: 16px;
  background: url(../img/mapmarker-dot.png) no-repeat 2px top;
}
```

The map marker dot is embedded as a background image, and the class l1 indicates location number one (dot to the right), while l2 indicates location number two (dot to the left). Absent are the location properties that position each marker on the map. This is because we dynamically position each marker as it fades in using an inline style, which for this particular marker is style="top: 61px; left: 53px;". That is, 61px from the top of the ul and 53px from the left of it.

The white background on which the tweet text rests is slightly transparent and has a drop-shadow on the left, right, and bottom edges. These two styles are accomplished using RGBa and box-shadow, respectively:

```
#voices ul li.l1 a {
    display: block;
    padding-left: 11px;
    font: 11px/14px Georgia, serif;
    color: #32312a;
    -webkit-box-shadow: 0 2px 3px rgba(0, 0, 0, 0.35);
    -moz-box-shadow: 0 2px 3px rgba(0, 0, 0, 0.35);
    background-color: rgba(255, 255, 255, 0.78);
}
```

As box-shadow and RGBa are covered in Simon's case study in Chapter 11, please refer to his text for an explanation of these two features. Note, however, that RGBa opacity differs from another CSS 3 feature called opacity. RGBa opacity can be applied to a specific property, such as background, and it will only affect that property. opacity, on the other, affects everything in the element it modifies, such as this:

```
#voices ul li.l1 a {
    opacity: 0.35
    ...
}
```

The values for opacity are similar to RGBa: 0 (fully transparent) to 1 (full opaque). However, I stress that this affects the entire element. Had we used it here, not only the white background would be 35 percent opaque but the tweet text, too.

When the user mouses over a map marker, the display of the marker changes, as shown in Figure 10-7.

*"L'Archetto di Cavour on
Via Cavour is one of the
best restaurants in
downtown Rome. Anything
on the menu."*

Figure 10-7. Full text is displayed on hover

This is where `text-overflow` comes into play. I wish I had a dollar for every time I could have used this feature in my career—by now, I'd be penning these words from a beach house in the Bahamas. The good news is that today it's fairly well supported across the major browsers. In fact, IE supports it better than Firefox, as does Safari. `text-overflow` clips a block of text that is too large to fit within its containing element. Using the value `ellipsis` appends an ellipsis (. . .) to the clipped text.

For each map marker, `text-overflow` is used to clip the text to one line:

```
#voices ul li.l1 a em {

  white-space: nowrap;

  width: 135px;

  overflow: hidden;

  text-overflow: ellipsis;

  -o-text-overflow: ellipsis;

  -moz-text-overflow: ellipsis;

  -webkit-text-overflow: ellipsis;

}
```

Because this feature isn't officially supported by each browser—even though all of the major browsers do support it—we've added the prefixes -o- (Opera), -moz- (Mozilla), and -webkit- (Webkit). Then, for the mouseover effect, we add the :hover pseudo-class to the element, change the height to 72px, and set overflow to visible.

```
#voices ul li.l1 a em:hover {

  white-space: normal;

  overflow: visible;

  text-overflow: inherit;

  -o-text-overflow: inherit;
```

```
    cursor: hand;
    cursor: pointer;
    background: #fff none;
    height: 72px;
    padding-left: 11px;
    padding-bottom: 5px;
    margin-left: -9px;
}
```

And that completes the effect—hat tip to CSS3.info for their `text-overflow` examples, which were inspiration for the creation of this effect. Other CSS 3 features can also be found at their website: `http://www.css3.info/`.

Font linking and better web typography

We could easily fill the pages of this book with techniques for typography on the web. In the brevity afforded by this case study, we'll cover only a few techniques here:

- Using px for `font-size`
- Hanging punctuation
- Multicolumn text layout
- Font linking and embedding

Setting font-size like it's 1999

For a number of years, px was the de facto standard for sizing text with `font-size`. It gave designers transferring their design from Photoshop (or other software) to HTML a consistent, absolute unit for text size. Then, as we became more knowledgeable of and concerned with accessibility, relative text size (em or %) gradually became the preferred unit. This enabled low-vision users, and really anybody, to change their browser's default text size permanently via the browser's settings or on-the-fly using the keyboard commands Ctrl+ and Ctrl– (Windows) or Command + and Command –.

Accordingly, and up until recently, all major browsers would scale up or down the size of the text while retaining the formatting and layout of the page. This is commonly called *text scaling* or *text zooming*. This adaptation required us to create markup that allowed for relative sizing of any elements containing text. For example, if a `div` contained text set atop a background image, we would have to either repeat the image as the `div` grew larger with text scaling or create the image larger than necessary to compensate for growth. This is something I covered in detail in my "The Highly Extensible CSS Interface" series of articles (see `http://cameronmoll.com/archives/2008/02/the_highly_extensible_css_interface_the_series/`).

However, recent versions of every major browser—Safari, Firefox, Google Chrome, Opera, and yes, Internet Explorer—now default to *page zooming* instead of text scaling for Ctrl +/– and Command +/– commands. Page zooming literally zooms the entire page—layout, formatting, and text size—in unison. Elements retain their size and shape, which greatly reduces the need to compensate for text scaling. In effect, the browser assumes the burden of relative sizing.

What does all this mean? It means px can again be considered a viable value for `font-size`. It also means the difference between setting text with absolute units or setting text with relative units may be negligible for users. For you and me, however, the difference is significant. The burden of calculating relative units throughout a CSS document is replaced by the convenience of absolute units—14px is 14px anywhere in the document, independent of parent elements whose `font-size` may differ.

Bear in mind this case study site is meant to be realistic but experimental, as well. I'm at liberty to explore and ask the questions "what if?" and "why not?". Your projects may not yield the same opportunity, so make the right choice for your audience. As with nearly all of the decisions we make as web professionals, you need to make the right decision based on *your* audience and users. That is the one constant that will never change with all the changes that have occurred and are bound to occur in our industry. In short, if relative sizing is the right choice for your project, no one else can tell you otherwise—including me.

For additional reading on the debate over px for `font-size`, check out these articles:

- **The Problem with Pixels**:
  http://www.wilsonminer.com/posts/2007/mar/16/problem-pixels/
- **IE 7 Does not Resize Text Sized in Pixels**:
  http://www.456bereastreet.com/archive/200703/ie_7_does_not_resize_text_sized_in_pixels/
- **Mezzoblue – Zoom**: http://mezzoblue.com/archives/2008/10/07/zoom/
- **Hello Old Friend**: http://orderedlist.com/articles/hello-old-friend

Hanging punctuation

Hanging punctuation is one of those subtle signals that a skilled typographer is behind the design. These feature is available in most of the Adobe family of design applications, but it's not available as a CSS property. *Not yet,* that is. There's actually a property called `hanging-punctuation` proposed in the CSS3 spec (see http://www.w3.org/TR/css3-text/#hanging-punctuation), but to my knowledge no current browser supports this property.

Hanging punctuation aligns punctuation marks outside the text block as to not disrupt the visual flow of the text. Figure 10-8 shows an example using quotation marks.

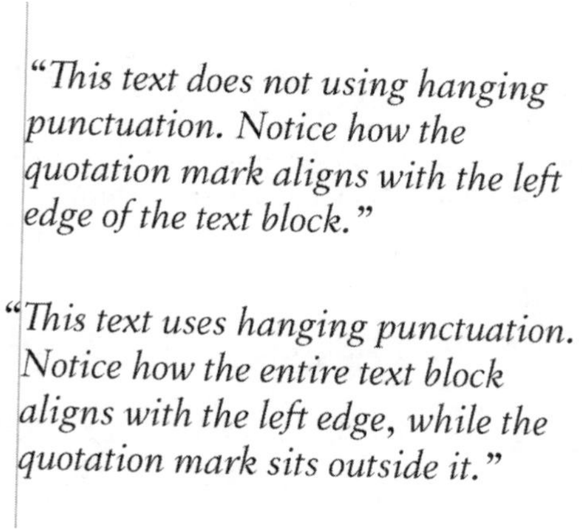

"This text does not using hanging punctuation. Notice how the quotation mark aligns with the left edge of the text block."

"This text uses hanging punctuation. Notice how the entire text block aligns with the left edge, while the quotation mark sits outside it."

Figure 10-8. An example showing how hanging punctuation (bottom) differs from punctuation aligned with the edge of the text (top). The latter is the default in most graphic design software, as well as text within a browser

This technique is used in three places on the home page: the first line of text beneath the Roma Moleskine heading (see Figure 10-9), the tweet text in the Voices Around the World map markers, and the orange quotation by the Venerable Bede. The last of these is an image, so we'll cover the first one. The same technique is used for the second.

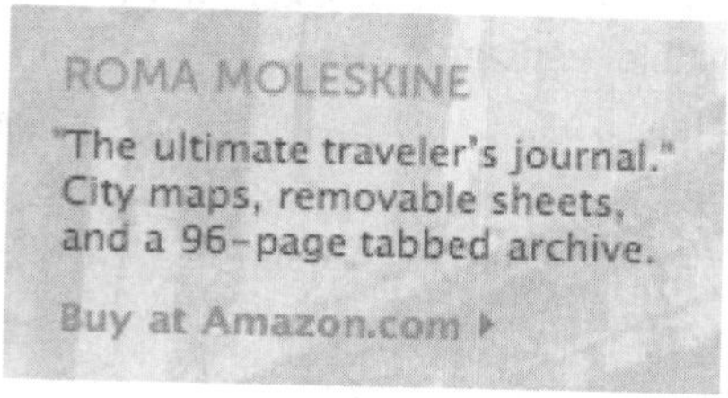

ROMA MOLESKINE

"The ultimate traveler's journal." City maps, removable sheets, and a 96-page tabbed archive.

Buy at Amazon.com ▸

Figure 10-9. Hanging punctuation implemented in Roma Italia

The HTML is straightforward:

```
<div id="featurette1">

  ...

  <p>

  &ldquo;The ultimate traveler&rsquo;s journal.&rdquo; City maps,
  removable sheets, and a 96-page tabbed archive.</p>

  ...

</div>
```

The HTML entities “, ’, and ” are *curly quotes.* These are not necessary for hanging punctuation, but they're yet another subtle signal of good typography. These entities make the source code appear a bit more cluttered to the untrained eye, but the adjusted punctuation rendered by the browser—and noticeable by trained eyes—makes up for the difference.

The CSS is where the magic happens:

```
#featurette1 p {
  text-indent: -.3em;
  }
```

And that's it. In your projects, adjust this value depending on the size and family of your typeface.

Multicolumn text layout

With a layout as wide as this one, maintaining a measure (or line length) that is suitable for readability becomes an issue. *Measure* is the width of a block of text, measured by the number of characters (including spaces) per line. There are countless studies and opinions about the optimal number of characters per line, ranging from 45 to 95 characters per line and varying depending on the medium. This section isn't a discussion about optimal measure, rather one about how to maintain a reasonable measure.

Because this layout is a full 1080 pixels wide, it provides an excellent opportunity to try out the multi-column text feature found in the CSS3 spec. This feature is currently supported by WebKit and Mozilla browsers. Other browsers render the text as a single column as wide as the columns combined.

Robert Bringhurst, in his exceptional and typographically replete *The Elements of Typographic Style* (Hartley and Marks, 2004), suggests 40–50 characters per line for text set in multiple columns. For the sake of convenience, I've followed his recommendation with this layout.

Shown in Figure 10-10 is a snippet from `video.html`.

Cameron Moll
Add as contact

Highlights from a recent vacation to Rome, Italy. Shot with a Canon HG10, edited with Final Cut Express. Music is First Breath After Coma by Explosions in the Sky. Typeface is Gotham by Hoefler & Frere-Jones.

I'm no video virtuoso. I only dabble with video as time allows, which it usually doesn't. But this is one short film I managed to get lucky with.

I've had a passion for film production ever since I was young. I saw myself first as a stuntman, then later as a film score composer. My time has passed on the first, but I hope I still have a shot at the second sometime in life. In more recent years, I've found myself behind the camera and in the editor's chair. I have much to learn about what it takes to shoot and edit and a great film.

If there's one thing I've done right since

purchasing my Canon HG10 last year, it's to shoot far more film than I think I'll need. That's how I got lucky with "Roma Italia". I shot more angles than I figured I'd need, and I left the camera running longer than I assumed was adequate. It paid off in the end, leaving me with five minutes of solid shots from a total of roughly two hours of footage.

I had no script for this piece, and there were only a few shots I planned beforehand to use in whatever the final film would become. The rest was editing mojo. I analyzed the material I had, pieced it together in way I felt told a compelling story, and added effects that complimented the storytelling. "First Breath After Coma", a moving and driving piece by instrumental rock band Explosions in the Sky, was a perfect fit. Not only is it the best song title ever, but its story matches that of "Roma Italia": One of awakening, surprise, and climatic rush and release.

In the end, I hope you enjoy the story. It's a chance to see the magnificent city of Rome through my eyes. Perhaps it'll encourage you to see it through yours.

Tags
rome (171)
roma (189)
italy (461)
italia (393)

Add a tag

Uploaded 2 weeks ago.

Figure 10-10. Multicolumn text layout on the video page

Notice the text is set in two columns. First, the HTML is standard stuff:

```
<div id="main-video">
  <h3>
  Highlights from a recent vacation to Rome, Italy. Shot with a...</h3>

  <p>I&rsquo;m no video virtuoso. I only dabble with video as time...</p>
  ...
</div>
```

The CSS, on the other hand, is anything but standard:

```
#main-video {
  float: left;
  margin: 40px 10px 70px;
  width: 520px;
  -moz-column-count: 2;
  -moz-column-gap: 20px;
  -webkit-column-count: 2;
```

```
    -webkit-column-gap: 20px;
}
```

Here again -moz- (Mozilla) and -webkit- (Webkit) are prefixed out of necessity. Notice there are two properties at play: column-count and column-gap. These properties are fairly easy to understand and to use—set a value for the number of columns you want, and select a value for the gap between them. The entire block of text is then automatically set in the number of columns specified. A third property, column-rule, allows you to add a border between the columns (e.g., column-rule: 1px solid #000;).

Questions about the practicality of multiple-column text on the web and issues with scrolling up and down the page are warranted, but I'm confident that in the hands of a skilled typographer, multicolumn layout has the potential to extend the typography options available to us on the web.

@font-face

The words of Jeffrey Veen, founder of Typekit (http://typekit.com/), are the perfect introduction to this section:

> The W3C recommendation for CSS web fonts [@font-face] will be 7 years old soon. Why, after all these years, has typography for the web not progressed further? Why haven't designers embraced linked, downloadable fonts in their designs?
> (http://blog.typekit.com/2009/06/02/fonts-javascript-and-how-designers-design/)

Excellent questions, Jeffrey. It's highly likely that by the time this book has hit store shelves and worked its way into your hands, Jeffrey's Typekit product will probably have resolved, in a big way, the very questions he's asking. Typekit attempts to resolve the implementation and security issues (discussed later in this section) with @font-face by hosting typefaces centrally that have already been approved by type foundries for font linking (see Figure 10-11).

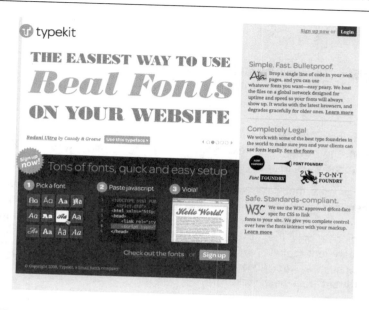

Figure 10-11. Typekit offers web font linking without the hassle of @font-face implementation and security issues

Simply put, @font-face provides us with the ability to use virtually any font in our designs *rendered as HTML text* without worrying about whether or not that font is installed on the user's machine. This is commonly referred to as font linking or font embedding. Instead of this at the top of our document

```
body {
   font-family: Georgia, serif;
   ...
}
```

we can do this

```
@font-face {
   font-family: "Garamond Premier Pro";
   src: url(fonts/GaramondPremrPro.otf);
}
```

Then, we reference the font-family as we're already accustomed to doing:

```
h1 {
    font-family: "Garamond Premier Pro", serif;
}
```

I get giddy just typing all this (geekness, I know). But imagine using *any* typeface you owned in your site's design and having your text rendered as real, HTML text—no sIFR, no Cufón, no images. You're probably just as giddy now, too.

Of course, if things were that easy, we would have been began using @font-face seven years ago. Indeed, there are caveats. First is—you guessed it—browser support. Safari 3 and newer and Firefox 3.1 and newer support @font-face. So does Internet Explorer 4 and newer. However, IE staunchly supports only the .eot (Embedded OpenType) format, which is essentially a Microsoft proprietary font format. .eot files can be created only from .ttf (TrueType) files, and other font formats such as .otf (OpenType) must be converted to .ttf to then be converted to .eot. No wonder @font-face hasn't taken off.

Second, type foundries and type vendors have been very apprehensive about font linking on the web, and their concern is twofold: because font files are stored on the site and therefore publicly accessible, they may be vulnerable to downloading and illegal use, and because many of their end user license agreements (EULAs) have not been updated to allow for font linking.

However, the good news is also twofold: new technologies are emerging, such as Typekit, that eliminate the two concerns just mentioned, and @font-face encourages the use of typefaces other than the standard set we're all used to (Arial, Georgia, etc.), which inevitably will increase the demand for commercial typefaces. Therefore, type vendors and foundries have a vested interest in seeing font linking and embedding flourish. In fact, during the course of writing this chapter, several foundries have announced new typefaces available for font linking on the Web, and even some have announced significant changes to their EULAs.

Museo Sans, see Figure 10-12, is a typeface by designer Jos Buivenga, released in 2008. In particular, Museo Sans 500 is free, and it's the weight I've used here. Best of all the EULA allows for font linking. (Note that Gotham, the typeface used in the logo and in the titles overlaying the fading feature images, would have been my first choice for font linking. Alas, their EULA didn't allow for it when this site was coded.)

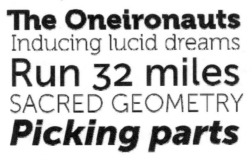

Figure 10-12. Museo typeface samples. Image courtesy of `MyFonts.com`

In *Roma Italia*, `@font-face` is used to demonstrate what is possible now and in the near future. In `screen.css`, you'll see the following code near the top of the document:

```
@font-face {
  font-family: "Museo Sans X";
  src: url(../fonts/MuseoSans_500.otf);
}
```

Museo Sans is used in several headings and in the top navigation (see Figure 10-13):

```
#home h3, #home h4, #home #header h2, #home #header ul a {
  font-family: "Museo Sans X", "Lucida Grande", "Lucida Sans Unicode",
    Arial, sans-serif;
}
```

Figure 10-13. Museo Sans is the typeface used in the top navigation

Notice that I've still indicated backup font choices in the event that the user's browser doesn't support `@font-face`. Also notice that the name of the typeface is Museo Sans X. When you establish `@font-face` in your CSS, you can name the `font-family` whatever you want. I could have used Musei Vaticani for all it matters as long as I reference the proper font file (`MuseoSans_500.otf`). Because Museo Sans is free, you may already have it installed on your machine. I specifically added the *X* to be sure you're seeing `@font-face` at work with my copy of Museo Sans and not a local copy on your machine.

Note that I've not converted the Museo Sans `.otf` file to `.eot` and therefore Internet Explorer will not recognize it. If you're seeing Museo Sans in Internet Explorer, you're seeing Cufón at work, not `@font-face` (see the next section).

For additional reading, see the following:

- Download a copy of Museo Sans at `http://myfonts.com/fonts/exljbris/museo-sans/`
- For an extensive review of `@font-face` and EOT, see Jon Tan's "@font-face in IE: Making Web Fonts Work": `http://jontangerine.com/log/2008/10/font-face-in-ie-making-web-fonts-work`

Cufón, an interim step toward @font-face

I've posted an extensive tutorial about Cufón on my personal website, which you can find at this address: `http://cameronmoll.com/archives/2009/03/cufon_font_embedding/`. Because of this, I'll offer only a cursory examination of Cufón in this case study. In short, Cufón allows you to render HTML text in the typeface of your choice without requiring any images or the use of `@font-face` (see Figure 10-14).

First things first. sIFR, as many of you may be aware, is a means of replacing "short passages of plain browser text with text rendered in your typeface of choice, regardless of whether or not your users have that font installed on their systems" using a combination of Flash and JavaScript (see `http://www.mikeindustries.com/blog/sifr/`). Shaun Inman, Mark Wubben, Mike Davidson, and several others put in many long hours developing and refining IFR and sIFR, and we all owe them our gratitude for moving forward in a big way the state of typography on the web. What `@font-face` lacked in browser support and type foundry endorsement over the years, sIFR made up for in the same period.

For many of us, however, the Flash part of these technologies often makes it difficult to set up and use. Cufón, on the other hand, can be set up and run on your site in about 5 minutes. Because of this, I personally see Cufón as an good interim step between sIFR and `@font-face` should you not have the option of font linking available to you.

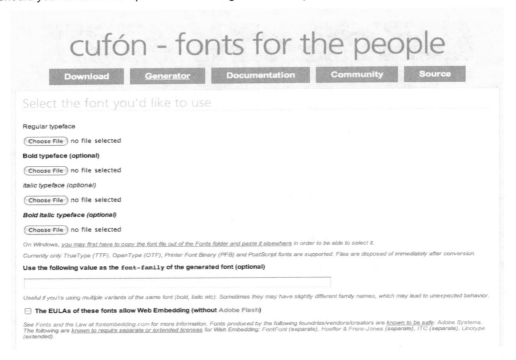

Figure 10-14. Cufón's typeface script generator

Here's how Cufón works:

1. Download the Cufón script file at http://wiki.github.com/sorccu/cufon.
2. Upload the typeface of your choice using the Cufón generator, which will provide you with a second script file.
3. In the head of your document, add references to the Cufón script and the typeface script provided by the generator, such as:

```
<script src="js/cufon-yui.js" type="text/javascript" charset="utf-8"></script>
```

```
<script src="js/Museo_400.font.js" type="text/javascript" charset="utf-8"></script>
```

Also add this just before the closing body tag to avoid a flicker issue in IE:

```
<script type="text/javascript">Cufon.now();</script>
```

Also in the head, indicate which HTML elements or selectors should be replaced with your typeface, such as:

```
<script type="text/javascript">
  Cufon.replace('h1');
</script>
```

or

```
<script type="text/javascript">
  Cufon.replace('h1')('h2')('blockquote');
</script>
```

4. Alternately, if you're using a JavaScript framework such as jQuery on the site where Cufón will be used (*Roma Italia* includes jQuery), Cufón will take advantage of that framework's selector engine such that you can call out specific selectors like this:

```
<script type="text/javascript" charset="utf-8">
  Cufon.replace('#header h2,#header ul a');
</script>
```

5. In your CSS file(s), modify any text replaced by Cufón the same way you would any other text—`color: #333;`, `font-size: 12px;`, `text-transform: uppercase;`, and so forth.

And that's it. Cufón is currently supported by IE 6, 7, and 8, Firefox 1.5 and above, Safari 3 and above, Opera 9.5 and above, and Google Chrome. In the case study site, I've included Cufón in addition to `@font-face`, so you can explore the two options. Be aware Cufón shares the same caveat as `@font-face` when it comes to licensing—the EULA for the typeface you choose must allow for font embedding on the web.

Note that I've wrapped `Cufon.replace` in a conditional comment because IE won't read the `.otf` font file we're using for `@font-face`. Therefore, Cufón becomes a replacement for `@font-face` in IE for the purposes of this case study. If you'd like to see Cufón work in any browser other than IE, simply remove the conditional comment, and it will override `@font-face`.

Adding interactivity with AJAX and jQuery

When I first spoke about AJAX in a workshop a few years ago, few raised their hands when asked if they had experience developing sites and applications that employed AJAX. If asked that same question today, it's likely many of you reading this would raise your hands. These questions would probably have similar results if asked about jQuery instead of AJAX.

Indeed, AJAX and jQuery have weaved their way into high-profile sites and weekend projects alike as the de facto twosome for producing rich interactivity on the Web. Of course, the two can be utilized independent of and separate from each other, but it's common to find them used in tandem. Emerging technologies such as Adobe Flex and Microsoft Silverlight challenge the pair's standing as king of the hill, but I suspect we will see AJAX and jQuery remain major players on the Web for at least a few more years.

This section is not meant to be an exhaustive lecture on these two technologies—there are plenty of great books, tutorials, and blog articles already available for that. Instead I offer a brief introduction (or refresher) to AJAX and jQuery and how they are each used in *Roma Italia*. If you're already familiar with these technologies, skip ahead to "Using AJAX and jQuery for the search feature."

AJAX

AJAX, shorthand for Asynchronous JavaScript and XML, typically includes at least three components:

- Asynchronous server communication, which is most commonly accomplished via `XMLHttpRequest`
- Manipulation of the Document Object Model (DOM) for dynamic display and interaction
- JavaScript to bind everything together

Asynchronicity is the key component of AJAX—or any rich Internet technology, for that matter— as it provides that native-application feel within the web environment. Instead of the traditional request and response model that fetches an entire page with a full trip to the server, asynchronicity means data is fetched only for a select portion of the page (e.g., user name availability when registering an account).

In *Roma Italia*, we fake asynchronous server communication for the purposes of demonstration by using a little JavaScript and by fetching data from a few static PHP pages:

- `imageLoad.php` for the large feature images that fade in and out
- `search.php` for the search field auto-complete feature

Faking asynchronicity merely allows you to download the code samples and open the interface on any machine running PHP, without requiring true server communication.

We'll take a look at the code for auto-complete feature right after the jQuery segment.

jQuery

Karl Swedberg and Jonathan Chaffer's very useful *Learning jQuery* (Packt Publishing, 2007) describes jQuery as a "general-purpose abstraction layer for common web scripting." I like to think of it as "JavaScript for scripting noobs like me."

jQuery enables you to do the following:

- Traverse the DOM
- Modify the appearance of a page
- Dynamically alter the content of a page

And it allows you to do all this without writing lines and lines of JavaScript. Even better, it leverages CSS syntax for using the selectors in your document as the hooks for creating interaction.

Let's pick apart a sample from another site I've coded to understand the components of jQuery. This is another fictitious site creating for instructional purposes and it can be found at `http://cameronmoll.com/articles/widget/`.

Figure 10-15. The Widget demonstration site created for my "The Highly Extensible CSS Interface" series

We'll use the Dismiss button located in the yellow notification bar at the top of the page (see Figure 10-15). When clicked, the yellow bar slowly slides upward until it is no longer visible.

Here's the code we add to the button's anchor tag:

```
$('#alert').slideUp('slow');
```

Following is a description of each component:

- $(): This basic jQuery construct (or function) is used to select parts of the document. In this example, we're selecting an element with the ID of alert.
- .slideUp: This is one of the many jQuery methods. Methods are essentially a shortcut for lots of JavaScript. It's quite obvious the method slideUp makes the element we're targeting (#alert) slide up.
- ('slow'): This predefined string establishes how the method functions. In this case, it tells the element to slide up slowly.

This code can be added either inline or in a separate .js file (or dynamically), the latter being the more optimal method. But here's the real kicker: I didn't have to come up with any of this code on my own. The construct, method, and string came prebuilt with jQuery. I just had to know I wanted the element to slide up slowly, and then I looked up the appropriate references in the jQuery library that corresponded with the animation and movement I was seeking. Boom. Done.

Using AJAX and jQuery for the search feature

Now that we've taken care of the instructional housekeeping, let's take a look at an example of AJAX and jQuery working together in *Roma Italia*. The feature we'll explore is the search feature. Earlier in this case study, we looked at how the attribute selector is used to target specific elements enclosed within the `form` for the search field. Now, we'll take a look at the other components at play.

The search feature is actually one of the most complex features codewise in the entire site. As a user types a keyword query, the magnifying glass icon is replaced with a loading icon and matching results are displayed. This is sometimes referred to as live search. Both AJAX and jQuery are hard at work bringing this interaction to life. Despite the complexity, piecing the components together is easier than it seems.

First, here's a review of the markup:

```
<form action="#" method="get" accept-charset="utf-8">
  <fieldset>
    <legend></legend>
    <label for="search-input">Search</label>
    <input type="text" id="search-input" name="search" value="" title="Search">
    <input type="image" name="" src="img/search-go.gif">
  </fieldset>
</form>
```

To swap in the loading icon, the most lightweight approach I could devise—and one I haven't really seen other sites do yet either—was to combine the background image for the `input` field and the loading icon into a single animated GIF (see Figure 10-16). CSS is used to position the image based on the state of the interaction, shifting the image up and down as the user types to toggle between the magnifying glass icon and the loading icon.

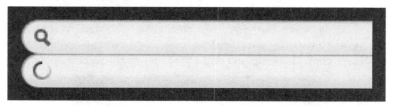

Figure 10-16. search-bg.gif, a single animated GIF that includes two states

Here's the CSS for the input field:

```
#header form input[type="text"] {
```

```
    ...
    padding: 6px 0 0 28px;
    height: 20px;
background: url(../img/search-bg.gif) no-repeat;
    }
```

By default, the background image is positioned at the top left, and we restrict the height to 20 pixels. Add 6 pixels of top padding, and this means only 26 pixels of the image are shown—exactly half the height of the image. Only the magnifying glass portion is revealed.

When the user begins typing, several things happen. First, each time the user types a character, four files are engaged: `autocomplete.css`, `jquery.plugins.js`, `jquery.autocomplete.js`, and `search.php`. As typing begins, `class="ac_input"` is dynamically added to the `input` field and then removed when the live search displays results. This selector is found in `autocomplete.css` and is styled as follows:

```
.ac_loading {
background: url(../img/search-bg.gif) no-repeat 0 -26px !important;
    }
```

Notice the background image is now positioned `-26px` from the top, shifting the image upward and revealing the lower half (loading icon). This indicates to the user that data is being retrieved asynchronously from the server (`search.php`).

Second, while the loading icon is spinning, data is exchanged with `search.php` to locate results matching the characters the user is typing. Open `search.php` and you'll see some of the terms I've populated the file with—Ancient Ostia, Ancient Rome, Arch of Constantine, and so on.

Third, matching results are delivered back to the page, and a `select`-like menu is shown beneath the `input` field with matching results (see Figure 10-17). This menu, which is really just an unordered list (`ul`), is generated by a combination of `jquery.autocomplete.js` and `jquery.plugins.js` and styled by `autocomplete.css`. The user can then select a match with mouse or keyboard, or continue typing and press the Enter key. This completes the interaction.

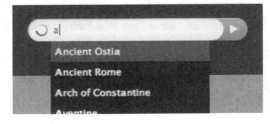

Figure 10-17. The completed search feature in use

Now, `jquery.autocomplete.js` includes several hundred lines of code, but that's another beautiful thing about jQuery—I didn't write any of this. It's a jQuery plug-in written by the community, and *many* such plug-ins are available. In fact, most of the jQuery in the case study comes from plug-ins. The auto-complete one is jQuery Autocomplete and can be found at `http://bassistance.de/jquery-plugins/jquery-plugin-autocomplete/`.

For additional resources and tutorials, check out the following:

- *Bulletproof Ajax* by Jeremy Keith: `http://bulletproofajax.com/`
- **Ajaxian.com**: `http://ajaxian.com/`
- **DHTML Site: Ajax Tutorials and Scripts**: `http://dhtmlsite.com/ajax.php`
- **Official jQuery site**: `http://jquery.com/`
- *Digital Web* magazine's jQuery crash course: `http://www.digital-web.com/articles/jquery_crash_course/`
- **Simon Willison's jQuery for JavaScript programmers**: `http://simonwillison.net/2007/Aug/15/jquery/`
- **Web Designer Wall's jQuery tutorials for designers**: `http://www.webdesignerwall.com/tutorials/jquery-tutorials-for-designers/`
- **Noupe's over 50 amazing jQuery tutorials**: `http://www.noupe.com/jquery/50-amazing-jquery-examples-part1.html`
- **240 plug-ins for jQuery**: `http://www.sastgroup.com/jquery/240-plugins-jquery`

Summary

You've now successfully uncovered many of the techniques used to code *Roma Italia*. There are plenty more—look under the hood, dive deeper into the code, and you just might find a few more gems.

Take note that the file sizes for this site are rather large, most notably the scripts and feature images. However, if this were a live, deployed site, we'd use actual AJAX to load images individually and we'd minify our scripts. For example, `jquery-1.3.2.js` is roughly 120KB, but minified and gzipped, it's as little as 19KB. (This compressed version is available for download at `jquery.com`.) These optimization techniques would dramatically reduce overall page size.

But the real beauty of what's demonstrated in this case study perhaps lies in the fact that the raw HTML markup is just as solid as the aesthetic design. If all styling is disabled, users should have no difficult reading and navigating the site. Though perhaps not beautiful to the web designer's eye, meaningful and lightweight markup is a real treat for screen readers, search engine robots, and the like. It's the best of both worlds—beautiful visual design coupled with elegant source code.

Chapter 11

Case Study: Climb the Mountains

By Simon Collison

In the previous edition of *CSS Mastery*, I introduced my More Than Doodles case study by talking about the "very rich palette" from which we designers can paint. At that time, we were reaching a period of critical mass, with web standards gaining ground across the industry. It was an exciting time, and we were having a ball with CSS 2.1, creating stunning layouts despite problems thrown at us by some of the older browsers.

More than three years on, we find ourselves increasingly comfortable with implementing techniques from the CSS 3 specification in our layouts. We can replace some decorative background images with combinations of CSS 3 rules such as `border-radius` and `box-shadow`, and we can achieve greater control of transparency layers without resorting to semi-transparent background images thanks to `RGBa`. Importantly, with progressive enhancement, we can still deliver a neatly constructed experience to those on browsers lacking support for CSS3 and its sweet little tools and techniques.

In this case study, you will learn about:

- HTML and CSS organization and conventions
- Grid flexibility
- Highlighting the current page based on body class
- Targeting elements with pseudo classes and adjacent sibling selectors

- Combining classes for extra power and flexibility

- RGBa, border-radius and box-shadow properties

- Positioning list items and revealing content

About this case study

This case study is built on a rock-solid XHTML structure — as lean, organized, and powerful as possible. Specifically, the XHTML does not contain any extra markup added purely for the purpose of hooking CSS onto it. No, what we have in the markup is what we need in the markup — and nothing extraneous. So, the aim of this chapter is to take what we have and use really smart CSS selectors to target specific XHTML without the need for extra divs, clearing divs or anything else that could be deemed unnecessary.

Climb the Mountains (herein referred to as CTM) is a fictitious web application dedicated to those hardy hill walkers, trekkers, and climbers out there who like nothing more than leaving the comfort of a warm home and spending hours, days, or weeks roaming the wildernesses in search of nature's pleasure. CTM is a social website with a strong community focus and networking opportunities between members (see Figure 11-1). A key feature is the upload and export of GPS routes to members' own GPS devices; this data adds detailed statistics to each archived route. Alongside this data, each route has accompanying photographs, maps, downloads, and associated information, and the information architecture (IA) is packed with data. This is where we can use some nifty CSS to bring things to life and ultimately ensure all copy and images are unsullied, and the whole layout can remain extremely flexible.

The design is broken up into numerous blocks of information, so that it is easier to focus on the area we're discussing, rather than mess around with layers of overly decorative styling. By analyzing a number of great techniques through this chapter, you'll hopefully see how these can be adapted and applied to your own designs, alongside others featured in this book.

Many thanks to my colleague Greg Wood for his considerable assistance with the Climb the Mountains concept. All of the photographs are from my own Flickr account, mostly taken in England's glorious Lake District earlier this year. The typefaces include various fonts from the Palatino family, plus more common flavors including Helvetica, Georgia, and good old Verdana, with defaults Arial or Times New Roman in the stacks.

The case study will remain online at http://www.climbthemountains.com/cssm/.

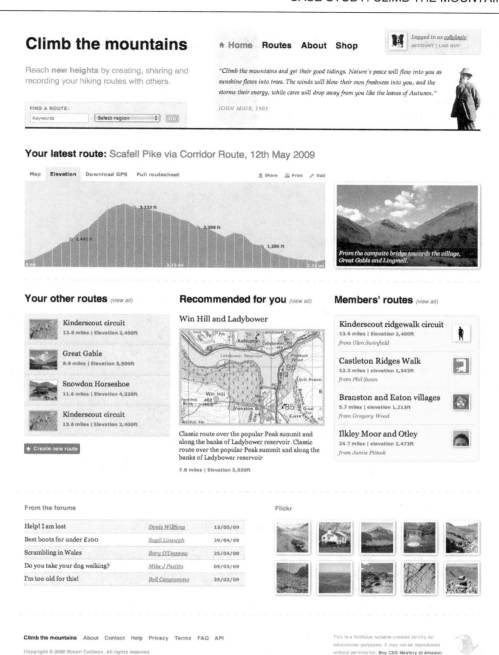

Figure 11-1. Climb the Mountains homepage

Style Sheet organization and conventions

Without question or compromise, every single website I'm involved with needs to be built with a solid foundation layer. This is a *conventions* package. Over the last two years, I have worked with my colleagues to develop a base layer of rules and conventions that act as starting points for HTML, CSS, JavaScript, and ExpressionEngine. It's a bumper compendium of connected CSS files, naming conventions, modules, plug-ins, and library scripts that ensure any project led or worked on by any member(s) of the team will stay on convention and be simpler for anyone else to step into and work with at any time (see Figure 11-2). Constantly evolving, the package is one of the most essential tools in our box.

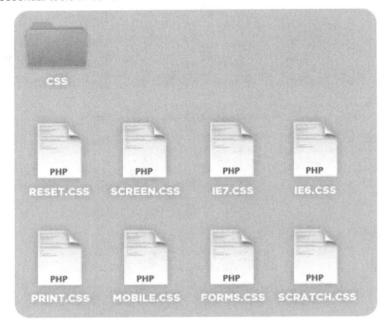

Figure 11-2. A typical set of style sheets from our basic files package

With specific regard for CSS, we have a set of cascading style sheets that work together to allow great flexibility and choice when it comes to browser irregularities, and enable the team to contribute via their own scratch files. With the latter, we use scratch files so that somebody can add their own CSS amendments or rules, and these will be rendered in the browser due to their place in the cascade. If the project director agrees to this CSS, it will then be taken from the scratch file and added to the relevant primary style sheet in place of any similar existing declarations. We also throw in very basic print and handheld style sheets, and a separate style sheet for any form styling. This is just our way.

The hard-working screen.css

The `screen.css` style sheet contains all declarations needed for the CTM case study if you're working in a Mac browser or in IE 8 or Firefox on a PC, alongside the `reset.css` style sheet. If you are working with IE 6 and/or IE 7, you'll also need the IE-specific style sheets described later in this section.

The `screen.css` file is linked as follows:

```
<link href="assets/css/screen.css" type="text/css" rel="stylesheet" media="screen" />
```

Many of the methods used in our `screen.css` style sheet will be familiar, but let's take a quick look at a couple of tools that I consider essential.

Describing contents

This tool is very easy to ignore or to dismiss as unnecessary. After all, your CSS will still work without such descriptive notes. Think again though. What if you are building a website as part of a larger team? What if your style sheets are often considerable in size? How do you ensure others can easily work with your designs, and also ensure that everything remains well organized?

This is where style sheet notes, and particularly a contents introduction can be immensely valuable. As a refresher, remember that any plain notes can be added anywhere in your style sheet by placing them within the following syntax:

```
/* I am a simple note */
```

So, we can use this approach to provide an up-to-date table of contents for the style sheet. This allows other designers and developers in the team to easily check that they are looking at the right sheet and to quickly check that the rules they want are there.

```
/*

CLIMB THE MOUNTAINS by SIMON COLLISON

VERSION 1.0


CONTENTS ----------

    1.BODY

    2.DEFAULT STYLING

    3.HEADINGS

    4.LINKS
```

```
    5.IMAGES

    6.LAYOUT

    7.BRANDING/MASTHEAD

    8.NAVIGATION

    9.SITEINFO/FOOTER

    10.GLOBAL ELEMENTS

        10.1 CAPTIONED IMAGE

        10.2 ELEVATION

        10.3 DISTANCE/ELEVATION PARAGRAPH

    11.HOMEPAGE

        11.1 CONTENT PRIMARY

        11.2 CONTENT SECONDARY

        11.3 CONTENT TERTIARY

*/
```

The exact layout is up to the individual or team. In the preceding example, I've used a structure made of returns and tabbing to create a very legible table of contents. The important thing is that you maintain the contents and constantly iterate it as you add rules to the style sheet, move rules within it, or remove rules from it.

Reset

The aim of a specific `reset.css` sheet is to create a level playing field across all browsers and devices. For example, some browsers have a default style sheet that might set different `margin` values, `padding`, heading font sizes, `line-height` and so on from other browsers.

We bring the `reset.css` sheet into the cascade with the following line in `screen.css`:

```
@import url(reset.css); /* RESET CSS */
```

This then gives us the confidence to move forward knowing that (in most `reset.css` cases) we are dealing with XHTML elements that have no `margin`, no `padding`, no `line-height`, no set font-size, and so on. We can now confidently work through `screen.css` applying the values that we want and not have to worry about inheriting values from the browser style sheet.

CSS wizard Eric Meyer provides what he calls a "starting point, not a self-contained black box of no-touchiness" at http://meyerweb.com/eric/tools/css/reset/, and this was my initial starting point for the CTM site, with just a few of my own minor tweaks and additions.

IE style sheets using conditional comments

This method of targeting specific Microsoft browser versions was introduced initially with Internet Explorer 5 and its point versions. Making use of XHTML markup wrapped in a conditional statement, inside of an XHTML comment, this special combination of syntax can be used anywhere in an XHTML document, giving us a brilliant opportunity to send certain information to certain browsers.

```
<!--[if IE 6]> Anything here is only seen by IE6 <![endif]-->
```

So, in the following example, we're using this combination of syntax to call three further style sheets should the user be viewing the site with any version of IE 6, IE 7, or IE 8.

```
<!--[if IE 6]><link href="assets/css/screen-ie6.css" type="text/css"↩
rel="stylesheet" media="screen" /><![endif]-->

<!--[if IE 7]><link href="assets/css/screen-ie7.css" type="text/css"↩
rel="stylesheet" media="screen" /><![endif]-->

<!--[if IE 8]><link href="assets/css/screen-ie8.css" type="text/css"↩
rel="stylesheet" media="screen" /><![endif]-->
```

The beauty of this approach is that we can avoid adding IE-specific hacks to our existing CSS rules in `screen.css` (which will be implemented by all other browsers) and instead create browser-specific rules in the relevant IE style sheets. This is the case for the CTM design, as we are calling a number of IE-specific amendments to the CSS, which we'll discuss later in this case study.

Grid flexibility

A grid acts as a solid foundation for any page in any website. Using a grid should liberate you, not restrict you. Never be afraid to break free from the grid and experiment. The grid acts as a reminder, a guideline, and a sense of reassurance.

Typically of a predetermined width and with a designated number of columns and optional gutters, the grid is your best friend, walking you through danger and mild peril. It acts as middleman between Photoshop and CSS, informing your initial layout choices regarding floats, positioning, margins, padding, borders, and so on.

Like many other designers, I work with a grid layer that I can turn on and off at will, regardless of whether I'm prototyping in Photoshop, Fireworks or the browser itself (see Figure 11-3).

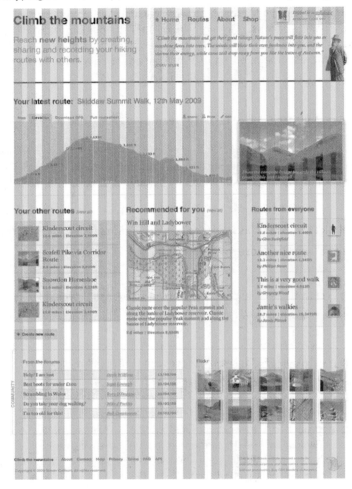

Figure 11-3. Climb the Mountains with its underlying column grid

How does the CTM layout work?

To bring all of this grid discussion to relevance, the Climb the Mountains case study layout is built on a robust yet flexible 1000-pixel wide grid. Within this 1000-pixel wide canvas, we have twelve columns, each separated by a clear gutter. Each column is 65 pixels wide, and each gutter is 25 pixels wide, as shown in Figure 11-4.

Figure 11-4. Column layout

Each column has its own structure also. Within the 65-pixel wide column, we have three subcolumns or widths (from left to right) 25 pixels, 15 pixels, 25 pixels (see Figure 11-5).

Figure 11-5. Internal subcolumn widths

These subcolumns allow us to work with a grid within a grid in some ways. They provide additional points of reference, something else to measure to or against when twelve columns might not be tight enough for what we need. Trace down the full screen grab example and see how items are sometimes aligned with the main columns and sometimes with the subcolumns.

Navigation control with body classes

We can use the value assigned to the body element to change page layout, control behavior, and make other significant changes with CSS. In the first edition of this book, I used a unique ID for the body element of each page to control layout, combining this with a class for location, such as `<body id="threeColLayout" class="home">`. This time around, I'm using only the class.

```
<body class="home">
```

It doesn't matter whether you use an ID or a class for this purpose; the power we get from this super-parent element is the same regardless.

Highlighting the current page

There are numerous ways of highlighting the page you are on, and many designers might use some clever PHP scripting to trigger the CSS, perhaps highlighting the Home link on the main navigation if on the homepage. That's cool, but it's just as easy with some smart CSS application reliant on pairing the body class with a navigation class. Let's take a look.

```
<body class="home">
```

```
<ul id="navigation_pri">
    <li class="nav_home"><a href="#">Home</a></li>
    <li class="nav_routes"><a href="#">Routes</a></li>
    <li class="nav_about"><a href="#">About</a></li>
    <li class="nav_shop"><a href="#">Shop</a></li>
</ul>
```

In the preceding code snippet, you'll see that the Home link has a class nav_home. We'll also add a body class to the Routes page, so we can test the behavior later on:

```
<body class="routes">
```

Next, let's use CSS to apply the styling to the navigation list. Note that we'll position the element absolutely, at specific coordinates from the top and left of the main container.

```
ul#navigation_pri {
    list-style:none;
    margin:0;
    position:absolute;
    top:0;
    left:415px;
    font-size:19px;
    font-weight:bold;
    font-family:Helvetica,Arial,sans-serif;
}
ul#navigation_pri li {
    float:left;
    margin:0;
    padding:30px 10px 0 10px;
    height:3000px;
}
```

```
ul#navigation_pri li a {
    color:#000;
}
ul#navigation_pri li a:hover,
ul#navigation_pri li a:focus {
    color:#333;
    text-decoration:underline;
}
```

This will give us the basic styled navigation shown in Figure 11-6, but without any indication of the page we are currently viewing. (note that we'll examine the blockquote that sits on top of the navigation layer later in this section):

Home Routes About Shop

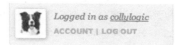

"Climb the mountains and get their good tidings. Nature's peace will flow into you as sunshine flows into trees. The winds will blow their own freshness into you, and the storms their energy, while cares will drop away from you like the leaves of Autumn."

JOHN MUIR, 1903

Figure 11-6. Basic main navigation

The next step is to use a selector to define a relationship between the body class and the navigation home class. Note that we have grouped two identical rules for the home page and the Routes page:

```
.home ul#navigation_pri li.nav_home,
.routes ul#navigation_pri li.nav_routes {
    background-color:#f5f5f5;
}
```

The first part of the selector .home or .routes sniffs to make sure we are viewing that page. The styling will only be applied if the ul#navigation_pri element is a child of .home or .routes. If a match is found, the action is performed. This will create the light gray background that fills the entire navigation tab area.

Next, we can define styles for the link behavior, again grouping the identical rules for .home and .routes:

```
.home ul#navigation_pri li.nav_home a,
.routes ul#navigation_pri li.nav_routes a {
    color:#278dab;
    background:#f5f5f5 0 center no-repeat;
    padding:0 0 0 20px;
}
.home ul#navigation_pri li.nav_home a:hover,
.home ul#navigation_pri li.nav_home a:focus,
.routes ul#navigation_pri li.nav_routes a:hover,
.routes ul#navigation_pri li.nav_routes a:focus {
    text-decoration:none;
    color:#000;
}
```

Thus, we get the blue text links we need. Finally, we can add some decoration only to the home page link. When the home page is in view, we'll display a small home icon to the left of the Home link:

```
.home ul#navigation_pri li.nav_home a {
    background-image:url(../images/site/nav_back.gif);
}
```

This results in the home page display shown in Figure 11-7.

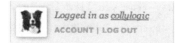

⌂ Home   Routes   About   Shop

"Climb the mountains and get their good tidings. Nature's peace will flow into you as sunshine flows into trees. The winds will blow their own freshness into you, and the storms their energy, while cares will drop away from you like the leaves of Autumn."

JOHN MUIR, 1903

Figure 11-7. The selected Home link

And Figure 11-8 shows our Routes page.

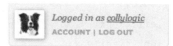

Home   Routes   About   Shop

"Climb the mountains and get their good tidings. Nature's peace will flow into you as sunshine flows into trees. The winds will blow their own freshness into you, and the storms their energy, while cares will drop away from you like the leaves of Autumn."

JOHN MUIR, 1903

Figure 11-8. The selected Routes link

Layering the blockquote

Now, back to that John Muir quote that sits on top of the main navigation. I truly love that quote – it inspires me to get outdoors regardless of the weather and blow off those web designer's cobwebs. Never forget to get out there, into the real world! On CTM, we could have rotating inspirational quotes in that part of the page to inspire the audience. Here's the markup:

```
<blockquote id="johnmuir">

    <p>&ldquo;Climb the mountains and get their good tidings. Nature's peace ↵

    will flow into you as sunshine flows into trees. The winds will blow their ↵

    own freshness into you, and the storms their energy, while cares will drop ↵
```

```
away from you like the leaves of Autumn.&rdquo;</p>
  <p><cite>John Muir, 1903</cite></p>
</blockquote>
```

Aside from using specific character entities for the quotation marks, there's nothing especially unusual there, and we can move on to defining the styling. Earlier, we positioned the ul#navigation_pri element absolutely with position:absolute, 0px from the top and 415px from the left.

```
ul#navigation_pri {
    list-style:none;
    margin:0;
    position:absolute;
    top:0;
    left:415px;
    font-size:19px;
    font-weight:bold;
    font-family:Helvetica,Arial,sans-serif;
}
```

We can now define the styling for the blockquote:

```
div#branding blockquote {
    width:505px;
    float:right;
    padding:0 70px 20px 0;
    background:url(../images/site/branding_johnmuir.jpg) no-repeat right top;
}
```

But, it sits behind the blue navigation tab area, as shown in Figure 11-9.

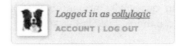

♠ **Home**   **Routes**   **About**   **Shop**

Logged in as collylogic
ACCOUNT | LOG OUT

untains and get their good tidings. Nature's peace will flow into you as
into trees. The winds will blow their own freshness into you, and the
ergy, while cares will drop away from you like the leaves of Autumn."

!903

Figure 11-9. The blockquote is partly hidden behind the Home link.

However, considering that the navigation is positioned absolutely, if we add position:relative to the blockquote, we can make it appear above the blue tab area:

```
div#branding blockquote {
    position:relative;
    width:505px;
    float:right;
    padding:0 70px 20px 0;
    background:url(../images/site/branding_johnmuir.jpg) no-repeat right top;
}
```

And with that, the blockquote will sit nicely above the main navigation, as illustrated in the earlier navigation examples, such as Figure 11-7.

Strategically targeting elements

Earlier in the case study, we examined the power of using descendent selectors to control the main navigation styling based on the body class of each page. Here, we'll look again at how a thoughtful approach to markup can afford greater flexibility and control through deep descendent selectors and how this forms a basis for even greater control through advanced targeting of elements.

Deep descendent selectors

First, let's lay the foundations. On the right-hand side of the CTM case study, you'll see the light yellow Members' Routes panel, featuring walks contributed by other users of the site. There's nothing especially remarkable about the markup, but let's examine it ahead of doing some selectors magic later in the section.

Notice how we group several elements such as h3, p, and img inside each unordered list item. I've often been surprised how many designers don't realize that you can add all sorts of interesting elements inside the li element. Often, you might only see a and maybe img inside the li element, but you can do so much more.

```html
<div id="others_routes">
  <h2>Members' routes <a href="#" class="more">(view all)</a></h2>
    <ul>
      <li>
        <h3><a href="#">Kinderscout circuit</a></h3>
          <p class="dist_elev">13.6 miles | Elevation 2,400ft</p>

          <p class="username"><a href="#">from Glen Swinfield <img ↵
src="assets/images/content/avatar_swinfield.jpg" class="avatar" ↵
alt="Glen Swinfield's avatar" /></a></p>
      </li>
      <li>
        <h3><a href="#">Castleton Ridge Walk</a></h3>
          <p class="dist_elev">12.2 miles | elevation 1,343ft</p>

          <p class="username"><a href="#">from Phil Swan <img ↵
src="assets/images/content/avatar_swan.jpg" class="avatar" ↵
alt="Phil Swan's avatar" /></a></p>
      </li>
      <li>
        <h3><a href="#">Branston Circular</a></h3>
          <p class="dist_elev">5.7 miles | elevation 1,213ft</p>

          <p class="username"><a href="#">from Gregory Wood <img ↵
src="assets/images/content/avatar_wood.jpg" class="avatar" ↵
alt="Gregory Wood's avatar" /></a></p>
      </li>
      <li>
        <h3><a href="#">Ilkley Moor and Otley</a></h3>
```

```
        <p class="dist_elev">24.7 miles | elevation 2,473ft</p>
        <p class="username"><a href="#">from Jamie Pittock <img ↵
src="assets/images/content/avatar_pittock.jpg" class="avatar" ↵
alt="Jamie Pittock's avatar" /></a></p>
      </li>
    </ul>
</div>
```

By building content in this way, we can collate blocks of information as lists, providing all the hierarchy and styling control that we know and love about lists.

It is then really easy to use basic selectors to target the unordered list within the others_routes containing div and the various elements within the li elements. Note that we're using border-radius, -webkit-border-radius, and –moz-border-radius rules to apply rounded corners to the ul element, and be reassured that we'll discuss these later in this case study.

```
div#others_routes ul {
    list-style:none;
    border:1px solid #dedeaf;
    background:#ffffcc;
    border-radius:5px;
    -webkit-border-radius:5px;
    -moz-border-radius:5px;
    margin:0;
    padding:10px;
}
div#others_routes ul li {
    margin:0;
    padding:10px 55px 10px 0;
    position:relative;
    border-bottom:1px solid #dedeaf;
    border-top:1px solid #fff;
}
```

327

```css
div#others_routes ul li h3 {
    margin-bottom:5px;
}
div#others_routes ul li img {
    position:absolute;
    top:10px;
    right:10px;
}
div#others_routes ul li p.username {
    margin:3px 0 0 0;
    font-style:italic;
    font-size:12px;
}
div#others_routes ul li p.username a {
    color:#666;
}
div#others_routes ul li p.username a:hover,
div#others_routes ul li p.username a:focus {
    text-decoration:underline;
}
```

In the preceding markup, we're targeting deeper HTML elements with some straightforward descendent selectors. For example, we can strategically target the link hover styling of the username link with div#others_routes ul li p.username a:hover, descending deeper and deeper with the selector until we define our target element—an element owned by every preceding element in the selector, resulting in Figure 11-10.

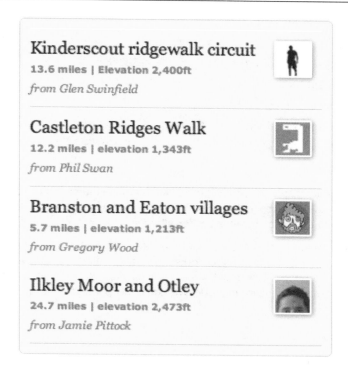

Figure 11-10. The initial Members' Routes container

Excellent. Our list of member-submitted walks and routes is shaping up nicely, and most might leave it as it is. It looks pretty neat and tidy. But wait! We are perfectionists, and we have powerful CSS at our disposal. Why settle for good when we could have great?

In the next two examples, we'll neaten up the top and bottom of the routes container using some nifty CSS tricks.

The :first-child pseudo-class

If you've ever wondered how a designer targets the first letter or line of a block of text, he or she is probably using a pseudo-class such as :first-letter or :first-line. These cool tricks enable us to style elements based on simple logic.

The :first-child pseudo-class targets only an element that is the first child of a containing element.

In this case study, I have my container of member's walks, with each item's detail added within an unordered list. Each li element has the same padding and thin border at the top and bottom.

```
div#others_routes ul li {
    margin:0;
    padding:10px 55px 10px 0;
    position:relative;
    border-bottom:1px solid #dedeaf;
    border-top:1px solid #fff;
}
```

This keeps the list content spaced evenly, but I'd like to reduce the amount of padding for only the top list item (in the example, this is the Kinderscout ridgewalk circuit walk). In fact, I don't want any padding at the top, and I don't want a border either.

So, bring on the pseudo-class. Here, we create a new rule, and we use the same selector to target the unordered list items inside the #others_routes containing div, but we add :first-child immediately after the li element, essentially saying "go in to the container, find the unordered list, and perform the following style override only on the very first li element you find."

```
div#others_routes ul li:first-child {
    padding-top:0;
    border-top:none;
}
```

As Figure 11-11 shows, the Kinderscout ridgewalk circuit item has no top border or top padding and nestles snugly under the roof of the parent container.

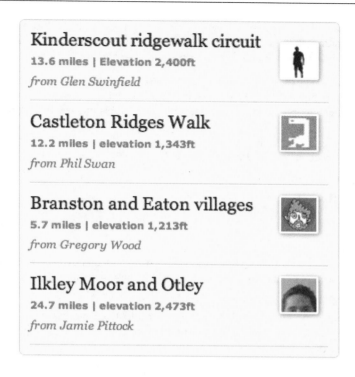

Figure 11-11. The top padding and border has been successfully removed.

It's as simple as that, but it's a very powerful method of targeting a specific element, with a million and one uses. And now that we've dealt with the top of our contained list, let's see what we can do with the bottom of it.

Adjacent sibling selectors

Having just introduced you to :first-child, now would ideally be a fitting moment to introduce the usefulness of :last-child, a method of targeting the last instance of a child element within a specific parent container. The approach is much the same as with :first-child, so feel free to experiment with this. Unfortunately, only recent versions of browsers such as Safari, Firefox, Google Chrome, and Opera support this method, so we need to be mindful of IE 6, 7, and 8 and employ an alternative approach, thanks to adjacent sibling selectors.

In this example, we now need to do the reverse of what we just did with the :first-child pseudo-class. As we previously discussed, each unordered list item has top and bottom padding and a top and bottom border. We successfully turned off these styles for the first li element, now we need to turn them off for the last element.

But how do we do that? How does the style sheet know which is the very last element in a certain group, and how can we accurately target it. This requires some kind of dark arts, right? Well, sort of.

Adjacent sibling selectors consist of several selectors separated by the + combinator. This matches an element that is the next sibling to the first element. Note that elements must have the same parent, and the first must immediately precede the second.

So, as with our :first-child example, we again target the others_routes parent div, and we then methodically drill down through the selectors until we hit the element we wish to style. Our unordered list will always only have four li elements, and that is the key to making this work:

```
div#others_routes ul li + li + li + li {
    padding-bottom:0;
    border-bottom:none;
}
```

So here, we've created a selector that thinks "Ah, when in the others_routes div, find the unordered list, count along until we match the fourth li element, and apply styles to that only." Simple.

Thus, the result, shown in Figure 11-12, presents the fourth li element without bottom padding or a bottom border, adding further neatness and attention to detail, simply by making the most of the CSS selectors at our disposal.

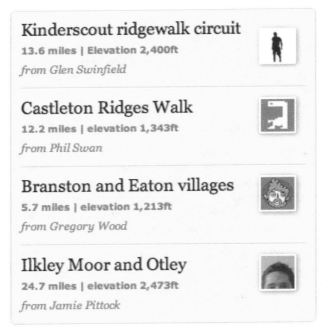

Figure 11-12. The bottom border and padding has been removed successfully

Transparency, shadows, and rounded corners

In the first edition of this book, my case study relied heavily on boxes with rounded corners. Everybody wants rounded corners at some point for a little visual flair, and well, right angle corners are just so easy, boring maybe.

Of the seemingly endless possible methods of creating rounded corners, I settled on one that used a fair amount of JavaScript in combination with several background image sprites and a reasonable amount of extraneous markup. It was weighty, clumsy, awkward, and there wasn't really an alternative.

Fast-forward to me sitting here typing this chapter, and I'm basically just going blue, wanting to shout "CSS 3!" as loud as I can. Things have changed: expectations have grown, and the tools have evolved. Sure, the browsers haven't all caught up (what else do you expect?), but as an industry we are braver and more willing to work with new ideas and push things forward.

In this section, I'll take one humble image and caption from the CTM homepage and do all sorts of lovely CSS 3 things to it, without any use of JavaScript, further graphics, or extraneous markup. Viva La Revolution!

Our aim

We'll being with one simple 310 × 185-pixel JPG named `campsite.jpg` (see Figure 11-13). Then, we'll apply a caption with white text onto a semitransparent grey overlay at the base of the image, and then apply a Polaroid-style photo border around the image, ensuring it has perfect rounded corners and a believable drop shadow. Thankfully, we can do all of that with CSS.

Figure 11-13. The initial campsite.jpg image

The markup is pretty simple. Our image and caption need to be contained within one div, named `captioned_image` for the purposes of this example. The paragraph is given `class="caption"`, so we can target it directly, and for now, that is it.

```
<div class="captioned_image">
    <img src="assets/images/content/campsite.jpg" alt="From the campsite" />
    <p class="caption">From the campsite bridge towards the village, Great ↩
Gable and Lingmell.</p>
</div>
```

With that markup in place, we can now experiment with three of the hottest CSS 3 techniques at our disposal.

Caption image overlay and RGBa transparency

Colors may be specified in a number of ways. Many specify color as an RGB triplet in hexadecimal format (a hex triplet). Others often use their common English names in some cases. It is also possible to use RGB percentages or decimals. The following examples are all valid for the color red:

```
color: #f00
color: #ff0000
color: red
color: rgb(255,0,0)
color: rgb(100%, 0%, 0%)
```

RGB stands for *red, green, and blue* and is a device familiar to most designers. RGBa introduces a fourth channel – an alpha channel that deals with transparency. The beauty of CSS 3 is that we can continue to specify color with RGB but also set the alpha transparency of that color with a fourth decimal value. We can use anything from 0.0 (totally transparent) through to 1.0 (totally solid).

In the following example, we again declare the color red with RGB, but also set a 50 percent transparency by declaring 0.5 as the alpha transparency.

```
color: rgb(255,0,0,0.5)
```

The RGBa value is assigned only to the element we declare, so any child elements will not inherit the transparency, which is a clear distinction from the opacity property, which will always be inherited.

So, for the CTM site, the following declarations will perform the first bit of magic for our photo and caption. We position the containing `div` relatively and then the caption absolutely, so that it can be positioned exactly where we wish above the image.

```css
div.captioned_image {
    position:relative;
}
div.captioned_image p.caption {
    position:absolute;
    bottom:0;
    left:0;
    margin:0;
    color:#fff;
    font-size:13px;
    line-height:16px;
    font-style:italic;
    padding:5px;
}
```

We next declare the RGBa value as `rgba(0,0,0,0.5)` where the first three values combine to give us black and then the alpha transparency value of `0.5` sets a medium transparency, which can be tweaked until we're happy with the overall effect.

```css
div.captioned_image p.caption {
position:absolute;
bottom:0;
left:0;
margin:0;
background:rgba(0,0,0,0.5);
color:#fff;
font-size:13px;
line-height:16px;
font-style:italic;
padding:5px;
}
```

This gives us the exact caption overlay we wanted, as shown in Figure 11-14.

Figure 11-14. The transparent caption in place

As with many exciting new CSS 3 techniques, some browsers are playing catch-up, most notably Internet Explorer (including the current IE 8), which will not render the alpha-transparency. For example, IE 7 will instead default to a reasonably acceptable solid layer, much like we'd see if serving a transparent PNG graphic without forcing alpha transparency support (see Figure 11-15).

Figure 11-15. The caption overlay as rendered by IE 7

IE 8, which still does not support RGBa, will simply render the caption text on top of the image without any kind of background. To get around this problem, we can add a rule to the screeni-ie8.css style sheet to ensure a gray background is placed behind the text.

```
div.captioned_image p.caption { background:#666; }
```

The important lesson is not to be put off by IE and its failings. I'd encourage all of you hexadecimal triplet lovers to start experimenting with the incredible flexibility of RGBa straight away, on a variety of elements within your layouts. You will never look back, and everything will be much clearer!

Combining classes

I'm still surprised when I speak to designers who aren't aware that classes can be combined to bring greater flexibility to elements.

For example, you might use class="profile" several times on any given page, assigning common color and layout information. However, let's say you wish to change only the background color based on a variable such as whether or not the user is a member or a guest. Instead of creating two profile styles just to supply different color references, you could simply keep colors as separate rules, and combine these with the profile class.

```
.profile {
width:300px;
margin:0 10px;
padding:10px;
font-size:11px;
}
.guest {
background-color:#ff9900;
}
.member {
background-color:#ff0000;
}
```

This style could then be applied using combined classes depending on user status. Any number of classes can be combined, simply by separating each with a space, as follows:

```
<div class="profile member">
<p>Member options…</p>
</div>
```

Bringing this to the CTM site, we can use combined classes to optionally add a frame around only certain captioned images. Notice that, alongside captioned_image, we have added the class polaroid:

```
<div class="captioned_image polaroid">
    <img src="assets/images/content/campsite.jpg" alt="From the campsite" />
    <p class="caption">From the campsite bridge towards the village, Great ↩
Gable and Lingmell.</p>
</div>
```

We can now define the styling for this polaroid frame, and that calls for a few more tricks from the CSS 3 specification.

border-radius

In the previous edition of *CSS Mastery*, both Andy and myself detailed a useful but somewhat laborious technique for adding frames and shadows to images. This involved a couple of divs and background images that needed to be very carefully styled and positioned. Yep, it was tough back in 2005.

This brings us to the border-radius property, which, essentially, brings rounded corners to elements using pure CSS declarations. Sadly, Internet Explorer (hello again) doesn't support this property at all, so IE corners will still be squared off, which seems acceptable to me. Currently, the same goes for the ever-evolving Opera browser.

At the time of this writing, no popular browsers are pledging support for the standard border-radius property, and so while it is important to include the declaration from a forward-thinking standpoint, we also need to add two further declarations in the short-term – one for Mozilla-based browsers such as cuddly Firefox and one for WebKit-based browser such as the ever-switched-on Safari (which also supports elliptical corners). For more information, examples and some cool tricks, view descriptions and examples over at http://www.the-art-of-web.com/css/border-radius/.

All three declarations are clearly defined here:

```
.polaroid {
    border:5px solid #f00;
    border-radius:5px;
    -webkit-border-radius:5px;
    -moz-border-radius:5px;
}
```

Seeing as white on white isn't exactly great for demonstrations, note that I have specified a temporary red border so that you can see what is happening in Figure 11-16. You'll see that each corner is rounded around a 5px radius. This is actually the radii of a quarter eclipse defining the exact corner. As with `margin`, `padding`, and `border`, there are four individual `border-radius` properties—one for each corner of an element—and one shorthand property.

From the campsite bridge towards the village, Great Gable and Lingmell.

Figure 11-16. Using a red border clearly shows the rounded corners

Now, how much easier is that compared with the methods we were describing back in the first edition? With our corners rounded, we can now think about applying a simple drop shadow to give the image some sense of affordance.

box-shadow

CSS 3 brings us a significantly simpler method of creating neat drop shadows for the Safari 3 and above and Firefox 3.5 and above browsers. The property takes three lengths as its attributes—these being the horizontal offset, the vertical offset, and the blur radius—and finally a color.

If we apply a positive value to the horizontal offset of the shadow, the shadow will be on the right-hand side of the element. A negative offset will put the shadow on the left of the element.

If we apply a negative value to the vertical offset, the shadow will be appear on top of the element, whereas a positive value would place the shadow below the box.

The blur radius is really handy. If the value is set to 0 the shadow will be sharp, and the higher the number, the more blurred it will become.

Adding this to our polaroid class, we can work with the four values to create a drop shadow that will be to the right and bottom of our captioned image, with a 5-pixel blur in a medium grey, as follows:

```
.polaroid {
    border:5px solid #fff;
    border-radius:5px;
    -webkit-border-radius:5px;
    -moz-border-radius:5px;
    -webkit-box-shadow:1px 1px 5px #999;
    -moz-box-shadow:1px 1px 5px #999;
}
```

Brilliantly, the box-shadow will respect the border-radius value we gave earlier, so that we have a rounded picture frame and complimentary shadow working in perfect harmony, as shown in Figure 11-17.

From the campsite bridge towards the village, Great Gable and Lingmell.

Figure 11-17. Our image now has a caption, frame, and rounded corners

Alas, this isn't yet the case in Internet Explorer, as shown in Figure 11-18.

From the campsite bridge towards the village, Great Gable and Lingmell.

Figure 11-18. Internet Explorer doesn't render the CSS 3 properties, but the result is acceptable

We noted the lack of RGBa transparency for the caption earlier, and you'll also see that our frame is rendered as a grey square frame. It has the same width (5px) but is not white and not rounded. Obviously, we're also bereft of that beautiful shadow. Remember, we have at least ensured the caption text sits on a gray background by adding a rule to our `screen-i8.css` style sheet. Oh well, maybe things will be fixed in IE by the time I have grandchildren.

Positioning lists and revealing content

For this chunk of the case study, we'll focus on the Your latest route area of the site, on the left of the layout. In a fully realized concept, this would be a selection of statistics, maps, and charts relating to a particular walk, each pane viewable via a different tab.

First, we'll begin by adding the navigation for the stats section of the CTM homepage. The markup requires two lists, one for the statistics tabs on the left, and one for the Share, Print, and Email options on the right:

```
<ul id="route_nav">
    <li><a href="#">Map</a></li>
    <li class="cur"><a href="#">Elevation</a></li>
    <li><a href="#">Download GPS</a></li>
    <li><a href="#">Full routesheet</a></li>
</ul>
```

```
<ul id="route_action">
    <li class="share"><a href="#">Share</a></li>
    <li class="print"><a href="#">Print</a></li>
    <li class="edit"><a href="#">Edit</a></li>
</ul>
```

Note that we've added class="cur" to the Elevation tab, as we'll want that to appear as selected throughout this exercise, and we can directly target that link with this additional class.

Due to our two unordered lists inheriting a few existing styles from elsewhere in the document, we have the basic blue link states and font-family and font-size rules shown in Figure 11-19.

- Map
- Elevation
- Download GPS
- Full routesheet

- Share
- Print
- Edit

Figure 11-19. The basic "Your latest route" navigation lists

Elsewhere, I've floated the Share, Print, and Email list to the right, with little extra of note. So, let's focus on the left-hand list from now on. We'll float that to the left and add a few basic styling declarations, including a bolder color for the selected tab:

```
ul#route_nav {
    list-style:none;
    font-family:Verdana,sans-serif;
    font-size:11px;
    font-weight:bold;
    float:left;
    margin:0;
}
ul#route_nav li {
    float:left;
```

```
        margin:0;
        padding:7px 10px;
    }
    ul#route_nav li a {
        color:#666;
    }
    ul#route_nav li a:hover,
    ul#route_nav li a:focus {
        color:#333;
    }
    ul#route_nav li.cur a {
        color:#000;
    }
```

This gives us our two lists as shown in Figure 11-20—one floated left and one floated right—with some initial styling.

Map **Elevation** Download GPS Full routesheet   Share   Print   Edit

Figure 11-20. The two lists floated left and right

We'll clear those floats by using clear:both on the statistics container that will follow this navigation. Next, we'll add a background color to the selected class:

```
    ul#route_nav li.cur {
    background:#dff1f1;
    }
```

This defines the exact area of the selected tab, as shown in Figure 11-21.

Map **Elevation** Download GPS Full routesheet   Share   Print   Edit

Figure 11-21. The two lists floated left and right with the selected tab highlighted

That's our basic Your latest route navigation sorted, but there's another neat CSS 3 trick we can pull.

Rounding the corners

Earlier in this case study, we looked at the CSS 3 `border-radius` property, creating a simple rounded-corner frame for an image.

Here, we will use similar properties to add rounded corners to a basic shape, specifically the selected list item in our navigation.

We're using browser-relevant varieties of `border-radius-top-left` and `border-radius-top-right` to only apply the corners to the top of the shape:

```
ul#route_nav li.cur {
    background:#dff1f1;
    -moz-border-radius-topleft:3px;
    -webkit-border-top-left-radius:3px;
    -moz-border-radius-topright:3px;
    -webkit-border-top-right-radius:3px;
}
```

This simple adjustment to the CSS will give us the subtle but sexy tab shown in Figure 11-22 in Firefox and Safari.

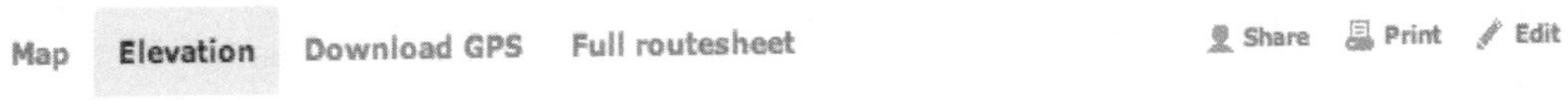

Map   **Elevation**   Download GPS   Full routesheet   Share   Print   Edit

Figure 11-22. The selected tab now has rounded top corners, using only CSS

With the navigation finally resolved, we can now move on to the altogether more juicy elevation data.

The main elevation chart

Below the Your latest route navigation bar, we'll now add the statistics pane that appears by default in the case study, the Elevation chart.

```
<div id="route_elevation">
</div>
```

The most important point to be aware of here is that (as mentioned earlier) we're using the `route_elevation` div to `clear` the floated navigation lists. So, you'll see `clear:both` defined for this `div` immediately.

```
.home div#route_elevation {
    clear:both;
    background:#dff1f1 url(../images/site/elevation_home.gif) 0 bottom no-
repeat;
    position:relative;
    height:195px;
}
```

We also position the elevation div relatively, as this will assist us later when plotting li elements (we'll add these shortly) on the chart. We also apply the background image elevation_home.gif (see Figure 11-23) with one shorthand rule for color, image, position, and repeat properties.

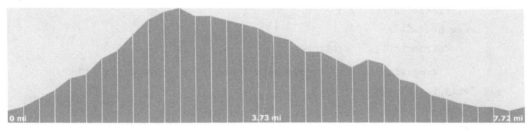

Figure 11-23. The elevation background image

This gives us the image shown in Figure 11-24 with the navigation data and elevation chart combined.

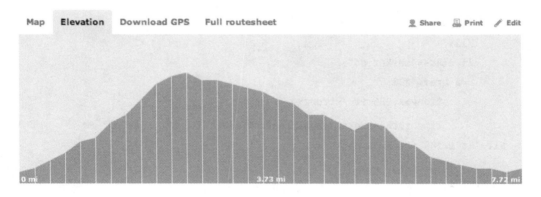

Figure 11-24. Navigation and elevation container combined

345

Next, we can create a new unordered list that will contain our elevation references. Each reference will feature a `height` and associated image from Flickr. Note that each list has a unique class, such as `marker_01` and `marker_02`.

```
<div id="route_elevation">
  <ul>
    <li class="marker_01">
      <a href="#">
        <strong>1,442 ft</strong>
          <img src="assets/images/content/elevation_photo_1.jpg" ↵
  alt="At 1,442 ft: Photo of the village" />
      </a>
    </li>
    <li class="marker_02">
      <a href="#">
        <strong>3,133 ft</strong>
          <img src="assets/images/content/elevation_photo_2.jpg" ↵
  alt="At 3,133 ft: Pennine Way" />
      </a>
    </li>
    <li class="marker_03">
      <a href="#">
        <strong>2,398 ft</strong>
          <img src="assets/images/content/elevation_photo_3.jpg" ↵
  alt="At 2,398 ft: Cup of tea" />
      </a>
    </li>
    <li class="marker_04">
      <a href="#">
        <strong>1,286 ft</strong>
          <img src="assets/images/content/elevation_photo_4.jpg" ↵
  alt="At 1,286 ft: Wool packs" />
      </a>
    </li>
  </ul>
</div>
```

We'll use these unique classes to define the display position for each list item on the chart, basing the coordinates from the top and left of the elevation chart container.

```
.home div#route_elevation li.marker_01 {
    top:123px;
    left:97px;
}
.home div#route_elevation li.marker_02 {
    top:50px;
    left:237px;
}
.home div#route_elevation li.marker_03 {
    top:95px;
    left:377px;
}
.home div#route_elevation li.marker_04 {
    top:137px;
    left:517px;
}
```

It is still early in the process, so all we have so far are a bunch of list items each with height and image snuggling up to the left of the container (see Figure 11-25).

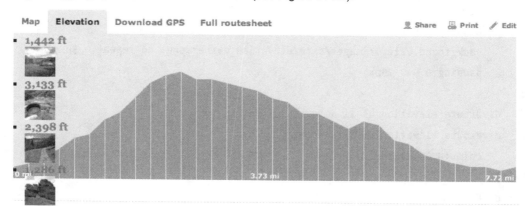

Figure 11-25. Our list items are snuggling in a line to the left

Before we force the list items to sit in their intended positions, let's first hide the images, and choose a more appropriate marker graphic. The graphic we'll use is the typical list bullet graphic shown in Figure 11-26 and named elevation_marker.png.

Figure 11-26. Our marker graphic

On to the list styling now, we'll set styles such as font-family, font-size, remove or define margin and padding, and so on. Importantly, we declare the elevation_marker.png background image for the div#route_elevation ul li element, applying a 15-pixel margin-left to create space between the bullet and the elevation height.

```
div#route_elevation ul {
    list-style:none;
    margin:0;
    font-family:Verdana,sans-serif;
    font-size:9px;
    font-weight:bold;
}
div#route_elevation ul li {
    margin:0;
}
div#route_elevation ul li a {
    color:#333;
    display:block;
    background:url(../images/site/elevation_marker.png) no-repeat 0 5px;
    padding:0 0 0 15px;
}
div#route_elevation ul li a:hover,
div#route_elevation ul li a:focus {
    color:#000;
}
div#route_elevation ul li a img {
    display:none;
}
```

Vitally, we have targeted the Flickr image thumbnails with div#route_elevation ul li a img, using display:none to prevent the images from being displayed.

The elevation chart now shows our list styled more suitably, but still snuggling up to the left of the container (see Figure 11-27).

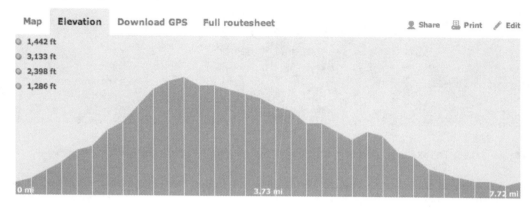

Figure 11-27. Our list markers are styled but still snuggling to the left

To make sure the list elements display according to their positioned coordinates, all we need to do is position them absolutely using position:absolute as follows:

```
div#route_elevation ul li {
    margin:0;
    position:absolute;
}
```

This repositioning works because the parent container is positioned relative to its own parent. If it wasn't, our absolutely positioned list items would base their coordinates from the top and left of the browser window, which wouldn't do at all. As Figure 11-28 shows, the elevation points are now plotted accurately on the chart.

349

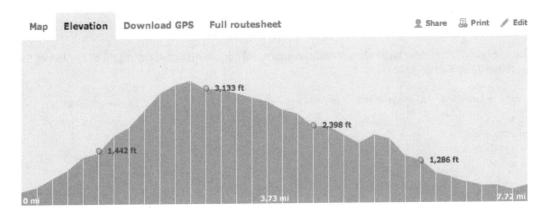

Figure 11-28. Thanks to positioning absolutely, the markers sit at the correct coordinates

We now need to deal with the images we hid earlier and bring them into view when we roll over each elevation point.

Our targets are the :hover and :focus pseudo-link states, and with control of those, we can easily apply declarations that will bring the images into view on rollover.

Notice that after setting height and width, we again position the elements absolutely, and we use negative top and right values to position the images exactly where we want them in relation to the list marker.

```
div#route_elevation ul li a:hover img,
div#route_elevation ul li a:focus img {
    display:block;
    width:40px;
    height:40px;
    padding:4px 9px 10px 12px;
    position:absolute;
    top:-16px;
    right:-65px;
}
```

As a result, on rollover, we get the thumbnail pop-up as expected, sitting just to the right of the marker. We added some padding around the thumbnail too (see Figure 11-29).

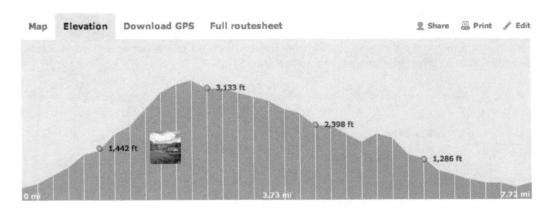

Figure 11-29. On hover, the basic image thumbnails appear

It is now time to make use of that padding and fit a neat frame and arrow graphic behind the thumbnail images. I'm using elevation_marker_image_bg.png here, which is shown in Figure 11-30. Note that the shadow is added to the graphic at Photoshop stage and it's exported as a transparent PNG.

Figure 11-30. Neat graphic to sit behind our image thumbnails

All that remains is to apply that background image to the CSS as follows:

```
div#route_elevation ul li a:hover img,
div#route_elevation ul li a:focus img {
    display:block;
    width:40px;
    height:40px;
    padding:4px 9px 10px 12px;
    position:absolute;
    top:-16px;
    right:-65px;
    background:url(../images/site/elevation_marker_image_bg.png) no-repeat 0 0;
}
```

If you're doing something similar, you may well need to fiddle with exact padding, positioning, and so forth, but the basic building blocks are all here. As a result of all the work we've done in this section, we now have a nicely executed Your latest route area of the page, with an interactive elevation chart plotting Flickr images, shown in Figure 11-31.

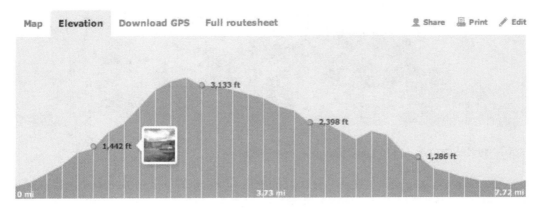

Figure 11-31. The completed "Your latest route" section with tidy image rollovers

Of course, all of this would ultimately need to be hooked up to a powerful CMS to really be exceptional, but well, this is a CSS book.

Summary

There you have it. This has been more of a brief weekend city break than two weeks by the beach, but insightful nonetheless, I hope. I've really enjoyed pulling the Climb the Mountains concept together for this second edition of *CSS Mastery*, especially with the freedom to cut loose with some fresh CSS 3 ideas.

Naturally, there are oodles more bits and pieces in the Climb the Mountains site that I'd love to have been able to walk through with you. Sadly, there just isn't enough space in one book to go into that level of exploration. Still, if you like a behavior or treatment in the site, and it isn't covered in this chapter, I think it should be easy to jump in, examine the source, and figure out how things work. I've certainly done my best to structure the source code with clarity and sprinkle in a number of helpful notes and references where possible.

Remember, the site will remain online at http://www.climbthemountains.com/cssm, and the source code is available from www.friendsofed.com. Do feel free to take it, examine it, rip it apart, put it back together again, and use it as inspiration for your own ideas and stunning CSS-powered masterpieces.

Index

Numbers & Symbols

+ combinator, 332
1-pixel transparent GIF, 5
960 layout, 281, 282
1020 layout, 282
1040 layout, 282
1080 layout, 281, 282

A

absolute positioning, 60–61
    description, 129
    in relative container, 269–270
:active dynamic pseudo-class selector,
        110
adjacent sibling selector, 29
:after pseudo-class, 68
Ajax, adding interactivity with, 304–306
almost standards mode, 22
anchor type selector, 109
annotating CSS files, 44
Asynchronous JavaScript + XML. *See*
        Ajax

attribute selectors, 30–34, 285
    determining external links, 116
    form layout, 190
        additions for advanced browsers,
            193
        browser support for, 191
    IE version support for, 118
autocomplete.css, 281, 306

B

background images, 71–74
background-image property, 84
background-position property, 84
bitmapped corner mask, 81
block boxes, 57
block-level elements, 57, 119
blockquote
    defining styling for, 324–325
    layering, 323–325
blur radius attribute, 340
body classes
    highlighting current page, 319–325
    navigation control with, 319–325
    overview, 319

pairing with navigation class, 319–322

body element
    adding class names or id attribute to, 38
    unique IDs for, 319

border property, 51

border-collapse property, 181

border-image property, 86, 87

border-padding property, 182

border-radius property, 85, 92, 338–339, 340

border-radius rule, 327

borders
    applying to isolate bugs, 254
    in li element, 329
    table border models, 181

box model, 21, 51, 52
    IE and, 53–54
    margin collapsing, 54–57

boxes, rounded-corner, 74–83
    fixed-width rounded-corner boxes, 75
    flexible-width rounded-corner boxes, 78

box-shadow property, 92, 339–341

box-sizing property, 54

branding element, 226

browser bugs, 246

browser modes, 21, 22

browser support, 271, 273

BUG keyword, CSS comments, 44

bugs, 245–273
    avoiding, 254
    common, 264–271
    fixing problems versus fixing symptoms, 256
    help resources, 256
    hunting for, 246–256
    workarounds, 260–264

bullet, custom, 134

button styled links, 119, 120, 128

buttons
    Pixy-style rollovers, 121
    rollovers with images, 120

C

caption element, data tables, 178, 182

captions
    image overlay, 334–337

RGBa transparency, 334–337

cascade process, 35, 39

Cederholm, Dan, 81

cellspacing property, 182

center keyword, positioning images, 73

centering designs, 210–211

check boxes
    form layout, 190
    multicolumn, 197

child selector, 28, 264

Clagnut.com, 91

class names, 8–10, 11, 12, 38

class selectors, 26

classes, combining, 337–338

classitis, 11

clear class, multicolumn check boxes, 199

clear property, 64, 65

clear:both property, 343, 344

Climb Mountains (CTM) case study, 311–352
    flexible grid use, 317–319
    modifying image with caption, 333–352
        border-radius property, 338–339
        box-shadow property, 339–341
        caption image overlay and RGBa transparency, 334–337
        combining classes, 337–338
        main elevation chart, 344–352
        overview, 333
        positioning lists and revealing content, 341–343
        rounding corners, 344
    navigation control with body classes, 319–325
        highlighting current page, 319–323
        layering blockquote, 323–325
        overview, 319
    overview, 311–312
    style sheet organization and conventions, 314–317
    targeting elements, 325, 332
        adjacent sibling selectors, 331–332
        deep descendent selectors, 325–329
        :first-child pseudo-class, 329–331
        overview, 325

col element, data tables, 179
colgroup element, data tables, 179
collapsed table border model, 181
colors, specifying, 334–335
column-count property, 236
column-gap property, 236
columns, in grids, 318–319
column-width property, 236
combining classes, 337–338
comments, 41–45
    conditional, 98, 260, 261, 317
    removing, 45
content area, 206, 207
contents, describing with notes, 315–
        316
conventions package, 314
corner mask, bitmapped, 81
corners
    drop shadows, 88
    mountaintop corners, 81
    rounded-corner boxes, 74
        fixed-width, 75
        flexible-width, 78
    rounding, 344
CSS (Cascading Style Sheets)
    history of, 6
    versions of, 17–18
CSS 3 columns, 236, 238
CSS extensions, 86
CSS frameworks, versus CSS systems,
        238, 243
CSS image maps, 150, 156
CSS opacity, 95
CSS sprites, 123, 125
CSS validator, 246
CSS2, advanced features, 284, 292
CSS3, advanced features, 284, 292
CSS-Discuss, 256
CSSDoc, 44
Cufón, 298, 299, 300, 301, 302

D

data tables
    caption element, 178
    col element, 179
    colgroup element, 179
    styling data tables, 176–182
        adding visual interest, 182
        data table markup, 179
        table border models, 181

    table-specific elements, 178
    summary attribute, table element,
        178
    tbody element, 178
    tfoot element, 178
    thead element, 178
date input, not displaying label for every
        element, 195
datepicker.css, 281
Davidson, Mike, 104
definition descriptions <dd>, 172
definition lists, 171, 172
definition term <dt>, 172
descendent selectors, 25, 325–329
display property, 57, 189
display:none property, 349
div element, 12, 13, 89
divitus, 13
DOCTYPE declaration
    browser modes, 21
    validating pages, 19
DOCTYPE switching, 22–23
documents
    applying styles to, 40–45
    downloadable, highlighting, 118
double-margin float bug, 264–265
downloadable documents, highlighting,
        118
drop shadows, 88–94
    Clagnut.com, 91
    coding for IE6, 91
    creating, 339–341
    using relative positioning, 91
DTD (document type definition), 19
dynamic pseudo-classes, 27

E

elastic layouts, 219, 220, 223, 226, 228
elements
    defining, 207
    HTML, 7
    naming, 10
    sizing, 258–259
    targeting, 325–332
        adjacent sibling selectors, 331–
            332
        deep descendent selectors, 325–
            329
        :first-child pseudo-class, 329–
            331

overview, 325
elevation chart, in CTM case study, 344–352
em layout, strong element, 193
email links, highlighting, 117
equal-height columns, 231, 236
escape characters, hacks and filters, 262–263
extensions, 86
external links, 115

F

Fahrner Image Replacement. *See* FIR
Fahrner, Todd, 103
faux columns, 228–231
feedback message, form layout, 201
feeds, highlighting, 118
fieldset element
    form layout, 186–188
    identifying purpose of, 186
    multicolumn check boxes, 197–198
filters
    band pass, 262–263
    conditional comments, IE, 260
    overview, 261–262
    using, 262
FIR (Fahrner Image Replacement), 103
Firefox browser, creating drop shadows for, 339–341
Firefox Web Developer Toolbar, 21, 247
:first-child pseudo-class, 329–331
fixed positioning, 61
fixed-width layouts, 219, 220
fixed-width rounded-corner boxes, 75–81
Flickr-style image maps, 156, 164
float model, 62, 69
float-based layouts, 212, 218
floated elements, 212
floated layouts, 258
floating, 51, 62, 69
    horizontal navigation bar, 142
    multicolumn check boxes, 199
:focus pseudo-class selector, 110
:focus pseudo-link state, 350
font linking, 292, 302
font-family property, 342
font-size property, 342
footers, tfoot element, 178

for attribute, label element, 187
form layout, 185–203
    additions for advanced browsers, 192
    attribute selectors, 190, 193
    basic layout, 187
    check boxes, 190, 197
    emphasizing field, 193
    feedback message, 201
    fieldset element, 186
    form elements, 186, 187
    form labels, 187
    grouping related blocks of information, 186
    horizontal form alignment, 194
    input element, 190
    label element, 187
    legend element, 186
    radio buttons, 190
    required fields, 193
    strong element, 193

G

gotchas, 44
gradients, background images, 72
grids, 282, 284, 317–319

H

hacks
    child selector, 264
    overview, 261, 262
    star HTML, 263
    using, 262
hard-working screen.css, 315–316
hasLayout function, 257
hasLayout property, 259
hAtom format, 17
hCalendar format, 14, 17
hCard format, 15, 16, 17
headers
    distinguishing from rows, 183
    thead element, 178
highlighting
    current page, 319–323
    downloadable documents, 118
    feeds, 118
    links, 115–117
horizontal form alignment, 194

horizontal offset attribute, 340
:hover dynamic pseudo-class selector, 110
:hover pseudo-class, creating rollover effects, 120
:hover pseudo-link state, 350
hProduct format, 17
hRecipe format, 17
hReview format, 17
HTML
    structured, 4
    versions of, 17, 18
HTML 4.01 Strict, 279
HTML 5, 279–280
HTML Validator for Firefox, 247

I

icons, external links, 115
id attribute, adding to body tag, 38
IDs, 8, 9, 11, 12, 26, 319
ie.css, 281, 286
IFR (Inman Flash Replacement), 104
image maps
    CSS image maps, 150
    Flickr-style, 156, 164
image-repeat property, 101
images
    background, 71–74
    gradients, 72
    modifying, in CTM case study, 333–352
        border-radius property, 338–339
        box-shadow property, 339–341
        caption image overlay and RGBa transparency, 334–337
        combining classes, 337–338
        overview, 333
        positioning lists and revealing content, 341–343
        rounding corners, 344
    replacement, 102–105
        Fahrner Image Replacement, 103
        Inman Flash Replacement (IFR), 104
        Phark method, 103
        Scalable Inman Flash Replacement (sIFR), 104
    rollovers with, 120, 121
    tiling images, 72

import (@import) rule, band pass filters, 262, 263
importing, 40, 41
indentation, lists, 134
inheritance, 39
inline boxes, 58
inline elements, 57, 119
Inman Flash Replacement (IFR), 104
Inman, Shaun, 104
input element
    form layout, 190
    name attribute, 187
internal links, 116
Internet Explorer (IE) browser
    box model and, 53–54
    bugs, 253, 256
        duplicate character bug, 267–268
        peek-a-boo bug, 268–269
    style sheets using conditional comments, 317

J

Johansson, Roger, 81
jQuery, adding interactivity with, 302–307

K

KLUDGE keyword, 44

L

label element
    for attribute, 187
    display property, 189
    form layout, 187, 189
    not displaying for every element, 195
:last-child pseudo class, 331
layering blockquote, 323–325
layout
    defined, 257
    effect of, 258–259
    problems with, 256–259
left keyword, 73
legend element, 186–188
li element, adding elements into, 326–327

lightweight markup, 277–278
line boxes
    clearing, 63–69
    inline elements within, 58
line-height attribute, 119
:link pseudo-class selector, 110
link pseudo-classes, 27
links
    styling, 109–130
        highlighting email links, 117
        indicating external links, 115
    turning off underline for, 111
liquid layouts, 220–223, 226–228
lists
    collating blocks of information as, 327
    definition, 171–172
    styling, 133–134
    vertical navigation bar, 138
list-style-image property, 134

M

main elevation chart, 344–352
margin collapsing
    box model, 54–57
    problems with, 249–251
margin property, 51
margin:auto declaration, 211
margins, centering design, 210–211
markup
    history of, 4–6
    important factors, 277–278
    meaningful, 7–8
max-width property, 227
meaningful markup, 277
microformats, 13, 17
minimal test cases, 255
mountaintop corners, 81
-moz-border-radius rule, 327
multicolumn check boxes, form layout, 197
multi-column layout, 295–296
multiple background feature, 285

N

name attribute, input element, 187
nav bars
    creating, 133

graphical, 141–144
highlighting current page in, 138–139
horizontal, 139–141
vertical, 135–138
navigation class, pairing body class with, 319–322
navigation control, with body classes, 319–325
    highlighting current page, 319–323
    layering blockquote, 323–325
nested boxes, 58
nonsemantic markup, 83
nontiled images, adding to page, 72
notes, style sheet, 315–316

O

opacity, 95
Orchard, Dunstan, 88
outline property, 52
overflow property, 67, 227, 234

P

padding, 134, 250, 329
padding property, 52
page layout, 205–243
    elastic, 223–228
    equal-height columns, 231–236
    faux columns, 228–231
    fixed-width, 219–220
    float-based, 212, 218
    foundations for, 208–211
    liquid, 219, 226–228
    planning, 206–208
page zooming, 292
parallax scrolling, 99
pattern portfolio, 46
Phark method, image replacement, 103
pixels, three-pixel text jog bug, 267
Pixy-style rollovers, 121–123
PNG transparency, 97
polaroid class, 338, 340
position:absolute property, 349
positioning, 51, 57–62
    background images, 73–74
    lists, 341–343
profile class, 337
pseudo classes, 27

Q

quirks mode, 21, 252

R

radio buttons, form layout, 190
rel attribute, 140
relative positioning, 59
    description, 60
    drop shadows using, 91
remote rollovers, 165–170
repeating patterns, 206
required fields, form layout, 193
reset.css sheet, 280, 281, 316
RGBa transparency, 334–337
rollovers, 120–121, 150
    with CSS3, 125–128
    Flicker-style image maps, 156–164
    graphical nav bar, 144
    Pixy-style, 121–123
    remote, 165–170
Roma Italia case study, 276–309
rounded corner boxes, 74–83
    expanding box horizontally, 78
    expanding box vertically, 75
    fixed-width rounded-corner boxes,
        75–81
    flexible-width rounded-corner boxes,
        78
    mountaintop corners, 81
    using CSS 3 multiple backgrounds,
        84
rounding corners, 344
rules, specificity of, 35
Rundle, Mike, 103
Rutter, Richard, 91

S

Safari 3 browser, creating drop
        shadows for, 339–341
Scalable Inman Flash Replacement
        (sIFR), 104
scratch files, 314
screen.css file, 315, 317
selectors, 25–36
    adjacent sibling selector, 29
    applying generic styles, 26
    attribute selector, 30
    child selector, 28

class selectors, 26
    to define relationship between body
        and navigation classes, 321
    descendant selectors, 25
    descendent, 325–329
    ID selectors, 26
    pseudo-class selector, 27
    rule specificity, 35
    selector specificity, 35
    sibling, 331–332
    simple selectors, 25
    targetting elements
        by attribute existence, 30
        by descendant, 25
        element children, 28
        with same parent, 29
        by type, 25
    type selectors, 25
    universal selector, 27
separate table border model, 181
shadows
    creating, 339–341
    drop shadows, 88–95
sibling selectors, 331–332
sIFR (Scalable Inman Flash
        Replacement), 104
simple selectors, 25
.slideUp method, 304
sliding doors technique
    expandable tabbed navigation, 144–
        147
    flexible-width rounded-corner boxes,
        79
sort order problems, 247–248
spacer GIFs, 5, 6
specificity
    problems with, 247–248
    rules, 35
    using in stylesheets, 37
Stackoverflow, 256
standards mode, 21, 252
standards-compliant browsers, 253
star HTML hack, 263
strong element, 193
structural areas, 206
style guides, 45–47
style sheets
    applying styles to documents, 40–45
    breaking down, 42
    comments in CSS, 41–45
    importing, 40

planning, organizing and
maintaining, 40–45
removing comments, 45
Styled fixed-width box, 78
styling
data tables, 176–185
forms, 185–203
links, 109–130
highlighting email links, 117
indicating external links, 115
lists, 133–134
Suckerfish drop-downs, 147, 150
summary attribute, table element, 178
syntactical errors, 246, 252

T
table border models, styling data
tables, 181
table of contents for style sheet, 315
tables, styling data tables, 176–185
Tantek Çelik filters, 262–263
:target pseudo-class, 114
targeting elements, 325–332
adjacent sibling selectors, 331–332
deep descendent selectors, 325,
329
:first-child pseudo-class, 329–331
overview, 325
tbody element, 178
text. *See also* captions
scaling, 292
zooming, 292
text-align property, 211
text-decoration property, 111
text-overflow feature, 288, 292
tfoot element, 178
thead element, 178, 183
three-column floated layout, 216, 218
three-pixel text jog bug, 265–266
tiling images, 72
TODO keyword, 44
tooltips, 128–130

transparency, RGBa, 334–337
two-column floated layout, 213–216
type selectors, 25
typographical errors, 246–252

U
underlines, 111–113
unique IDs, for body element, 319
universal selector, 27
username link, 328

V
validation, 19–20, 21, 246–247
vertical navigation bars, 138
vertical offset attribute, 340
:visited pseudo-class selector, 110
visited-link styles, 113
visual formatting model, 57, 59

W
W3C validator, 19
Web Developer Toolbar, topographic
view, 250
Web Standards Group, 256
webkit-border-radius rule, 327
-webkit-gradient value, 126
websites
style guides, 45
uniformity among browsers, 285–
287
Wubben, Mark, 105

XYZ
XFN format, 17
XHTML 1.0 Strict, 278
YUI Grids, 238